STARVING

A Memoir

By Christen Bensten

D1400777

To Brent

Starved; starving: to suffer extreme hunger: to suffer or perish from deprivation: to deprive of nourishment

-MERRIAM-WEBSTER DICTIONARY

Barn's burnt down

Barn's burnt down --
now
I can see the moon.

- Mizuta Masahide

Author's Note

I acknowledge that the reader will take away what they will from my memoir. However, my desire, my wish, would be that you see my story through an empath's eyes. I felt incredibly misunderstood in my early childhood and into my teenage years because I was so quiet, so fearful. I didn't have the tools or courage to advocate for myself and I was often dismissed. I didn't know how to ask for what I wanted and even if I did, there wasn't space in my world for me to exclaim my deprivation and hunger for emotional and physical support.

I was alone for so very long.

I have finally arrived at a place that feels like the right time to tell my story. I have always wanted to open my mouth and speak and clarify and tell and be seen. I believe we all want to be seen. Writing my memoir is part of being seen, part of my healing process. It does not come from a reactionary place, but one of truth. I feel like I've been given time on this earth to tell my experience as an adult; as someone who has fought for her own freedom. This is what I offer in this story. This is an opportunity for those that know me to understand me and for those that don't know me to see a girl that fought for her own, personal health because she knew that it was God-given, and she deserved it. Like we all do.

Thank you for reading.
In truth,
Christen

PROLOGUE

I was stuffed.

I was filled to the brim with scripture, cautionary tales from the Old Testament about floods and earthquakes, and shame. I carried shame inside my body like a hostile, cancerous tumor, the kind that grows to the size of a grapefruit before its existence is discovered. The cells dividing and dividing, unrelenting like a little gremlin, his fingernails pressed into my soft interior parts, his weight so heavy that moving and breathing and growing became labored. He is a monster that refuses to be cut out completely, evicted. Shame rides shotgun, always the observer, and rejoices in sneaking up on me when I think everything is safe, when I beg to be left alone in the sunshine. He metastasizes when I show up in the world too confident or comfortable. Big.

Growing up, I watched the world from my bedroom window too afraid to participate in what was going on outside my haunted house. The holy trinity – my mother, my school and my church all surrounded me like bullies on a playground, picking on the small kid, and it didn't take long before I realized there was no authority I could run to for help. They were all on the same side, with the same mission. Bring her down. Cut her at the knees. Snuff out any God-given agency and keep her tiny at all costs.

They had me surrounded.

If I was scared of my mother that meant I was scared of God because she was the one on her knees praying for two hours every morning on the living room carpet. And when I was at school, being a good girl meant being a quiet girl. The loud girls and boys were the ones that got publicly punished and it wasn't worth speaking up just to be misunderstood and hit with a paddle. Church. Well, my church just perpetuated my state of confusion about love and God and the world. The people were odd, speaking in tongues felt phony and friends my age being slain in the spirit was terrifying. As Brené Brown would say at the beginning of the COVID-19 pandemic, "When are the parents coming?

I had no one to run to for help.

My body was the first to recognize danger. Bodies are so smart that way. I read somewhere that I should call my body a "she" as if my flesh were personified. It helps me love her more. I hated her for so long because she wasn't big enough, wasn't old enough, run-away enough and fight-back enough. But she was damn good at keeping that little light ablaze inside, warming her hands by its fire and waiting until the time she was grown, able to nourish herself and walk away.

There was a time before I can remember that I decided the best way of managing the empty pit in my stomach was to stop needing. Quit asking for all those practical, little things like sharp pencils for school, clean laundry, a ride home and a tuck-in at night. And when I discovered that I could use the same little bar of soap on my body for weeks if I stretched it out, I could also stop asking for an after-school hug or a kind word from my teacher. I realized quickly that there was something about asking for what I needed that seemed to upset everyone around me. The look I received from all the adults in my life when I had a request was anxious, annoyed or too busy to be bothered. So, I shut down the piece of myself that required hugs and a soft, warm space to land. It wasn't available anyway.

And instead of understanding that it was the limitations of those around me that kept me from receiving the love I deserved, I thought it was me. I was too dumb, too ugly, too little, too freckly, too curious, too sensitive, too much.

The seed of anxiety started in my belly, and purging every day became part of my routine before school. I lost weight. When my peers were growing into teenage bodies, my body refused. It was safer that way. I stopped eating to control my nerves and the fear that my stomach could rupture at any time and spew vomit. I stopped growing. My foot size stalled, pants slipped off my thin waist, my hair fine like a baby's and my wrists and ankles so small they often ached with use. I was terrified to develop physically. I feared being noticed and shamed for the audacity of my body, so I let myself curl into a tight little ball of self-protection and starve.

Mine is a painful story filled with misunderstanding, confusion, heartache, death and a lot of puking. I looked everywhere for some to care for me, to water me like a little seedling until I was old enough to nourish myself.

I found out later on, sometime during therapy and adulting that there wasn't enough to go around. All the resources around me were limited. They were dry wells. And even though that makes me grieve for the little she, it also flamed the fire that no one noticed burning in me and keeping me alive. Not with food or love, but with something innate. Something that I was born with, pressed into my flesh like a nail in a hand on a cross. There was so much of me, a little blonde fleck of a girl, that withered away and died. I mourn for her. But what she didn't know, and what her mother, her school and her church did not understand was that she was built to withstand starvation.

When the time was right, she uncurled her body and went out into the world. She expanded; she grew. She was reborn, raised from the dead and she fed off the fruit that was saved for her, the nourishment that was her birthright.

1

The rules in my household were unwritten and often unclear. I wish there were just one more chapter in the Bible that could have explained what I was doing wrong or why I was so wrong, I would have committed it to memory. Instead, I found myself in a confusing, familial maze. If I rushed into the kitchen with good news, I was shut down hard. Too excited, too much. If I was quiet and snuck up to my room, I was aloof. When I cried, I was too sensitive. When I was frustrated, I was too angry. If I wasn't grateful enough it felt like I was on the verge of being discarded from the house altogether.

I needed a clear step by step manual so I could get it right. And by right, I mean not just accepted as the second daughter, a sister, but poured into. I may have been filled with warnings and rebukes, but I was empty of what I needed. I wanted to be filled emotionally with all the love and support I could possibly handle. I wanted effusive embraces, cuddling, warm chocolate chip cookies, watching movies under a blanket, Saturday morning pancakes with loads of maple syrup, my crayon drawings hung in prominence on the refrigerator, and my little poems framed. Oh, especially those poems. If shame were a knife, my mother wielded it and sank the weapon deep into my flesh that Mother's Day morning when I gave her "The Nightingale."

"She didn't even spell nightingale right." I overheard her say it from her bedroom and I pictured her pursed lips, the paper floating into the small, woven trashcan.

Her world was black and white, and everything had to fit into one of the two, Good or Evil. I wanted to know how to land in the light. I wanted to be holy. And when I didn't know if she was irritated that day or feeling prayerfully peaceful, I hedged my bets and locked myself in my bedroom where I knew I would be safe.

I learned to ignore the growling of my stomach when the smells of dinner wafted under my door. It wasn't worth it. I would eat tomorrow or if I was really bold, I would sneak down after they all went to bed and nibble on the orange block of cheese that always seemed to be in the fridge.

My home life was inconsistent, and it terrified me.

I can't help but wonder if life were that way from my very beginning. Was I was just as offensive as a newborn?

I often wish I had a video, even little snippets, from when I was a baby. All those things that are impossible to know or remember in my infant-mush of a brain. I have a guess though. Eleven years of therapy, reading about attachment issues and experiencing panic, sweat-inducing nightmares that still startle me awake, quite paralyzed, must be filled with truth.

The image I have of myself as a baby is of a sweet, blue-eyed thing, all peachy opening her eyes and looking up to the ceiling, wanting. She paws at the air and smacks her lips, noticing the pit in her stomach is starting to actually hurt, cramp. And that's when she starts the crashing waves of crying. They grow and move and turn violent. Wailing too big for tears. A rupture - hot face, bleeding lungs and the silence outside in the hallway. The baby in such distress that she can't even understand what needs to happen next. But when nothing happens and the belly-upset numbs, she is surprised. The hour of hysteria calms. There is still pain and her lungs burn more intensely now. She whimpers, hiccupping in air, wondering about this new sensation. There is a calm in the room and for a moment, a few minutes even, she doesn't notice that no one has come to fill her belly.

I continue to imagine myself as a toddler, a growing child, because I can't help but be curious about where it all began. I've come to speculate that it wasn't my ugly baby-ness that was offensive, but a part of my mother that really wasn't able to offer more of herself. I have a suspicion that she needed to be mothered before she could mother. And unfortunately for both of us and our broken relationship as it stands at present, that still hasn't happened, and I'm stuck with blistering nightmares and self-loathing, silent messages dispensed into my soft, porous head.

So, I think of myself as this baby. I am in a playpen. My sister is there. I hear her chatter somewhere beyond the netted walls of the soft cage. She is able to travel, move at will. I am too small, too wobbly. She knows it and every so often comes over to peer through the holes at me. I am sitting, chewing a book with hard edges choosing this instead of the soft animal that has also been tossed at me from above.

I haven't seen her in what feels like a very long time. I haven't seen the woman that changes my diaper. I worry because I am wet and soggy. I think about the relief of dry backside, when my skin is not pruned and crinkled. It is disgusting and I can tell she thinks so too by the way she pinches her nose and turns her head away from me.

I'm not sure if such things happened. I will never know, but I can imagine this is where it all started. These scenes would fit into the puzzle nicely.

The most circulated photo from that time, which even made it onto a plastic keychain, is the image of my big sister holding me in her arms as an infant. Christmas is in the background or maybe Abigail is wearing something red. I look like an enormous, a mummified body, stiff with eyes closed.

The other photos I recall are still stuck to the gooey carboard album pages behind the peel away plastic protective sheet stacked in my parents' basement along with Gram's china and the Singer sewing machine that my dad keeps trying to give me. Most of these include both of us, "the girls." There is one image that feels very familiar, the picture where I am playing alone. A toy house, me outside on the back slab of concrete, picking at what looks like a doll in the kitchen of the blue plastic home. The sun setting, the shadows coming up the house in the background and I look content, unbothered. I remember being out there on the patio and the stuffed blue elephant I went to bed with. I must have sucked on him nightly because his fur was crusted and discolored. He smelled like old breath and I loved him for it. That familiar stench that was mine and took me home to dream land every night.

"You loved playing by yourself. You were just like a little doll."

My mom told me this when we had that knock out fight in my kitchen a few years ago, when she got on her knees next to the dishwasher, begging me not to yell at her.

A doll.

"I asked God for a baby that looked like me. Abigail was more Italian-looking, like dad's side of the family. I wanted a baby under the Christmas tree that year that was fair and blonde."

She got me.

Unfortunately for her, I wasn't born a doll. I didn't sit still on the shelf with a painted pink smile on my face ready to be picked up when she was ready to play. I was a healthy, curious human child. Maybe in the beginning I learned not to fuss when she was pre-occupied making lists and puttering around the house. But, when I started to do that thing toddlers do like walk off just far enough out of reach and then look back to make sure that mom was watching vigilantly, that was when I imagined her disappearing into the kitchen. Poof! There one moment and gone the next. Like Peek-a-Boo with a harsh ending. And I'd cry. She wasn't watching. I couldn't find her. There was something about me – this developmental phase that seemed to bring out the monster in her - that made her dig her feet in more and shake her head at my audacity, punishing me for my curiosity. I remember this feeling.

I recall moments from preschool. It was sweet. There were other adults there that recognized me as a real girl with her own ideas. The moms came in one day and sat on the round, braided carpet. I'm not sure how I felt about my mother being there, but I do remember her leg hair poking at me the way sharp, cold wind bites in the wintertime. I was annoyed. I was uncomfortable on her lap. I wondered why she didn't shave, and I couldn't stop grabbing at her face and turning it towards me, "Your legs hurt me." Shave. It seemed like such an easy adult-woman thing to do. She laughed it off. I probably embarrassed her. She was so busy looking at the other faces.

"Chrissy loves little things." My preschool teacher with the short red hair called me Chrissy and I liked it. It felt softer. She was the first one to recognize my individual taste. It made me feel seen. She remembered what I had brought in for show-and-tell a week before. It was a tiny plastic toy in the shape of a chocolate cookie that opened to reveal a tiny home. It was little. I was little. I knew the detail of the doll's sticker interior, the little toaster and bottle of jam. I pretended she made herself breakfast every morning on her own like a big girl.

I was reminded all the time that I was not a big girl nor was I Chrissy at home. I was the youngest in the house – the younger sister, the baby. But not even this birth order position gave me shelter. I remember turning to my sister for comfort. There were times she seemed to be on my side and times that her instinct was to punish. It probably wasn't her fault. It's what she witnessed. I'd like to think that at least.

Abigail told me I could pee in the bathtub, the one in which we bathed together every night and fought over the toy boat with the big yellow bird. It was mine, in truth, given to me as a birthday present, but she never acknowledged that when she demanded it first. First, we played for a bit and when I was ready and just like she offered, I let go and peed. The warm urine filling what had become a cool tub of water. I knew something had gone terribly wrong when she screamed and stood up yanking herself over the impossible wall of the porcelain tub, causing pools of water to spill over onto the tile.

I told my therapist a million years later when we were doing that thing that therapists like to do where you reprocess painful memories by saying what you wish had happened. The new memory went like this: My mom comes into the bathroom to see my sister pointing at me, the little one still in the tub, screaming at how gross I am. And instead of raking me out of the tub and placing me to the side to clean out the dirty tub with all the urine in it, sprinkling copious amounts of powdered bleach so my breathing becomes stifled, in my new, manufactured memory, she wraps me in a dry, white towel and carries me to my bed. There she dries me off, petting my hair in a gentle downward motion telling me it's ok. And just in that little motion I feel like I am not the most disgusting human on the face of the earth. I even dare to imagine her sending Abigail to her room for being so insensitive.

In reality, I don't remember what actually happened after I was shamed out of the bathroom, leaving my mom highly irritated that she had to get on her hands and knees and clean out my mess, but I imagine I went into my room dripping wet and pulled my nightgown with all the itchy pills over my head and let the stick of the water sit against my skin as I climbed into bed. I probably turned off the light and closed my eyes, my hair in wet clumps soaking into my pillow.

We were in the same bathroom when we were given the Cabbage Patch Kids, which in my mind are synonymous with spankings. We hid in the steamy bathroom from my dad. My mother was fresh out of the bath and if Abigail and I sat in there long enough, my dad would cool down. Little did we know that we were not in fact in trouble or getting our pants pulled down and our bottoms hit, but we were getting a present that she had stood in line to buy for us. It feels very contrary that they would want to get us this gift that was sold out at every toy store and popular, which was often a sibling to sin itself.

We were gifted Ned Gill and Howard Luke in the living room where all precious moments happened like birthdays and

Christmas and reading the Bible as a family. I was confused after peeling Ned from the plastic still wondering if we were getting a spanking. Did they want to scare us before lavishing us with these dolls? It felt that way. It felt like there had to be a sacrifice before a gift. Pain and pleasure. It soured the gift, and I took it out on Ned Gill, letting his head scrape again the wall, leaving a white stain on his forehead. I equated him and his blue eyes with some kind of threat that I didn't quite understand.

I hugged each parent and went up into my room before they remembered the spanking. I sniffed his bald head that smelled like plastic and real live baby powder before putting a band aid over the fresh mark. I placed Ned Gill under the covers and wondered how he would mingle with the five stuffed animals I had tucked in my bed at the time. I didn't want them to feel inched out by this baby doll even if he was packaged in the fanciest box I had ever seen and came with his own birth certificate. Cupcake, the dog I bought with my own money from that one lonely section of the grocery store, still deserved a prominent place on the pillow next to me and no doll was going to demote him.

2

I remember promising myself that when I entered my first-grade classroom I would scout out a private corner where I could suck my thumb in secret. Maybe in the little toy kitchen area, behind the pink, plastic stove at recess when there was more movement in the classroom. I knew I couldn't pacify myself in front of the other kids especially if they had abandoned the self-soothing technique. I don't think I spied a single kid with their thumbs or fingers in their mouths and I was watching. Maybe if I discovered another little girl who also had saliva-salted fingers I would recognize a kindred spirit, someone frightened like I was. But, as I recall, everyone seemed at ease, playing in the stations around the classroom as if they owned them. The reading station, the art station, the kitchen station. There was no one else that looked as petrified as I felt. They all looked kind of entitled, in fact. Like they were meant to be there and were free to move and play at will. I did not feel that way and the generalized anxiety that came up during each assignment made me feel like I did at home - one wrong move and that wide smile on the teacher's face would disappear.

I stopped sucking my thumb that year. Either I was too ashamed that I was still doing baby things, or I completely forgot to take a few sucks in hiding. The need dissolved. I forgot all about it and that made me feel like I had one less thing to set me apart from the rest of the kids. I already felt different from all of them. We weren't the same just like my family wasn't the same as our neighbors and the people at the grocery store.

I could usually guess the kids at school that didn't go to church. They were the ones with divorced parents and wore the latest tennis shoes. They were the ones dropped off at the pool for the entire afternoon without supervision and allowed to walk to the drugstore to buy candy. There was a girl in my neighborhood like this. She lived with just her mom. Her bedroom had yellow walls and on one of them opposite her canopy bed was a poster of Michael Jackson, his black curled hair contrasting against the pastel wall color. She played *Thriller* in her basement, and I was both scared and intrigued. What did that say about me? Was she going to Hell because her parents were divorced and she listened to Michael Jackson? If I was paying attention at home and church then, yup, she sure was. I still loved riding my bike over to her house on the hill, the one with the long driveway. Shortly after my mom saw me trying to figure out how to moonwalk on the linoleum floor in the kitchen, I was told I couldn't go over to her house and play.

I realized when I was an adult that it was shame that made me hide my drawings that year, hooking my arm up and around my paper and leaning my head forward to create a little cave only I could see into, but I feel the clench in my belly almost forty years later thinking about the teacher or the other students leaning over and saying, "Let me see."

The audacity!

And then the question, is it me or is it them? Confusion. I could not imagine showing the crayon marks and design I had created in case it was atrocious compared to my neighbor's cat or rainbow drawing. It was most definitely worse than anyone else's house or farm landscape. My sister was the artist, not me. My dad was the designer, not me. My mom could even draw a pretty cute frog like the one she sketched out on a note she left at the kitchen table for us to read when we got home from school.

I imagine a hot flash of anger surfacing in my cheeks at the little, hovering inquisitor. It was invasive and none of their goddamn business what my fish looked like. We probably didn't have to turn the piece into the teacher, and I can image crumpling the paper into a tight little ball and putting it in the bottom of the trash can so no one would ever see it.

I did things like that all the time. Hiding things that I didn't want people to see. My parents probably thought I was sneaky, but I felt like I was keeping myself safe from all the critical glances. No, I wasn't sneaky, I was learning the system I was born into and doing a damn good job of finding ways to keep myself from depletion.

The pretty Asian girl with the long, straight black hair who always seemed a little scattered, her desk a mess, didn't seem to care one way or another who saw her picture. I recall almost daily, the girl coming up behind me, poking my shoulder and whispering, "Can I borrow your crayons?" I wanted to explode on her. Was hate too strong a word for how I felt? Because it really felt like hate. Maybe if she only wanted to borrow, say, five crayons from my full-sized crayon box and certainly not ask for the favor every day, I would have felt more generous of spirit. But I was the one who took out five crayons and gave her the rest of the box. I don't know why I did this, but I'm sure it had something to do with Jesus and what we were taught in Sunday school. But, when she returned them having rubbed the perfect points all the way down, I'm positive I wanted to scratch her eyes out. Instead, I'm sure I just accepted them back and kept my mouth shut because she poked my shoulder again the very next day.

I remember this being a really big deal and every day when the bus picked her up, I looked for a brand-new box of crayons in her hand to replenish my supply. Maybe an apology note too. I remember hoping that she would notice what she was doing and when she didn't, I really wasn't sure how to manage the situation. There was no way my parents were going to buy me a new box and frankly she was the one that was taking advantage of my generosity. I didn't have words to express my frustration.

It was during this struggle that I realized I had lost my voice completely. Probably long, long ago while still carrying around that baby fat in my cheeks. I imagined other kids would have said something to the effect of, "Stop wearing down my crayons, Jen" or "No, you are ruining my crayons." I didn't know how to start or finish these sentences. I don't remember feeling like I had the words or the right to be so mean. It would be mean to refuse her, right?

I never yelled at the crayon-annihilator, so I imagine what I did was negotiate with myself. I would swallow the anger, loan her my crayons, but next time, like if she wanted to borrow my glue, I would make up a lie and say that I needed it all. Yes, I could live with that untruth and still make it to Heaven.

I thought I was in trouble when my parents pulled me from the little neighborhood public school and made me repeat first grade at the Christian school. At least my teacher was not the round woman with the tight curls and bad breath. She was the kindergarten teacher in the room where there was an entire wall lined with a photo of a forest. It had faded with the sun coming through the window and for some reason I was willing to go to the school as long as I didn't have to be in that room with the woods.

I learned quickly that my new school was different. There was no cafeteria with warm pizza smells filling the halls or a jungle gym in the back of the school. There were no coloring pages or crafts to be done after lunch. No one to read us from a book as we sat in a circle. We didn't even need a fresh box of crayons at the beginning of the year because we didn't use crayons. I don't remember much color at all. Our uniforms were navy with little, skinny red and yellow lines creating a plaid pattern in the dress.

I thought my new school was just fine until I saw the first boy in my class get paddled. I had never seen anything like this before and it was a new threat that I needed to be aware of. I had to be very careful and even smaller so no one would notice me, so no one would think I was a bad girl and hit me.

I wasn't quite sure how to do this at the beginning of the year, but I quickly found that if I moved slowly and said nothing all day except at lunch outside to the other little girls, then I would be safe.

Unlike the sunshine that seemed to sparkle through the windows at my neighborhood public school, this small, darker building exclaimed that we were not permitted to bounce from station to station. In fact, there were no stations. There were desks for the students and a teacher's desk and that was it. No little round carpet on the floor for morning meetings and no colorful posters on the wall with a snuggly kitten hanging off a tree encouraging us to hang in there.

In this school, I was not only limited by my own fear, but by the threat of punishment. I needed to figure out how I was going to survive this place and that meant keeping my head down and staying small. It would also do me well if I could be cute. A little, cute girl meant a good girl, one that wouldn't cause trouble.

I remember my mom tying pigtails in my hair. I allowed myself the pleasure of feeling cute. So, when picture day came along, I begged for her to brush my hair and put it into pigtails. She put a little red sweater around my shoulders. I looked like a doll. I needed to be a doll for the next five years. I looked as innocent as I was. The photographer must have thought so too because he put me in the very center of the class picture where I held the sign that read: Hope Valley Christian School, First Grade.

I was surprised by how well the photo turned out. You couldn't even see the freckles that were starting to crawl up and around my face. They were the same kind that my mom had all over her arms that I saw her try to sweep away with a hand when she looked into the mirror.

3

Church felt just as inconsistent and intimidating as home and school. It was the third wall of the triangle that kept me from feeding on the fruit of curiosity and exploration. I went to see an art exhibit in high school where the artist set up an interactive installation of a room with tilted, yellow walls. I walked into the space and at once felt disoriented, trapped and angered all at once. I was never sure if it was the walls or the violent, yellow stain that evoked such a strong reaction. But, if I had to describe my life at this point, around age ten, I'd say it was like this. Except there was no door, no way out that I could see.

My church took the frigid, emotional neglect from my home and the crippling fear of my new school and dumped in a heavy dose mortality. Life and death. Heaven and Hell. I was taught that I was going to one of these places for all of eternity, which mean forever and ever and ever, so I better button up and shut out anything about myself that was contrary. To be honest, it was all very confusing and if I had to sum up the general idea of what I was taught it was that God was big and could destroy me with a natural disaster, Jesus was kind but was murdered, and Satan was real. Maybe he didn't have horns and a pitchfork - now that would just be silly - but he was watching me and ready to find a foothold.

Shut it down.

Don't be like those people on the outside, out there in the secular world. They aren't going to party in Hell. No. Those kids with the bright, new shoes will be clawing and gnashing their teeth and ask you for a drop of water on their tongue. Make sure you are going to be on the right side because Death with a capital "D" is coming and you won't know where or how, but if you are not right with God and you are in a car accident that smashes the life out of you, you may not make it to one of the rooms that God says He is building for you.

Fuck, that's scary.

I was already voiceless and small. The conduct and rules of my church – which now that I look back as an adult seem to have a dose of cult-like tendencies - left me panicked. And I didn't need anyone scaring me anymore than I already was. I wanted someone to fill me up, comfort me and tell me it was all going to be okay. If I had to put it into words now, I could either show up as I was and risk going to Hell or I could put myself into a self-induced coma and be saved. I chose the latter.

But what I didn't realize at the time, was that there was a part of me that refused to comply. A defiant, feisty nymph, a fighter that was keeping an eye on things until I was older and could make my own choices apart from all the scary ultimatums. I like to think that she knew a way out, a trap door, that would bring me to safety.

So, before this becomes too depressing, stay with me. We are going down a dark, wooded path, but there is a pinprick of light I see ahead, and I promise the light is worth the years of darkness.

The clear message was that the stakes were really, really, really high – life and death high. God didn't mess around if He was upset with you. There were demons and fire and floods and lions and deserts and torture. I needed to be an extra good girl to avoid all of this. I studied my pastel pink Bible nightly and came to the conclusion that if I followed the long list of rules, if I didn't murder, steal, become an adulterer or wear black, I wasn't going to Hell. I think that last one about wearing black was my mom's rule, but she was definitely closer to God, so I assumed that all the rules merged. I thought if I could abide by all of these, I would make it into Heaven by the skin of my teeth.

I truly believed that my church was the only real church. I believed that only real churches were three hours long, and only real Christians spoke in tongues and if you wanted to be close to God, you had to get there by our pastor laying hands on you until you fell backwards and spent some time passed out on the red carpet. I recall thinking that all the bodies up by the altar were lifeless and imagined someone having to scoop them all up and put them in the ground behind the church parking lot. All those other churches out there were doing their best, but we were the ones riding the clouds straight to the shores of Heaven.

I thought it was normal.

I also felt like I was going to puke every time we rounded the corner where the car dealerships were, approaching the building. For so very long I thought it was me. My anxiety, my puking, my displacement. But, looking back with adult eyes, it was terrifying.

However, at the time, if someone questioned me or rebuked the exorcisms or the Christian rock band, I would say, you are unfortunately very far away from God. I will pray for you. I will invite you to pray. I will witness to you like we were taught. I will feel bad for you. Oh, and you are going to rot in this awful place called Hell if you don't do what I say.

It wasn't until Peter came along that I was jarred from my self-righteousness. I wiped the mud from my eyes. I took a good look around me and realized that there was something terribly wrong.

That's when I realized I was the one that was naked, exposed. Shit. I had spent every ounce of energy absorbing everything I was taught and now something felt wrong. Was it me? Was it my church? How was I going to sort this out? How was I going to love God and love Peter? Would God punish me, make the earth quake under my feet? Was God going to withhold love like my mom? Most importantly, was I not going to Heaven because I still loved the gay boy at church?

4

I went along with all of it. The procession of robed men, the clumsy hand-made flags that bobbed unsteadily forward, carried by fathers from the congregation and the monish man that led them all up to the painted plexiglass cross made to look like raw wood. They were making their way to the altar, carpeted red like a movie theater, but instead of watching a movie, our attention was on the classroom-like pull down screen manned by a projector from a little upstairs room, like Oz behind the curtain. Looking back, it reminds me of a pageant wagon with graceless costumes and awkward props. I remember feeling so disoriented, pulled to participate, but also too embarrassed to close my eyes and lift my hands.

I was a teenager when I started to process the awkward fanfare at church. It was asking a lot from a self-conscious, painfully shy skinny girl to digest. I was also navigating pimples and braces, new boobs. I didn't even feel comfortable in my own clothes. The maroon skirt my mother had picked out for me was too short and revealed my splotchy, purple cobweblike marks on my opaque skin. My thighs like thin cut slices of deli salami. Fatty meat. Abigail was sure to make fun of my boney chicken legs that I left bare. I didn't own tights. I could be wrong, but I don't remember there being tights in my top drawer next to the cotton underwear. I also don't recall sweaters or an alternative pair of shoes when I opened my closet. I remember separating the two doors and hoping I'd see a basic sweater hanging amongst my uniforms.

Sitting on the carpeted floor was the only pair of shoes I owned, the brown leather loafers I had to wear to school, laces like a bee's body. Yellow and black. We learned to wind them up with a pencil and tie them off to look cool. I needed a pair of basic black, fancy-like shoes that I could wear to church and all those funerals we seemed to go to when I was little. Oh, and I needed jeans. I didn't own a pair of jeans until I was dumped back into public school. But by then, I was too far behind. I would never feel like an insider. I needed so many things – a curling iron, those white flat sneakers, and I definitely had to find out who Madonna was if I wanted to fit in.

My mom bought us a few items when she took us back to school shopping in late August. But, like most things, shopping with my mom made me nervous. I said yes to everything she liked. She would pull out hangers of the ugliest turtlenecks and itchy sweaters. I would lie and say I liked them because I was too scared to upset her.

My sister, a few aisles away, would beg for the loud-colored shorts that were popular at the time. I have no idea how she knew what was trendy because she also wore uniforms every day, but she was right. The ugly, board shorts were damn popular as I would come to find out. What I wanted to say to my mom was that I wanted everything Abagail was getting but in my size. Please and thank you.

It didn't work like that. I watched how Abigail navigated my mom. Unlike me, she was able to express her taste without upsetting her. I was so jealous at how she bluntly said "no" and "I want this." How did she get away with that? She was clearly unafraid and more concerned with going home with a brown shopping bag full of items that she truly wanted. And she did. She asked for what she wanted, and she got it. I, on the other hand, went home with the ugly maroon skirt and a tight-necked, white turtleneck that exposed my budding nipples.

The procession was still moving, urged forward by the sway of the congregation. I didn't mind this part because there was so much to look at and notice. The clergy, nestled in the middle of the line, was my favorite part. They were like angels in their ethereal beauty, gliding down the far left-hand aisle like Moses crossing dry land in the middle of the parted Red Sea. They always made their march down the aisle that we in. We were so close to this holy parade that we could almost reach out and touch the hem of their garments like a bleeding woman touching Jesus' cloak in order to be healed.

There were two pastors, each one a beautiful angel dressed in white robes with a white rope tied at the waist and a hood sewn at the back of the head. The men looked just like Jesus if he were dipped in white, shiny paint. Each Sunday they wore a different scarf-like banner around their necks, the ends cut like a ribbon on a Christmas wreath.

John Stuart Mills was our main pastor. He was the one that came to us when we prayed. He moved to Virginia with his quiet wife and two children just for our church. I hope we looked as good to him as he did to us. The other pastor walking next to him was tall with a soft smile like a shepherd, Brian Lockheart. It wouldn't be until I saw a woman years later on the altar that I would consider how these beautiful white men floating on air were just that, white men. Once I saw a woman pastor, a black woman leader, dressed in the same white robes. She was silent and stood almost hidden at the back corner. Her presence was quietly pronounced, and I thought to myself how beautiful she was with her dark skin and puff of hair swept up like a crown. My mom did not seem to like her though and I wasn't sure why. Did my mom understand something I didn't?

Then one day the woman was gone. No one told me where she went, and I didn't ask. Was she kicked out? Was she only visiting? Did people complain? Did my mother complain? It was as if she were there one moment and then sank back into the shadows as quietly as she appeared.

I found out later that my mom and other congregants didn't believe that women should be pastors. It made sense based on what I had already learned in Sunday school.

*"Wives, submit to your own husbands, as to the Lord. For
the husband is the head of the wife even as Christ is the
head of the church, his body, and is himself its Savior."*

- Ephesians 5:22, 23

We were taught that God came first, then the husband who
was the head of the household. The wife was to be obedient, but
she was prone to mess things up just like Eve, the evil, naked
sinner who couldn't keep her grubby hands off the one tree God
told Adam and her not to eat from. She was born from Adam's
rib as a companion for her husband and it didn't take long for
her ruin their lives. The rest of us would suffer because of her
carelessness. Women were told that they would suffer in child-
birth because of her grave mistake. It made me hate Eve. It made
me hate being a woman.

John Stuart said the same prayer he did every Sunday. He'd lift
his arms to the Heavens, the sleeves of his robe naturally falling to his sides like wings. He smiled with his eyes and looked
around the congregation before bowing his head. "Dear Heavenly Father. Thank you for bringing each one of us here this
morning. Bless us as we worship you. Help us to hear your voice
through the noise and the chaos of our world. Shine Your Light
down upon us as we praise your name."

The service was starting, and I was at the mercy of. No turning back now. The piano would come to life and lyrics appeared
on the screen. All the people in all of their out of tune voices
sang or pretended to sing.

I actually enjoyed the music. It was the playlist of my childhood. I can't sing along to "Livin' on a Prayer" when my girlfriends join in unison on a mom's night out because I don't know
the words, but name a Jesus song from the 80s and I know it by
heart. The songs were the same week after week. My mom sang
them at home, lifting up her hands in the kitchen or when her

Bible study came over. It was one of the ways I knew that the waters were calm in the house. When I heard her sing it was a siren at peace.

My mother participated in church like her life depended on it. There were those in the church that seemed distracted and stared around the room and those that looked like they were filled with the Holy Spirit. My mother's arms flew up into the air as if pulled by strings from the ceiling. People closed their eyes, more arms lifted, and voices filled the room. I watched as the skinny woman with short brown hair rocked her body back and forth in rhythm to the music. Her hips were mesmerizing, and I found myself staring at her throughout most of the worship time.

I let myself people watch during worship. We were a collection of misfits – people that did not fit in the outside world and gathered in this room to learn how not to screw up our lives and end up in Hell. Or at least that's what I assumed. Why else would we all be doing this?

My sister and I grew up around the people who sat in our section of church near the exit door where the remainder of the communion wine was poured out after each service. I thought about the blood of Jesus bubbling and soaking into the crab grass by the storm drain.

I hated where we sat. I hated that we had no friends or no one to say hello to besides the random single person looking lonely at the end of the aisle. I wasn't sure why we were so quiet and aloof. I followed my parents' lead. It felt like they wanted to be a part of things, but just didn't know how. We had been at the church for years and it still felt like we were outsiders. Now isn't that something. Outsiders in church, outsiders out of church. We should have been sitting in the front row, clapping and going out for Sunday brunch with our pastor.

Our church didn't have money for formal, wooden pews and even if it did, I think everyone would still vote for the ugly 1970s inspired plastic and metal chairs in orange, brown and black. We didn't even use the word church to describe our building. It was called "The Gathering Place." There was no grand steeple rising up to the heavens, no heavy double doors to welcome its guests or wooden pews to slide into. It looked like a small, dismal warehouse with grey metal paneling and few windows.

My church mirrored the message my parents and school taught me. There was something wrong with progress, something wrong with consuming and moving into the world, participating and expanding. There was something shameful about embracing anything new or evolved. It didn't make sense to me why the church didn't want to hide the regrettable appearance of the building with a coat of paint or why my parents refused to trade in the big blue station wagon that had the same urine stain on the front passenger's side seat for the last five years.

The people who went to my church were equally dated and a bit odd. They didn't match the type of people that I saw at the grocery store or the mall. They dressed funny and seemed like they didn't care about fitting into the bigger world outside the Gathering Place. And they didn't. They, we, lived by a completely different set of rules. We were taught to be humble, never self-promote, always turn the other cheek, never gossip about others, never call attention to ourselves with luxury items - God forbid a Louis Vuitton entered the church doors. We were called to not watch secular television or listen to FM radio, do not say God's name in vain, do not vote democratic. If you were a woman, you let you husband do the leading – the driving, the thinking, the praying for your family. Women cook, clean and take care of the children, cleave to their husbands. Then there were the obvious rules – no cussing, no adultery, no sex before marriage, no porn, and no homosexuality. These last few would get you a ticket straight to Hell. As for hurricanes, earthquakes, fires and other awesome acts of nature, it was my understanding that those were God's way of punishing His people for mistakes they had made. An earthquake was never just an earthquake. It was a loud and clear message to change your ways or God was going to shake the ground beneath you.

Fear. It was a lot of fear.

In front of us sat the same small family. A disheveled mother with large brown glasses and a father with oversized, worn blue pants. I heard my mom call him droopy drawers one time in the car on the way home. Disheveled Mom and Droopy Drawers had two small disheveled, droopy-drawered children. And since we sat behind them for years, we watched them grow up. The children year by year looking more like their parents and narrowing the odds that they were going to make it out of here as anything less than nose-picking, thrift store wearing oddballs.

Abigail referred to the little boy as Bob Dylan because of his mess of curly hair. He turned in his plastic chair so that he was sitting crisscross and stared at us, snot dripping ominously from his nose. The mother wore the same pair of coral polyester pants that were two sizes too small, her stomach spilling out over the elastic band, and passed the boy pieces of dry cereal, licking her fingers each time he sucked one from her paw. I wondered why neither parent took a tissue to Dylan's nose and wiped up what was becoming a small puddle near his mouth.

My anxiety had picked up through the years and I often found myself in the tiny, cream-colored bathroom at church standing over the toilet waiting for my stomach to erupt. Breathing in the faux floral mist of the bathroom spray was enough to at least make me gag. I'd wash my hands and plug my nose on the way out, moving slowly so as to kill time. If I excused myself during Sunday School, then I moved extra slow. We were taught the same Bible stories over and over and then asked how these stories related to our lives. My Sunday School teacher didn't remember my name and I never raised my hand to offer my insight. I didn't know how the burning bush related to me and my life or if God would save me from a lion's den, but I was put on high alert that God at any time could steal me from my bed and turn me into a pillar of salt.

We were usually invited to go to our Sunday school classes after a few more songs and Bible verses. We were stuffed into a back room and forced to study scripture. The one teacher that I remembered looked as terrified as I felt to be stuck in the room and have to actually discuss things out loud instead of just sitting in the church listening.

Sometimes we were asked to do stupid things, elementary school things, like act out a scene from the Old Testament. I laugh when I think of how Grace orchestrated our performance of Abraham and Isaac. She told me that I would be Isaac because she would be able to carry me up to the mountain the front desk) to kill me. She was so quick-witted and asked me just to play along. No problem. I was too quiet to cause trouble.

She put me on the desk and raised her hands as if holding a knife and without hesitation brought it down to my chest, killing me. The punch line that she ended the piece was, "Sorry, God, I didn't hear you in time. He's already dead."

It was brilliant. When we performed it, the class agreed, offering loud laughter and clapping.

I did my part and pretended I was dead as I lay on the desk in front of the class. Grace was right, it was rather risky of God to call upon Abraham to stop the killing of his son at the last minute like that.

5

It was Peter.

Just as I was making eye contact with Ester in the front row, ready to be excused to our classrooms, John Stuart made an announcement that our age group, ten and up, were to stay in the service for a special speaker.

I sat down, slightly relieved and rubbed my hand back and forth across my marbled flesh. I snaked a frigid leg behind the other, trying to make myself smaller.

Once the room was cleared of all the babies and small children, John Stuart invited Peter to come to the altar. I watched closely as he climbed the steps of the altar, his foot catching on the red carpet making his body jump forward slightly. He had on pleated khaki pants, oxblood Doc Martins, a red shirt with a collar that refused to fold over neatly and instead bent awkwardly like a strip of wavy bacon. His bangs fell in a curved, ocean wave and covered his left eye. He stared downward, letting a small shadow cross the rest of his face. He looked nervous.

Peter was the senior high youth group leader and if Jesus walked on water, so did he. The older teenagers talked to him like he was their trusted friend and all the younger kids, like me, wanted to be in his holy presence. We loved Peter. We interacted with him during the large group portion of Sunday School when all the kids in the church congregated before splitting up into age-appropriate classrooms. He was the cool older brother, confident and good-looking. Peter was funny when we needed levity but could drop into seriousness like any good Christian leader the moment it was called for. He quoted Bible verses from memory and could recite almost the entire book of Matthew.

Why did he look so nervous? He rung his hands together and refused to lift his head. My stomach popped and pinched with unsettled energy. I rubbed it softly hoping my sister sitting next to me didn't overhear my seeping nerves.

I watched with blistering curiosity as Peter scanned the crowd like a scared fawn, paralyzed in the moment. All was too silent. It must have taken him some time to get through what he had to say. I don't remember it. I don't remember all the words that he used, just the big ones like conversion therapy and homosexuality. I witnessed the nods around the room, the congregation urging him on in what felt like a more patronizing way rather than compassion.

He told the people he was struggling; he was gay. He went to a place that helped make him un-gay. Later on, in the car, I must have heard my parents discussing him because it became clearer. He liked boys and the Bible said that was a sin. I don't know who sent him away because I don't remember ever seeing his parents. Maybe someone caught him being gay with another boy and told the people in charge he needed to change.

He looked so small all the way up there from where I was sitting, my hands pressed underneath my thighs so I could absorb the coolness from the chair. I remember being confused and telling myself that I had to think long and hard about this because I wasn't sure I wanted to let go of what I thought about Peter. He was so good. He was so cute with his sandy blonde hair. I was nervous now that no one would like him. Because even though there were a lot of "Amens" coming from the crowd, I didn't trust the woman with the short hair in the center aisle or the family with the two blonde girls that snuck in late every Sunday, to forgive him. If they didn't forgive him and embrace him, then what?

My stare broke when John Stuart put an arm around him to pray over him. We all reached out our arms as far as they could go, a gesture of laying hands on him. Afterwards, I watched him make his way back to his seat in the front row. I remember desperately wanting him to sneak out the side door, take a huge breath and walk out the church doors.

I looked at the back of his head wondering if he was going to sit there for the rest of the service or if he was biding his time until he could get up and run to the bathroom. I imagined him slamming a stall door and letting his tears out with a great push of air from his lungs. I thought about what it would look like if I met him there, excusing myself for being in the men's bathroom but wanting to see if he was ok. But Peter didn't move during communion or the remaining worship songs at the end of the service. He sat with his back to the people where we couldn't observe his expression.

I was afraid of what my mom would do if she ran into him in the narthex. It wasn't that long ago that she questioned the boy in the grocery store who was bagging our groceries. He had an earring and my mom without hesitation asked him if he were gay. I was scared of her hurting Peter like she did with that boy.

Abigail remembers too because sometimes we talk about how mortifying it was. Being at the grocery and watching as my mom asked the teenage boy with the earing checking us out if he were gay.

He was rather calm about it, because I think I would have punched her in the face if I were him. He asked her why she thought that, and she said because of the earring and then proceed to tell him that being gay was a sin. In all honestly, I don't remember if this happened before or after Peter, but I connected the two eventually. I realized at that my mom had the potential of going around asking people if they were gay and if she thought they were presenting as such, she could just right then and there witness to them or shame them – sometimes they are both one in the same.

To the boy at the checkout, she said it with all the confidence of the whole damn church behind her and she said it with disgust in her voice.

I wanted to die. I didn't care if the boy was gay or straight or from another planet. This was the worst thing that could happen. My mom was unhinged. It felt okay to hear about these things in church and with our Christian friends, but she was bringing God and the word sin into the grocery store. I was mortified. This was the first time I recalled my mom transforming into a born-again out in public and confronting the world around her like a hurricane– her target just a young boy a few years older than Abigail.

What was happening? Why was she being so mean?

I wanted to smooth things over and apologize to the boy on behalf of my mom or tell him I liked his jacket and just to ignore the woman in front of him and finish bagging our groceries. 'Look over here! Look at me! I'm little and blonde and won't say anything offensive to you!'

I felt embarrassed to be associated with my mother and yet burdened at the same time. Were we supposed to be witnesses for Jesus out in the open like this in such a hateful way? My mom seethed at the boy as he looked down and put the mayonnaise in a plastic bag. He didn't say a word and waited while my mom wrote out a check. She continued to glare at him until I thought he would catch fire under her stare right in front of me. Was she able to do that? I looked to the boy who glared up at her one last time before we took our leave.

I was in such shock that I don't remember getting in the car and driving home. My mom didn't say anything about what had just happened. Abigail and I just sat there listening to Christian radio on the way home, probably Sandy Patty or something. *"...over and over like a trumpet underground, did the earth seem to pound..."*

It was in this unassuming boy that I found out that my mom hated gay people. I thought of Peter. God must not like gay people either.

6

I don't remember seeing Peter after that service. Maybe he was there or maybe he had left like I imagined. I think I would have liked him to leave for his own safety. Not that anyone would hurt him, but I can imagine people that were his friends and allies looked at him differently. The church was like that.

I was confused.

When I no longer saw him in the narthex before the service or after, I assumed he was gone for good. Shortly after Peter's disappearance a new youth pastor arrived. He was older, doughy around the middle and wore open toed sandals that showed of his crusted heels. He brought with him a wife and an infant son, which conveyed that he was super out of touch with anything that the church youth was experiencing. He was from Texas and he asked us to call him Pastor Ben.

We were usually dismissed from church at the same time. John Stuart would tell us to go out into the world and make disciples of ourselves. But, by that time of day, I was only feeling one thing and that was hunger. My stomach releasing uncontrolled growls and all I wanted was to stop at McDonald's on the way home. It's what I wanted every Sunday as a little treat for being so good at church. It was never something that we consistently did like many other families that I knew for a fact ate at the pancake restaurant each week. I wished we were one of those families. I would have ordered a huge stack of blueberry pancakes and sausage on the side like in the commercial.

My family had to wait for my mom to make her way through the narthex. She waited in the small circle surrounding John Stuart, waiting for a chance to talk to him or at least get some face time. There were a few years there that she was a part of the Vestry and I knew that was a big deal for her. I don't know exactly what they did, but I think they got to make decisions and vote on things to do with the church and my mom must have loved that.

Often times, Abigail would beg to wait in the car, listening to Nine Inch Nails or WHFS, alternative FM radio. I would pretend to be occupied by looking at pictures on the walls of all the missionaries. They were faded and old. I'm sure the ones with the white kids from the missionary family standing next to the brown and black kids were all grown up. My dad was somewhere close by, perusing the bulletin board, maybe taking another look at the Men's Retreat sign up flyer.

My mom was never quick. My belly was empty because I didn't eat before church in case I had to puke. The only morsel of food I had Sunday mornings was the sweet lump of communion bread. I would have been more than happy slicing up the rest of it with some butter. I imagined the monk-man wasting it, breaking it up in the side yard so it could return to the earth like the red wine.

When my mom was finished pursuing John Stuart like a wanting child, she collected my dad and me. She would comment on the missionaries as she passed the images, stating that when her and my dad were retired, they too were going to become missionaries and move to Honduras. I heard this all the time and it made me feel like I was holding her back somehow. I tried to imagine my mom in the jungle, her hair cut short and surrounded by children, their little, dirty hands all over her, grasping for her face. Would she let them handle her and fight over who got to sit in her lap? Would she like them better because they were brown and poor?

I was dying for a hamburger and was willing to break my silence for one. There was an urgency to my hunger. What I really wanted was the Big Mac and fries, but we were never allowed. Abigail and I knew that the rule was to keep the cost as low as possible so as not to stress my parents out. So that meant ordering the hamburger even though I'd at least choose cheeseburger, but that was more money. Again, if I knew that my dad wouldn't flash his jittery eyes or gawk at the green numbers on the cash register, I would get a two all beef patties, special sauce, lettuce cheese, pickles, onions on a sesame seed bun.

The idea of the sauce alone made my mouth water. I would gear myself up to beg even though this felt risky. There were only so many times I would ask before I would receive a sharp look from my mother.

We made it to the car. I asked once in the parking lot.

Abigail was waiting, staring out the window. The noise and the heat mixed with my hunger and made my head want to explode.

"Keep the window closed!" My dad yelled. "The A/C can't work if the windows are open."

"Can we go to McDonald's?" I tried again in sweet, softer voice still waiting for a definitive reply.

I looked over at Abigail for support. "Don't you want to go?" I whispered hoping she would be on my side.

"I don't care."

Abigail looked out the window. It felt like she saw my desperation and intentionally acted as if she didn't care. Something about me trying to meet this need was offensive to her. How could she not be hungry? Why didn't she want McDonald's? Why was I the only one starving?

Abigail was older by two years and always had the ear of my parents. She had them wrapped around her finger and I learned that if I really needed something, if it was imperative, I had to get my sister on board. Every so often she'd throw a curve ball and would show me some kindness and help me with my cause. Sometimes she'd even wrap her arm around me and pull me in for a tight hug.

"You aren't hungry?" I looked over at her in the seat next to me. She kept her eyes on the flow of people still exiting the church and getting into their cars as we pulled out of the parking lot.

"I ate breakfast." She said without turning her head.

I was screwed. My dad would never agree if it were just me asking.

"Mom, do you have any gum?" I tried.

She dove a hand into her purse, rattling through the contents. I heard plastic against plastic. A compact rubbing against a brush scratching on her wallet, keys, lipstick, a few pens.

She tore a stick of wintergreen in half with the silver wrapper still on and handed it to me. "We'll make something at home. I just need to stop at Shoppers for a few things."

I succumbed to the weight of my body, letting my head fall to the back of the seat. A trip to the warehouse grocery store after church was never less than a two-hour event. I leaned my forehead against the window and tried not to cry out of hunger pains and frustration.

It was Abigail that was the last one to slam the car door with a "What's wrong with you?"

I slid my feet under the seat in front of me and kicked them up and down in a rapid pattern. I wasn't taking in regular breaths and my headache grew worse. Tears streamed. Rage. I told them I was staying in the car with the windows down.

I was silent when they finally made their way back to the car one hour and forty-three minutes later. I wanted them to notice how silent I was. I wanted them to feel my anger, my eyes burring holes in the backs of their heads.

No one said a word to me.

We drove home in silence, the anger still boiling inside of me as I considered the confines of the back of the car. I had sweated through my shirt and felt frustrated enough that I started pushing on my mom's seat in front of me with my foot.

"Stop pushing my seat!" She snapped.

I pushed one more time.

When we got home, we had to put away the groceries. I looked for any treat to satiate my hunger and anger, but it was the same old stuff – oatmeal, bread, orange juice, apples, lettuce, mustard, mayonnaise, canned beans, canned green beans, canned peaches, canned tomatoes, canned chicken noodle soup, canned tomato soup, canned tuna, coffee grinds, coffee filters, dish detergent, toilet paper, and one box of All Bran.

No chips. No cereal. Never any snacks.

My mom made tuna sandwiches.

"I hate tuna." I said to her face with a scowl. I was angry and hoped it felt like a slap.

I grabbed an apple from the plastic grocery bag, turned from the kitchen and went to my room. I shut and locked the door. The tears streamed again as I bit into the red, sour apple.

Sundays were the hardest day of the week because I would spend hours upon hours in my room. I wasn't sure when I would emerge. Today my pride would not let me. I would wait for dinner. I would shut down my stomach and wait.

I finished the apple and placed the core in my trashcan. I hoisted myself onto the big bed and lay down facing the headboard that reached almost all the way to the ceiling. I rocked my body like a fish starting at my arched back, to my head and back down letting the momentum I created smash my heels on the headboard creating a loud thud. I did it over and over and over again until I wasn't able to feel the anger in my throat.

This exercise quieted me down and I fell asleep. When I woke up, the daylight from the windows was fading. I could smell something cooking and promised myself that even if it was liver, I would eat it. I opened my bedroom door and emerged. I was going to try again.

I walked down the stairs and into the kitchen, relieved at a different view than the four walls of my bedroom. I had been in my room for almost an entire day. I never heard anyone coming or going from beyond my door. My face was numb, my eyes puffy from sleep and crying and my chest felt heavy with sadness that no one came to check on me.

My mother stood at the counter by the phone in a pink polyester slip. Bare legs, bare arms, bare feet and a pit of cleavage. She was casually laughing with someone on the phone.

I felt my throat tighten as I looked at the lace trim on her bedroom attire and felt my body stiffen. On Sundays my mom and dad would go into their bedroom and lock the door. The house was quieter than usual at this time and I felt the awkwardness in the air. She would come out after an hour and traipse around the house in whatever silk thing she had put on.

I was sickened by her immodesty. It made me feel like we were all in compliance with what I thought was obviously meant to be private. She brought it out into the open belly of the kitchen, and I seethed at her dripping with post sex bliss. My mother followed her own rules.

She hung up the phone and pecked away at her sticky notes with a pen.

I looked at her with disgust, "What are you wearing?"

I wanted her to acknowledge how uncomfortable I was. I wanted her to see that this was not appropriate. I wanted her to go up and put on some pants.

She laughed and looked up from her scribbling.

"What?" she said.

I wanted to rush her, push her to the ground and start beating her smiling face. Instead, I turned around, gripped my stomach and went back up to my room. When Abigail knocked on my door to tell me dinner was ready, I told her I was not hungry. She shrugged and walked back down the hallway. I heard them talking and laughing together and realized they did not miss me.

7

I threw up every morning before school.

After putting on my uniform and brushing my teeth, I walked down the carpeted stairs and even before stepping on to the linoleum flooring, I felt the upset coursing through my body. It would start at my neck, grow with a stubborn heat up my face and head, throwing me off balance and then shoot straight back to my stomach. My palms would sweat as I scurried to the bathroom just off the kitchen. I would fling the toilet seat up with the clink of porcelain on porcelain, bend my body over the bowl and retch until my eyes watered and sweat gathered at my temples. This happened every, single morning for an entire school year.

I couldn't remember how it all started. I imagine one day I just feel queasy after breakfast. The first few times I was late for the bus and felt the eyes of all the kids on me, watching me carefully with questioning eyes. I slid into my seat as quietly as possible.

"Why are you so late?"

"I'm sorry. I know."

It was Gregory, a fourth grader. I was so painfully shy that the question and attention mortified me. I would not let it happen again. The next morning, I got up ten minutes earlier and made myself a bowl of cereal. I felt a pinch in my stomach and anxiously checked the microwave clock. I analyzed the feeling of the milk making its way down my esophagus. A twinge of a cramp and the texture of the wheat in my teeth sent me running to the bathroom. I let myself cry at the shock that this was happening again. The mess before me floating in the water, brown and sticky. The appearance of the contents of my stomach made my belly pump. I leaned over and fought with my body willing it to stop. It didn't. I vomited again before running out into the hallway to see if the bus was there outside the window. It was just pulling up. I heard the squeak of the breaks as I slid my backpack on.

My mom was not out of bed yet so there was no one to say goodbye to. I shut the door quietly and walked up the drive, trying to push down the nausea. I could not throw up on the bus. I will not throw up on the bus.

The next morning the same thing happened. I realized it was now a vicious pattern that had blown so big and out of my control. I didn't know how to stop the beast inside of me that was clanging to get out.

I prepared myself to throw up in any setting or circumstance. I kept a plastic grocery bag in my pocket knowing how embarrassing it would be to pull out and use but eased by the comfort that I could contain exposing my disgusting insides. I started chewing my cheeks until they bled.

Every morning I counted the houses on the way to school to try to occupy my brain. I knew every turn and every bump the bus made. I knew the stop lights and the traffic patterns. I hyperfocused on the kids near me and made-up stories about their home lives. I made up the rule that if I could make it through the bus ride, I could make it through school.

Nick and Hunter were the best distractions. The bus driver, Mrs. White, would pull up to their house and honk, knowing that the brothers needed the reminder. They were clearly still sleeping when we arrived, and I watched as the upstairs bedroom light would flick on. I could see inside. Bunk beds and sheets and two boys tearing around the room. I smiled, loving how they collected themselves in such a rambunctious and chaotic manner while I was now getting up an hour early to make time for my morning purge. Sometimes Nick would sit next to me, shoving a frozen waffle into his mouth.

"Hi." He'd say swinging his backpack around and onto his lap.

I heard rumor that he had a crush on me. He was in my same class at school and I would always seek me out during a break to work on a puzzle with me and a few of the other girls. Nick was a gem and although I didn't like him like him, I loved the attention and kindness he offered me.

I was curious by the clear lack of structure at his house and wondered what it would be like living there. He was the only kid I knew that had divorced parents. He lived with his dad and his older brother. And although there was no parent there to wake the boys or ensure they caught the bus to school, I imagined there was also freedom behind the front door that allowed for waffles and bunkbeds.

Nick was a constant during those elementary school years. He had started at Hope Valley in kindergarten, a year before me. I considered him a neighbor even though we were not in the same neighborhood. However, we both in lived in Great Falls, a twenty-minute bus ride from our school, which was equal to another planet away.

"How did you do on that vocabulary test?" Nick asked.

"I don't remember." I said looking down at my hands. I certainly did remember. Six out of ten.

"I hear Mrs. Ericson is going to come in today to talk to us."

"What? Why?"

"No idea. She smells though."

I laughed out loud. "She does smell."

"She smells like onions."

I laughed again and my whole body warmed. I loved Nick for the distraction. I saw him looking down at my hand on the pleather, brown seat and wondered if he wanted to touch it. I would have let him.

I looked back out the window as I felt the bus turn left at the stop light. We were only a few blocks from school.

The bargaining about not throwing up on the bus had worked. If I made it to school without getting sick, I would be able to get through school without getting sick. I convinced myself of this and committed myself to it. This belief was the only way I made it through the fifth grade and the rest of my stay at Hope Valley.

8

Hope Valley Christian School. That was the full, proper name. It was a conservative Christian school started in the home of Mary and Paul Ericson. When the couple outgrew their space, they bought a building and turned it into a school with the help of the teachers and the students' parents, who were required to dedicate one weekend a month to maintain the property. I recall my dad painting the hallways with a can of white paint and my mom scrubbing the brown baseboards with a yellow sponge.

The school had a front office and several classrooms that ran along an L-shape, each one with big, bright windows. The back yard had several picnic tables, one swing set and a basketball court. There was also a small blacktop at the bottom of a grassy hill that we were allowed to play kick ball on.

There was no art classroom, no music classroom, no gym and no cafeteria. We were required to bring our own lunches, with the suggestion that they were to be healthy. There was something eerily quiet about the school with its white walls. The hallways were dark and the only natural light came in from the windows in the classrooms and I craved it like water.

The teachers were mostly women that had the same, sterile straight mouths as my mother. They all wore skirts that went past their knees and were required to teach us reading, math and science. Mrs. Lynch would come into each classroom starting in first grade to teach Latin.

Each classroom sat about twenty students in desks attached to a seat by a metal pole, a cubby underneath to store books and notebooks. At the front of each room was a modest desk for the teacher and a blackboard that covered the entire wall behind her.

When I first started Hope, Mrs. Ericson came into the class every other week to work on reading with a small group. I remember sitting next to her reading from a red weathered, cloth-bound book with tiny print. I was so nervous and read slowly in order to get every, single word correct. I was distracted by the wooden paddle that hung by the door and was unclear when they would use it on us. Would I get paddled if I missed a word? Five words? How many mistakes did I get before I would be hit?

9

My morning ritual of vomiting grew worse week by week. It became a horrible, dark secret. There were times that I fanaticized about someone coming to my recue and making it all better and other times I agonized about someone finding out. I felt out of control, like I was dying. I didn't know how to stop. I didn't know how to tell my parents. My morning purge had become a shameful secret and I was suffocated by embarrassment. What was wrong with me? Why couldn't I control my body? Would I ever stop throwing up?

My mind went down a long and winding road of panic at the thought of throwing up at school, at the grocery store, at church, or at a friend's house. Vomit was everywhere with its large, loose chunks and offensive stench. I wouldn't be able to go anywhere ever again without the threat of my insides coming out. I didn't know how to fix this.

I hid it for months, shutting the powder room door and running the faucet to drown out the noise of my heaving. I prayed to Jesus and God and the Holy Ghost for my stomach to settle. My weight dropped considerably. My uniform was loose, and the skirt refused to stay put and I was forced to hold it up on the playground at recess. I waited for my mom to notice and come to my rescue.

It was January when I decided to tell my parents. The weight had become too great to face alone and even though I dreaded the conversation, I could not keep the pain in my stomach a secret any longer. I was scared that my mom was going to be angry and I worried about upsetting my dad. She was working as a teacher at a preschool in Vienna during the day and when she came home, she didn't want to be bothered. My dad talked about his commute around the beltway and came home each night, put his briefcase with the pig-skin lined interior in the hallway and watched the news until dinner. There was no time for my throw up.

I decided it would be easier if my mom discovered my retching on her own. Then she would believe me. She'd take me seriously. She would know that I wasn't a liar or a fake. On Monday morning I left the bathroom door open so she could hear me from upstairs.

Maybe she would come running to my side if she heard it herself. Maybe she would be able to fix the problem that had taken over my life. I waited, hanging over the toilet. I wiped the bile from my lips, shut off the bathroom light and went to sit on the stoop to wait for my bus. She didn't hear me. I wasn't loud enough.

On Tuesday I slammed my hands on the toilet seat and groaned.

On Wednesday I was nauseous, frightened of telling her and angry that she had not come rushing to me to hold back my hair.

"Mom?" I said quietly as she stood by the phone in her pajamas.

"Mmm."

"I don't feel well."

She reached her hand out and put the back of it to my forehead without lifting her eyes. "You don't feel warm."

"No, I'm sick to my stomach."

"Oh?"

She looked up, her mystic green eyes staring with the small black part in the center beaded like a bullet pointed right at me. I waited and grew anxious.

"I threw up."

"Where?"

"In the toilet."

"Show me."

"I flushed it."

"Ok, sit down at the table until the bus comes."

"I keep throwing up. Every day."

"What's wrong?" She stared at me, bullets poised to strike. "Are you ok?"

I was scared to tell her I wasn't OK. I didn't know if I was OK.

"I'm throwing up every morning before school." I said quietly looking down at the floor.

She sighed, put her pencil down and sat across from me on one of the kitchen chairs. "Are you nervous about something?"

"I don't know."

"Do you think you're sick?"

"No."

"Did you eat anything?"

"Mini wheats at the beginning. But, now I can't eat breakfast."

She stared at me like she was waiting for an answer to come to her or through me or from God above.

"Ok." She said still staring.

I broke eye contact and glanced up at the microwave clock. I looked back at her hoping she had something to offer me, an answer. My eyes pleaded with her eyes. I needed her to understand my urgency without having to explain my desperation. I needed her to sit down me, cancel her day, cancel school, wrap me in a soft blanket and lay me down. I wanted her to pet my hair and tell me that she would do whatever it took to find a solution to my pain. I needed rescuing.

"Well, let's pray about it. Then I'll walk you out to the bus."

10

On Thursday I threw up. I didn't flush the toilet so I could show her. I felt braver and walked into the kitchen. She wasn't there. Instead, there was a note on the table that read:

> *"The Lord is my light and my salvation; whom shall I fear? the Lord is the strength of my life; of whom shall I be afraid?"*

It was printed neatly in my dad's all caps handwriting, bold and black and written on graph paper torn from the pad he carried in his briefcase. My mom told my dad. She probably talked to him about it at night while in bed. I often heard them whispering in the dark hours and could imagine her telling him about my stomach. I felt betrayed. It was my shameful secret that I shared with only my mom, and she exposed me by telling my father. I felt blinding anger, the heat incinerating any trust I had in the woman I thought could reach down into the canyon, pass me her hand and pull me up to safety. Not only did she not save me inches from my death, but she passed off my rescue to my dad who tried saving me with a Bible verse. I didn't want a Bible verse and I didn't want a prayer. I wanted to stop throwing up.

I read the passage and waited for my stomach to settle. I was willing to see if the words were magic. I wanted something to change. If they both now knew, I would accept all help. I wanted someone to talk to. I wanted someone to take me seriously. I wanted a doctor. I wanted the hospital. I wanted help. I wanted breakfast. I wanted to eat something and fill my belly so I could rid myself of this empty feeling.

I picked up a small, plastic card that was laid next to the verse.

Take this card and hold it dear.

When you read it know He is near.

The capital "He" was God. It was from God delivered through my parents. It looked like something she had pulled out of the onion sliced pages of her Bible. The corners were worn and the plastic coating pealing. I didn't even know if she meant to give it to me. I didn't ask for permission to take it, but I did. She didn't tell me the little card was a gift for me, but I knew it was the only thing that I was being offered and I dared to hope it would work. I grabbed the card and slid it into the front pouch of my backpack. Maybe the card was magic.

11

It was February and I thought God was preparing me for death. Every night I would make sure my underwear was folded neatly in my bottom dresser drawer and my journal tucked safely underneath my mattress. I would go to bed thinking I'd wake up in Heaven. I didn't mind the idea of it. I had recently been asked by a neighbor if I could take care of their Doberman pincher in the afternoons and if death didn't come to me while I slept, it was sure meet me in the yard when I was trying to play fetch with the temperamental canine. I thought waking up on the beachy shores of Heaven would be a relief. My parents would have come in and see me all blue and dead, but I think me being far away in Heaven would be best for them too.

And yet, every day I woke up.

Sometimes there was a new Bible verse scribbled on another full piece of graphing paper on the kitchen table and other times it was the recycled one from the day before. I read the passage, threw up in the bathroom, rinsed my mouth out at the sink and went outside to wait for the bus. Day after day I did this. Read the passage, threw up in the bathroom, rinsed off and got on the bus. Twenty-seven minutes later and we arrived at school.

Mrs. White parked the bus, which was actuality a work van spray-painted school bus yellow. However, it was embarrassingly small and looked nothing like a school bus. I'm not even sure it was legal when they pulled out the forward-facing seats and installed two parallel benches in order to fit more kids.

The "bus" door opened and one by one we were let off and funneled into the school. My fifth-grade room faced the parking lot and I was grateful for the two large windows that looked outside into a forest that opened up under the cool blue sky.

My teacher's name that year was Mrs. Brayburn and she was new. Her hair was short and curly, the kind of curls that appeared while catching the breeze on a sandy beach. It was a shade of red that reminded me of cherry-flavored, translucent Jolly Ranchers and only came from a box at CVS. Mrs. Brayburn was the only female teacher I knew that wore make up at Hope Valley. And not just make up, but green eyeliner. When I got close enough to her face, I could see the perfect line she had drawn from the inner pink corner of her eye across the lid to the opposite side. She stenciled a similar green line just under the short lashes.

She smiled too. She had big, white teeth and rose-tinted cheeks that sparkled slightly under the florescent lighting. Sometimes I would go up to her desk just to get close enough so I could smell the floral perfume that danced around her body and hung on her clothes. If I closed my eyes I could imagine her putting her arms around me, rubbing my back until I let out the breath I was holding.

Mrs. Brayburn's daughter, Peggy, was in our class, creating an interesting dynamic. There were times that I think Peggy forgot she was at school. We laughed when she called Mrs. Brayburn "Mom" and braced ourselves when she lost her temper, her face burning red, with her mother. It was a welcomed distraction from the tense environment that the rest of the class was used to.

We started each day standing to the side of our desks and singing three songs. We were allowed to request our favorites, but they were limited to those we had learned growing up at Hope. It always felt too early in the morning to sing and some of us would just pretend and mouth the words hoping they would not get caught. Others, like Peggy, belted out every single syllable in order to let her neighbors know that she was the best at singing. I thought singing at school was weird and I hate the songs. I felt like singing next to our desk was a lame excuse for a music lesson. The songs themselves made me feel like I was a toddler. They were baby songs. Joshua and Jericho and hand movements.

When we were a few months into school, Mrs. Brayburn taught us a new song called, *"If I had a Hammer"* and it was definitely was not a Christian song. It was a pleasant song about kindness and hammers, but I got the feeling that if Mrs. Ericson ever knew we were singing songs about peace and love she would not approve. I worried that Mrs. Brayburn would get fired if someone heard us singing from the hallway.

Mrs. Brayburn also never paddled anyone in our class or sent a child to see Mrs. Ericson in the principal's office or duck taped us to our chairs like all my other teachers. I watched her closely to see if she ever grew upset enough to threaten these things and when she didn't, I thought it might be nice to even go home with her. What was she like at home if she were this nice at Hope?

Once the songs were sung, we said the Pledge of Allegiance and then Mrs. Brayburn lead us in a prayer for the day. We were then allowed to sit. My desk was behind Becky Wallinsky, who was blonde and much taller than I was. I was so tiny that there were third graders that were now taller. I was reminded of my unacceptable height on picture day when we had to line up by size. I hated picture day and I wanted to scratch out the eyes of the kids at recess that yelled, "Back to back," expecting me to press my back against another student to see who was taller. Why were people so surprised that I was short? Why did it matter to them? Was something indeed wrong with me?

I sat in the second row and felt a bit of shelter behind Becky. The wall was to the left and May, who rode my same bus, sat to my right. In the mornings, she would lick her hand and pat her younger brother's rough hair down. It was motherly and kind of gross at the same time.

May was the smartest in the room and knew the answers to all the questions. She was always reading books on Hitler that were twice as thick as any of the books that the rest of us were reading.

"Hi Becky." I said walking by her desk.

"Hi," she sighed.

I said it every morning and every morning she signed back to me like all of this school-business was my fault. She always looked tired and kind of sad. Maybe she didn't like me, but I always got the feeling that she was upset even before she made it to her desk in the morning.

"How was your night?" I pursued.

"Fine." She sighed and put her head in the palm of her hand ending our conversation.

Becky was new to our class and I wasn't used to her. I was used to the small, sweet, quiet kids. Becky was different. She didn't care about our unwritten rules.

Most of the kids in my class had been together since first grade. There were a few that wouldn't come back the following year and we usually added a couple each year, but there was a core of ten of us, that had been together for the last five years and we were tightly bonded. We knew everything about one another. We went to each other's birthday parties and knew each other's secrets. We cheered each other on when we were favored in class and feared for the one that held the teacher's ire for the day. We all thought we were going to marry one another and never imagined leaving each other. Ever.

We knew Megan got in trouble for talking too much and often had her nose put in the corner, Samuel was the boy that was always in trouble and paddled more times than I could count over the years. His father was also the fourth-grade teacher at Hope, Mr. Wagner. We knew Matthew liked Wendy, and Stacey was always apt to cry and repeat "sorry" too many times when she was anxious. Patrick was the cutest boy in the class, Jacob Miller was the second and the new boy, Aaron, was probably third. Melen, the only black student in our class, was the fastest runner in kickball and Mr. Wagner used to say she ran like a jackrabbit. Nathan always had boogers in his nose and smelled so much that no one wanted to stand near him. Jonah was the boy that kept getting out of his chair in third grade and Mr. Wall duck taped his wrists to the desk so he couldn't move. Katie Harper was the tallest girl with the long, straight hair and also had six siblings. She had huge birthday parties where her mom let us stay up all night long without supervision if we wanted to. Chrissy's house smelled like oregano and she lived with her grandmother who always wore slippers in the house. And then there was Dove, my best friend. Tall, blonde, blue-eyed, beautiful best friend.

I was the shortest girl and felt loved by the boys and cherished by the girls. My friendships kept me alive. We were each other's entire world and we couldn't imagine this changing. Ours was a deep love, but this was the first year that things seemed different. Something was in the air and a shift was happening. Next year was sixth grade and we would be in a different hallway. Mrs. Lynch taught sixth grade and the idea of moving closer to a full day alone with her felt like edging our way out to the guillotine. I didn't know how I would survive her. I wouldn't survive her.

12

"Pull out your *Learning English* workbooks, Class," Mrs. Brayburn said. "We are going to work independently on pages 41 – 49. You have about an hour to complete these pages and if you don't it's homework."

The class worked quietly, driven to finish before the hour was up. The only student to move was Samuel, who had trouble sitting still. For the last five years, he would get up in a frenzy, dropping books, tripping over feet and stumbling to the bathroom located near the front of the classroom. He would have to get up numerous times, but no one was distracted by it anymore. Megan sneezed and Grace blew her nose. Otherwise, we were as quiet as mice, trained to be that way.

I thought about lunch for the entire morning like I did every day. The clock above the door was the only thing besides the chalk board that hung on the bare, cream-colored walls. I looked at the time and watched the second hand slowly creep toward the six. Lunch was at twelve-thirty.

"Ok, lunch time. Bye." She called out.

We each reached into our desks to grab our lunches, climbed out of our seats and fled the classroom by way of the door at the back. I grabbed my brown, crinkled bag greedily. It wasn't until I was outside and sitting next to Katie on one side and Godslove on the other that I felt the weight of the sack. It was cold and wet and had a tear in the bottom. I lifted my fingers to my nose to smell the liquid that had pooled and realized in an instant what the offensive smell was. Pickle. My mom had packed pickles again. No amount of baggies, without the precious zip lock, kept pickle juice from escaping.

"Eww. What is that?" Katie asked.

I had eyes staring at me for both directions, their lips twisted in disgust as they peered over at my soggy bag.

I grabbed the spears dripping their sour liquid over my palm and ran them over to the trash can. I rubbed my hands together anxiously, hoping at all costs that the smell would dissolve. It didn't. I went back to my seat and peeled open the rest of the bag. There was no napkin. I knew there wouldn't be. I could have gone back into the classroom and into the bathroom to wash my hands, but I did not want to risk losing my seat in the middle of the gaggle of girls who were loitering near our picnic bench ready to slide into an empty spot.

I fished around in the wilted, torn bag until I felt the sandwich and a small bag of carrots. I pulled the half sandwich from the folded baggie and peeled the two pieces of wheat bread apart. Mayonnaise. No turkey, no cheese, no lettuce, and no tomato. It was a mayonnaise sandwich. I was equally embarrassed, but my huger won out and I shoved the stiff bread into my mouth and then the carrot sticks one by one trying to fill my stomach so as not to feel the pinch of hunger pains that afternoon. I felt a pang of sadness thinking of my mom having to peel and cut the carrots. I know that took her extra time, but I was equally disappointed that she wasn't willing to buy the deli turkey from behind the counter that I craved. I didn't know what it was like to have a turkey and cheese sandwich. If I wasn't given a mayonnaise sandwich, she packed egg salad with its weird mustard color or grape jelly and cream cheese that refused to spread and instead lay like chunks of lard on the same crusty bread. Each sandwich variety carried its own disappointment.

My only hope was Katie Harper. I don't know if Katie felt sorry for me, or if she wanted to be my best friend, or if I just looked like a sad puppy dog, but she always gave me the last square of her microwave cheese pizza. Always. Every day. She'd unwrap the foil revealing four squares of cheese pizza and ate all three leaving behind a red stain from the sauce on her lips. I sat as close to her as possible and smiled my brightest.

"Do you want this piece?"

She'd hold up the fourth square to me.

"Are you sure you don't want it?" I'd ask shyly as my mouth watered.

"No, take it. I'm full."

I died a little as I reached for the piece and ate it slowly, letting it melt like butter on my tongue. It tasted like the Tombstone frozen pizzas that my mom would buy for special occasions. The crust was white and thin and the sauce salty. The cheese was shredded and melted in little strips across the slice. It was a piece of heaven in my mouth and I loved her for it. Katie shared this fourth piece of microwave pizza with me every day from first grade until I left Hope at the end of fifth grade. She had no idea how she saved me for all those years. I always felt like I owed her more than I could repay.

13

"Well, now, that's just a stupid answer."

I knew I had risked everything when raising my hand. I also knew that ten students ahead of me had answered the Latin questions correctly and were invited to go up to the front of the class and finger pick a single jellybean from the same cellophane bag and she brought back class after class. If you were invited up to the front it was like you won an Emmy. A Nobel Peace Prize. The Lottery. It was never about the jellybean. It was about the walk past the desks, past the classmates and standing opposite Mrs. Lynch to pick a candy. The student had one moment face to face with her and if you were one of the lucky ones, you needed to make it count. She didn't remember names, but she remembered the faces of the smart kids.

My eyes dropped to my hands resting in my lap. It would be the last time I would ever raise my hand in a classroom until my senior year of college.

I thought I had the right answer. We were reading Virgil's *Aeneid* and interpreting it line by line. I raised my hand when we made it into Book 2. My palms were sweating, and my heart beat faster as my hand climbed into the air. This was the line I had been waiting for.

"I rejoice with the Greeks."

It was as if she reached out her hand and pounded me in the face with her fist. Her words hurt with physical pain. I never would have raised my hand if I thought I was so wrong. She was right, I was so stupid.

"Anyone else?"

May raised her hand and answered it correctly, "I fear the

Greeks, even when they bring gifts."

I felt like May had betrayed me by correcting my mistake. I watched her walk up to the desk for the second time that period and pick out a jellybean. She even had the confidence to *choose* a flavor. I would have just grabbed whatever was on the top and been grateful.

Even my mother didn't trust Mrs. Lynch. That's how scary she was. My mom had pulled Abigail from Hope before sixth grade, knowing that she was going to have her the following year. We had not discussed it, but I knew she would move me too to public school too. I don't know what I was more scared about. Leaving Hope to go to the local public school five-minutes from our house or graduating to Mrs. Lynch's class. Both felt like a death sentence. I would do anything to stay out of Mrs. Lynch's gaze. She was tiny with curly black hair and pale skin, perpetuating the rumor that she was part vampire. Her mouth curved downwards, and I was always shocked when I saw her smile or even laugh when speaking to another teacher. The expression looked so foreign on her face, like a tiger trying to smile and only able to bare their teeth. I also wanted nothing more than to impress her. If I were smart, she would like me. If she liked me, I would be safe.

Every day after lunch Mrs. Lynch would walk into our classroom carrying her leather bound, navy grade book in hand and throw it on the desk. Slap! The book hit the wood and we all sat up a little straighter.

"Pass your homework to the person on your right."

The class shuffled papers and I waited for the far-right aisle to bring theirs to our side of the room. I stared down at Megan's Latin vocabulary. A huge wave of relief washed over me as I looked at her penmanship and the spaces where she was missing answers. She had even written the words out in blue ink instead of pencil. It was worse than mine. May had my homework in her hands and carefully checked off each word that was correct as Mrs. Lynch called out the answers. We were asked to define twenty Latin words as well as look up and find another word that came from the Latin root word with definition.

I was always excited when I saw the same word in Latin as I did in English in the *Webster's Dictionary*. It was a match! May raised her hand.

"What if the person wrote the same word as the Latin word?"

"Well, now, that's just stupid." Mrs. Lynch said. "Minus one."

May used a red pen. She was on Mrs. Lynch's side. When it was time to pass back our papers May had written a large "-20" on the top of my paper and circled it twice. I took the paper in my hands, glanced at the corrections and folded it in half so no one would see. Becky turned around in her chair, "What did you get?"

"I don't know."

"Show me."

"It doesn't matter."

I pulled my stomach muscles in and wished that she would just turn back around.

"Moving along." Mrs. Lynch picked up the grade book. She went alphabetically student by student, calling out their names and asking for the grade they had just received. I bowed my head and waited for her to call my name. She never got it right and I never corrected her.

"Christian?"

"-20." I said.

"F."

"Becky?"

"-25"

"Seriously? How does anyone miss almost the entire assignment?"

"I didn't have time to finish." Becky said.

"Well, that will do it." Mrs. Lynch moved on. She didn't care and either did Becky.

14

My first crush was on a boy named Jacob Casey. He had six brothers and one baby sister - Simon, Joseph, Jacob, Matthew, Micah, Able and baby Ester. There was a handful of kids that came from large families at Hope and I remember feeling that they were embraced by the Ericson's, the founders, more than the rest of us.

Jacob Casey made me laugh. He made me feel seen and when we had to stand in line by size and I had to stand in the very back, he always came to tell me a joke, but I think he was really checking on me. He was silly like the other boys and ran as fast as he could down the lawn when we were released at recess. But he always found his way back to the swings where I was playing with the rest of the girls. He was sweet with big brown eyes. He wrote me notes that he folded in little, complicated triangles that I had to work to open.

At recess, Jacob Casey would invite me behind the tall trees that lined the fence near the side of the school. He'd hold my hand and even though his was sweaty from the heat of the day, I liked it. He told me what his room was like at home and how he shared it with four of his brothers. He didn't seem to mind though. Jacob Casey didn't seem to get worked up about anything. He didn't even cry when he was told to go to the front of the room for a paddling last year. I remember wanting to scream out at Mr. Wagner that he wasn't the one that had used the bad word on the playground. It was Samuel.

"Turn around." Mr. Wagner said calmly as he grabbed the wood paddle off the wall where it hung on a nail. I looked into my teacher's eyes and thought I saw delight, a smirk tickling his lips.

Jacob Casey turned around and put his hands flat on the desk, his backside to the rest of the class. We all grew silent and braced ourselves for the two slaps as if we were all being hit at the same time.

He didn't do it. He didn't do it. It was Samuel. It was Samuel!
Slap!
Slap!

Mr. Wager said nothing. Jacob Miller said nothing. I said nothing.

I saw Jacob Casey's head bow as he worked his way back to his desk. He was not silly that day. He packed up his bag when we were released and left by the back door out to the parking lot where his mother and brothers gathered to be taken home. I wanted to run to him and ask him if it hurt and tell him I knew it was Samuel and I was so so sorry. I should have said something. I should have told Mr. Wagner. I should have opened my mouth and yelled, "He didn't do anything wrong!"

Jacob Casey's face crushed me.

I'm not sure Mr. Wager enjoyed it, but he certainly didn't seem affected by spanking someone else's child. He had done it enough times to Samuel and a few of the other boys, but never Jacob Casey.

"This is what happens when you choose to disobey God's rules."

As if God wrote in the 11th Commandment, do not say "shit" when you miss a basket on the basketball court at recess.

Mr. Wagner was also the teacher that told us never to drink soft drinks even though we watched him crack open a fresh can of Coke every day after recess. He would flick a few peanuts in the can and jerk his head back, swallowing hard. He said soda would rot your teeth and even brought in a few of Samuel's back molars that he had lost and performed a little science experiment with them by leaving the teeth in a plastic cup of Coke for six weeks until they, indeed, turned black and rotted out.

One day in the spring of our fourth-grade year, Jacob Casey

was gone. He left a note on his desk saying he'd miss us all and the teacher told us that he had moved to another school. We looked around at each other sad and confused that we had lost one of our own, that he had left our little island either for safety or for another private school. He didn't tell any of us he was leaving. He didn't tell me. The other boys in the class were quick to try and give me the same kind of affection, but they were not Jacob Casey. I felt a sense of loss, like something had been stolen out from under me.

Jacob Casey was the sun shining through the window and giving me hope in what was a very dark prison. Something fell apart in me when he left, and I didn't know how I was going to put it back together. I felt like I was left on an island in the middle of the sea and the winds were whipping uncontrollably around me. A ship came to steal him away in the night and take him far away. I never heard from him again.

15

I climbed down the stairs of the bus and scurried down the long driveway with excitement. No one was home after school most days. I opened the door with the key from my backpack and felt the air conditioning with welcomed relief. I was starving and almost giddy that I had the entire house to myself. I made my way to the pantry and pulled out a crinkled, half eaten bag of tortilla chips, pushed up onto my tippy-toes and turned on the broiler on the top oven pushing the knob until it clicked. I watched as the spirals went from a matte black to burnt red before grabbing the salsa and shredded cheese from the refrigerator.

I found the same little baking sheet I used every day in the drawer below the stove and began placing the triangle-shaped chips in clean rows, careful not to overlap. I used a tiny spoon made for sugar and put a dollop of salsa carefully onto each chip. The cheese was sprinkled last and I could feel my sore stomach growling with anticipation. I dragged the kitchen stool over to the stove and cautiously picked up the little tray and slid it into the hot oven. I clicked the interior light on and watched as the cheese melted into a gooey layer. Just when the edges of the chips began to brown, I turned the broiler off, put on an oven mitt and delicately pulled the tray from the heat. It took every ounce of patience to wait for my precious snack to cool and most of the time I burned my tongue willingly by taking a bite. The salt from the salsa and chips and the cozy cheese met me with the same comfort every time. I closed my eyes and crunched each bite with religious gratitude. My breath came back to me and I mellowed into the quiet of the house. I had exactly an hour before Abigail would walk through the door and my mom following in a bustle of chaos. I didn't want to think about it their impending arrival. I wanted to savor every minute of quiet and cool the house had to offer.

I went and sat on the bare floor of the family room, its walls blanketed in honey wood paneling, and turned on the tiny television that sat on a gold-colored TV tray by the brick fireplace. It was a small black and white television with silver bug antennas that I had to maneuver back and forth to eliminate the fuzz on the screen.

I found *Lavern and Shirley* on Channel 5, crisscrossed my legs and placed the tray of chips in front of me. I was still in my uniform, the wool scratching at my bent knees, but I didn't dare move and waste my solitude.

My stomach felt warm and soothed from my snack. I pushed my legs out in front of me and leaned back on my arms, satisfied for the first time that day. A smile crept to my face every time I saw Laverne in a shirt with her trademark "L" on the corner. Whose idea was it to put an "L" on every shirt she wore? I had never seen this before or since but loved that she claimed the "L" it as her own. There was no mistaking who she was. Lavern with an L.

I was nearing the end of *The Andy Griffith Show* when I heard the scratch of a key in the door. Metal on metal.

"Why did you lock the door?!" Abigail yelled from the foyer.

I jumped up from my spot on the floor and flicked off the television. My heart beat quicker and I lost the steady pace of breath that settled me in that solitary hour.

I raced into the kitchen and placed the tray in the sink.

"I always lock the door." I said back.

"If you hear me trying to unlock it come open it!"

Her voice was harsh and impatient. I didn't know if I feared her face more or my mother's coming through the front foyer. Abigail dropped her backpack and stomped upstairs to change. I tip-toed up the stairs after her and went into my room, closing the door quietly so that she wouldn't hear.

I looked around my room. I took in the king-sized bed with the large, horizontal wood headboard that went almost to the ceiling fit for an actual king. It was so grand and matched the other pieces of mission-style furniture that my grandfather gave to my parents when they were first married. I inherited the pieces as a toddler only because they fit into the room that I was given near my parents' bedroom. The dresser was enormous. It had a mirror that swung on its hinges and was so large that I couldn't see my own reflection without standing on my trash can. It didn't fit me. The only piece that was the perfect Goldilocks size was the desk. It was the smallest piece in the room with three drawers down the side and a little cubed space for a small chair. I hid treasures in each drawer. The smallest, littlest toys and treasure that I could acquire. In the bottom drawer was the little yellow plastic bear that I stole from my last year at preschool. I never took it out to play with because of the guilt that I felt from stealing it from the bucket full of primary-colored bears. I was so ashamed and sure that God was going to punish me somehow, but I didn't know how to return it. I couldn't throw it away and I couldn't confess what I had done to my parents. The little bear would have to live in the shadows of the desk until I could find a way to destroy it.

I raked open the massive oak dresser drawer with two hands to keep it from falling off the track. I picked out a soft cotton dress that was so thin I could just about see through it. The dress was faded light green like grass found in a meadow with brown dots. The feel of the fabric on my hands was so soothing that I found myself taking in a deep breath of air.

I pulled at the straps of my uniform and unzipped the side of the pleated skirt. I threw it into the corner by the door and began unbuttoning my white Peter Pan collared shirt. Each button could not unfasten fast enough. I was rough and reckless with the garment. Once I was relieved of its hold, I quickly pulled the dress over my head letting it baptize me. Its softness felt like someone had dipped my body in a cool pool in the unbearable heat of summer. I climbed onto the absurdly large bed and placed my head onto my pillow. The pillowcase was even softer than the dress, speckled with little pink and yellow flowers. I never washed it. I never washed the dress either. I was too scared it would never make it back to my room from the loads of laundry washed and folded by my mom.

I pulled my book from the round, antique nightstand that I had discovered in the basement and asked to have in my room. It was black with delicate gold leaf painted in the ridges and one tiny drawer with a round brass pull. I felt grown up with the table next to my bed and loved looking at the vignette with my books stacked on its surface.

I was reading *Wuthering Heights*. I had taken a break from the Nancy Drew books that were lined on the bookshelf in the family room. They were my mom's, cloth bound and tattered at the corners. I had read every one of them and was in love with the mystery and suspense of the stories but forced myself to put down *The Ghost in the Attic* after only three chapters. I loved the story and wanted to find out the ending, but the nagging feeling that God was going to be mad at me for reading about ghosts was too much to bear. It was painful to stop reading the rest of the series, but God would know if I kept up with them and risking that wasn't worth it. God, forgive me.

I read for over an hour, sensing the light dim outside my windows. It was drawing in towards evening time. My mom had come through the door not long ago and I stayed in my room until dinner time. The thought of opening my door and going down into the belly of the kitchen during this dizzying late afternoon timeframe was terrifying. Abigail would be there and make fun of me for wearing the same, old dress. She'd ask when I had washed it last and turn her mouth down in disgust at the thought. My mom would be behind the counter combing through her sticky notes or maybe on the phone.

My Dad walked through the door next. I watched his car pull into the driveway from my bedroom window. I heard the mumblings of voices below me and smelled dinner. I was growing hungry when I had a terrible thought that it could be liver. I prayed we were not having liver. My mom made me sit at the table with the kitchen lights off the last time I refused to eat it. I eventually gave up, plugged my nose and force the grey, bumpy meat down my throat so I could go to bed.

The smell tempted me out of my room. I made my way down the stairs and found the family in the kitchen.

"Why doesn't Christen have to set the table?" exclaimed Abigail.

"She'll clear."

"You better wipe down the table." She glared at me as she put the plates down. "I don't want to see crumbs all over when I do my homework."

I walked over to the stove top and asked my mom what she was making. She looked down at me and stared. I wasn't meant to ask.

"I'm making dinner and you should have a grateful heart."

"Sorry."

I snuck away after taking a look into the metal skillet bubbling with ground meat and noodles. Stroganoff. Phew.

I walked into the living room so as not to get caught doing nothing. I found Minnie basking in the sun. Abilgail's cat was a gorgeous black barn cat that we had brought home from the place where my friend's family boarded her horses. My mom fell in love with the baby kitties and let us take one home. Abigail and I fought the entire way home when Abigail refused to let me hold Minnie.

I saw Minnie lying peacefully near the window in the evening sun and grabbed her, slapping her repeatedly on the hind leg, listening to the satisfying thwomp of my hand against her. I flipped her upside down so I could get a good look at her face gazing up towards me with fear in her eyes. I stuck my fingers in her mouth and pulled at her paws until she meowed in pain.

"Put her down! Put her down!" Abigail screamed.

I glared at my sister and dropped Minnie and remarkably the cat landed on her feet.

"You are so mean. You are going to kill her. What is wrong

with you? Mom!" Abigail screamed, picking up the cat and carrying her carefully into the kitchen.

When Abigail wasn't around to rescue Minnie, I'd throw her down the basement stairs and watched her fly through the air.

"You have to be nice. You can't do that to her." It was my dad. He always said things like this to me about the cat. I think he was the only one that thought me capable of hurting her. I don't think I wanted her dead, but I did want to punish her or maybe I was trying to punish Abigail.

"Dinner's ready!" My mom sang.

We all clambered to the table, scooted in our wood chairs and tried to align the pulled the heavy wood tabletop, which was not secured to the base. I had no idea why this was the case.

"Christen, why don't you pray?" It was my mom asking, a kind of warning in her voice.

I bent my head and closed my eyes.

"Thank you, God, for this day. Thank you for this dinner. Please bless our week. Amen." I ended the prayer and looked up. My mom and dad's eyes were still closed.

"Dear Heavenly Father," my dad interrupted the movement I began to make towards my fork. "Please bless us, Dear Lord. I ask that you bless the work of my hands and mom's hands. Bless the girls. Please guide us and help us to learn your ways, Heavenly Father. We pray these things in Jesus name, Amen."

My prayer was clearly not good enough. It would not make it to God's ears. I was not as close to God as my dad. But I also wasn't convinced that he said anything more than I had. We all began eating mostly in silence. My dad slurped his noodles next to me. I hated the sucking sound and clutched my fork tighter trying to squeeze out the noise with my hand. The noodles were overcooked and fell apart on my fork. I tried to scoop up the ground meat and sauce, letting the pasta slip back onto my plate like a wet slug.

"Mr. Grey pulled me aside at the end of class and said I should sign up for advanced math."

"That's great, Abigail." My dad said looking up at her.

"Wonderful, Hon."

"He said Ashley and I are the best students in the class."

Abigail was naturally smart. She was always a straight A student, tested into the Gifted and Talented program and made middle school sound like a breeze. She never seemed to need help with her work unlike me who could read the same directions over and over and still feel confused. I always found myself rushing to finish my homework just for the relief that came with its completion. I felt my teeth clench and a headache begin behind my eyes with the conviction that I was not smart like my sister. I would never be in GT and would never know that glow on my dad's face. I wanted to finish my food and go back upstairs.

I tuned them out and looked up at my reflection that formed in the window parallel to the kitchen table. It was dark outside, and I could make out my long, blonde hair and the shape of my face. I smiled at myself and tucked a curtain of hair behind my ear.

"See something?" My dad noticed me looking at my reflection and I felt the heat rise to my cheeks in embarrassment.

"Just looking outside." I lied clearly looking at myself, but not wanting to admit it. He too knew I was checking myself out and I felt the familiar sense of shame rise like it had after my sorry attempt at saying grace.

"Christen has to clear and do the dishes." Abigail reminded the family as she got up, scraping her chair along the linoleum flooring. I said nothing, but started clearing the plates, scraping ceramic against ceramic.

I was still hungry but didn't want to go look into the pan on the stove for any scraps. I knew it would be scraped clean except for beads of sauce. I promised myself that I would return to the kitchen for a snack that night when everyone else had fallen asleep. I stacked the dishes on top of each other and grabbed at the forks. I worked in silence until the mess was cleared.

My mom stood at the sink that she had filled with water and a few drops of dish soap. She was careful to clean each plate before setting them on the drying rack on the counter. We had a dish washer right below, but it had been broken since last summer and there were no plans to fix it.

After dinner was cleaned up and my dad had taken out the trash my mom would pronounce, "The kitchen is closed."

The announcement meant we were not allowed back into the kitchen to make a mess. I'm not sure what the punishment would be. I never risked it.

My dad snuck into the family room and turned on the news. Abigail went up to shower and my mom sat down in the living room with a book she was reading for her women's group at church. I slunk back up to my room and started my homework.

I pulled out my math workbook and picked at each problem for way too long. I didn't know my multiplication tables and struggled to finish without looking at the back of the book where the answers were written. It was getting late and I just wanted to be finished so I could sleep. I copied to rest of the answers from the back and slammed the book shut.

I climbed up to my bed and picked up my book preferring to get lost in my novel to thinking about Grace's red marks at school the next day. I read until it was black outside my window refusing to close the shades of the night sky's offering. I head Abigail use the bathroom that we shared across the hall and return to her room, closing the door softly. We used to brush our teeth and wash faces at the same time, but recently I grew self-conscious as she started pointing out the little pimples on my chin or how tangled my hair was.

"Why don't you take care of your hair?"

"I'm growing it out. I want it to be long.

"I know, but you don't even brush it. It's all knotted at the bottom."

I did brush it. I didn't argue back, though, because I knew it wouldn't change what she thought about me or my hair. And maybe I wasn't good at taking care of it. I did know that I wanted to grow it as long as I could, though.

By nine-thirty I could hear the faint snoring of my dad in my parent's bedroom at the end of the hallway. He had come up after Peter Jennings and fell asleep hours before my mom. I was relieved that there was one less person to worry about.

I snuck down the stairs, hoping the last step didn't creak. The lights were all off except for the basement where my mom would exercise down in the main room on the carpet. I was almost giddy as I made my way to the refrigerator. I peeled open the door and let the light stream onto the floor of the kitchen. I pulled out the block of cheese from the vegetable drawer and unwrapped it from the baggie. I retrieved a sharp knife from the lower cabinet where my mom insisted on keeping all the sharp knives, I assume so no burglars could have easy access to them. I pulled out the paring knife and cut three thick slices. Feeling like I had just gotten away with something, I quickly wrapped up the cheese and put it back in the refrigerator. I grabbed the slices and put one in my mouth as I crept back upstairs to my room. The salt from the sharp cheese bit my tongue and soothed my stomach. I would be able to sleep.

16

"Oh Boy."

It was Dad. I could hear him from my room.

"Oh Boy. Oh Boy." He said it over and over again. It was Saturday morning, and he was still in the bathroom. "Oh Boy."

I carefully peeked around my mom's long dresser to see what he was so distressed by. I couldn't quite see into the bathroom, but I imagined him standing in front of the mirror picking at his hair and trying to cover the bald spots. My dad used to ride motorcycles in the desert before we were born. He worked on submarines and helicopters. He loves talking about his days at Sikorsky and how he managed to stay alive during flight as he rode in the little cabin at the bottom of the aircraft. He stopped and they moved when they had babies. He said it was too dangerous.

He sounded so upset.

I was so upset just hearing him. I desperately wanted to make it all right and to fix it. I knew then that if he felt this way inside of his bathroom, he might feel this way outside of his bathroom and if that was the case, then there was no way he was going to see or hear me. My needs wouldn't get met with his being so loud.

"Hi Dad." I yelled out into the hallway when I heard him pass by.

"Hi Chris." He stopped.

"Do you want to see my room?"

"Sure."

He was pleased at my invitation. I showed him my books perfectly lined up and my collection of tiny ceramic animals. My desk was neatly adorned with several notebooks and journals and I had several posters on the walls, including a *Phantom of the Opera* one that he had given me.

"You have done such a nice job in here."

"Thanks, Dad." I smiled at him with affection. I was proud of my space and wanted to show it off.

I pulled out the black jewelry box that he had given me a few years ago and opened it revealing my rings.

"Ahhhh, those need a good polish, don't they?"

"I think they look okay, but if you want to."

"Why don't you pick out a few and we'll put them in the tumbler."

"Sure. I was also hoping that we could work on the Mexican Opal ring later."

"Yes! Let's do that. Let me check with mom to see if there's anything I need to do after the dump."

"Sounds great. Love you, Dad."

He offered his cheek to me and I kissed it.

It was Saturday and on Saturdays I excitedly cleaned my room. While the neighborhood kids were out biking and playing, I stayed inside powdered my carpet, vacuumed and changed my furniture around. I did all this while listening to *Odyssey*, a Focus on the Family radio program.

Mr. Whitaker owned an antique shop in a small town and each story involved an adventure with some younger kids, a problem to solve that would come full circle back to a relatable *Bible* story.

Odyssey aired on the same Christian radio station that my mom listened to. I would tape each broadcast and listen to them over and over again, sometimes just to hear the friendly voices in the air.

My favorite episode was on, the one where Mr. Whitaker time traveled with some church kids to Bethlehem. I pressed play and record simultaneously on my boombox tape player to record the episode and looked around my room. The sun came streaming in my three windows and I took a deep breath in, appreciating the space. Abigail's room was at the end of the hall and she never let much time go by before complaining that I had the bigger room. The downside was that I was right across the hall from the bathroom and I had little privacy unless my door was shut.

I looked at the king bed by the window and decided I wanted to see what it looked like by the door. I planned to move the dresser with mirror to where the bed was.

"Well, kids, you are sitting in a barn because this is where Jesus is going to be born." I heard Mr. Whitaker's soothing voice talking to the kids in the tale.

I went over to the window, put my back to the side of the bed with the headboard, braced my feet on the wall and began to use my legs to push. The bed moved inch by inch. I then moved over to the dresser and did the same thing, pushing with my body to move it past the bed. It took me two hours and some buckles in the carpet, but when I was done, I savored the idea of redecorating in the newly formed space.

"What did you just do?" It was my sister at the door. "Why did you move your furniture?"

"I wanted a change."

"I want your room. Why do you get the big room? I'm going to ask mom if we can trade. It's not fair."

"Get out."

"You're so mean. What is your problem?"

"Get OUT!"

I pushed her by the shoulders and pressed the door to squeeze her out. She pushed back until we were both using all our strength.

"Get out, Abigail!"

"Stop being such a brat!"

I pushed the door as hard as I could to no avail and stepped back letting it fly open with a great force. It slapped me in the lip.

"Owwww." I screeched and put my hand to my mouth. I looked at the blood on my fingers. The sight seemed to scare her more than it did me. Tears flung to my eyes not from pain, but frustration. I slammed the door in her face and locked it.

I cried for a few moments on the floor before picking myself up to look in the mirror. I looked at my face and wiped away the blood with a tissue that I pulled from a box sitting properly on the dresser. I saw the scrape on my lip and bared my teeth, pressing them until I was convinced that they were not loose.

I sat back on the floor and allowed myself to cry. A note slid under my door, folded into an intricate pattern. I unwrapped each section until the paper was unfolded into a square. I wiped down the creases and what she had written.

I am very sorry that I hurt you, but you were being mean. I will pray for you. I hear the mouth is the fastest body part to heal. Please don't tell mom. Sorry.

Love, Abigail.

Pray for me? It sounded like my mom, like something that we were supposed to say. It made me cringe and wish we could just fight, hit, scream and then make up. Did she say this so she could tell my mom that she was praying for me? Or so I wouldn't tell my mom that she hurt me? I honestly didn't care. I just wanted to be left alone.

I pulled myself off the floor and sprinkled the Arm and Hammer carpet cleaner around the room. The scent filled the space and made me feel like I was creating a beautiful, serene environment for myself. While it sat for twenty minutes, hopefully penetrating the ugly brown piles, I made my bed, pulling the rainbow comforter up to the pillow-line. I carefully tucked my precious stuffed animals into the left side of my bed. Abigail made fun of me constantly for sharing the space with toys, but I delighted in Duchess, Peachy Puff and Cupcake having a cozy spot next to me while I slept.

"Chris, ready to tinker?" My dad yelled up the stairs. "I found the opal and think I have enough wire for a setting.

"Oh great! I'll be right down."

I quickly vacuumed up the powder, breathing in the floral smell. I looked around my room and admired the new configuration. With my bed near the door and my dresser by the window, there was a new common space in the middle. I dreamed of what it would look like to buy a small, woven run to lay down over the brown carpet and the possibility create a room that was even more cozy. I heard kids screaming outside and looked out into the yard where my sister and her friends were playing. My desire to move around furniture and design my space on a Saturday morning seemed to confuse my family. They didn't understand why it was so important for my room to be just so. But creating a space based on my own taste smoothed down the edges of my anxiety and allowed me to feel a sense of control that I couldn't grasp at school or church or in the kitchen of the house.

I took one more look around my room at the doorway feeling satisfied. A part of me always knew that I wanted to be as close to the windows as possible so moving my bed back felt inevitable. But, for this moment, everything felt brighter, and I was hopeful.

I hopped down the stairs and quickly moved through the hallway so as not to be seen. My dad was in his studio, which was the back, unfinished room in the basement.

I approached his workbench which was sprinkled with silver wire, a variety of colored precious and semi-precious stones, unfinished bezels, at least four sets of pliers, a skinny maroon torch, a soldering block and two toolboxes filled with the similar supplies. At the back of the workbench were three unidentified glass jars, one of which contained a liquid that made a sizzling noise when a steaming piece of metal was dropped into the vessel.

I sat quietly at his side, participating in the reverence for the process. I was about six when I started to recall the rhythm of this tradition. Dad bringing up the ring sizer and a variety of stones. He would ask my sister and I our finger size. And when we had friends over to play, my dad asked them their size. "I'll make you a ring!"

He was endeared for his generosity. My dad would go down to the basement and bring up armloads of zipped baggies containing smaller zipped baggies of sterling silver jewelry made by him and his father. This was not even a quarter of what he had stored in the walls, behind drywall, the cubbies under the bathroom sinks and even buried in the yard. He would pull out rings upon rings. Too many to count. Some with stones – precious stones, glass stones, cabochons, square, rectangle, tear-dropped in all colors - sapphires, star sapphires, rubies, cat's eyes, moon stones, opals, pearls, cameos, carved coral, jade, amethyst, onyx, and then all the glass stones in greens, blues, reds, yellows that Grandpa George had purchased in bulk.

The bags also contained unfinished rings and pendants just waiting for us to pick out a loose stone to be glued and soldered into them. My friends wore these pieces for years, proudly displaying my dad's hand-crafted work. They were bonded to me and my dad in this way and I recognized that my dad understood this connection superseded jewelry just as it did for my grandfather.

"I used to stand by my father's side while he worked. Ah, my dad. You know, he never complained. He was in a wheelchair for most of his life."

I heard the sadness his voice as he talked about Grandpa Sergio. The story was folklore. Grandpa Sergio worked as an electrician in Flushing until he contracted spinal meningitis. He had eight surgeries, the last one experimental and left him paralyzed from the waist down. He was fired from his job for being a "cripple," and jewelry is what saved him. There was an occupational unit at the hospital, and those nurses taught him how to design and create jewelry. He worked every day, all day at his workbench, selling his work and supporting his family. He bought a home in Queens and built a wheelchair ramp and an elevator. And what set him apart from other men? His love of the Lord, as my dad always said, and his generosity. I always imagined Grandpa George sitting on a little white cloud up in the heavens, smiling down on my dad as he carried on the jewelry-making tradition like it was a holy anointment.

"He'd make penny rings for the whole neighborhood and just give them away."

My dad talked about Grandpa Sergio all the time. He'd give and give and give. It sounded like he gave more penny rings than Jesus gave miracles when my dad told the stories.

My dad tinkered for hours and hours on the weekends in his basement studio. It wasn't until later in my life that I realized my dad going down to his studio was a version of me going to my room to read book after book. He was escaping from the energy in the house. He was going to his own, private space to think and create. He was happy there, alone with his thoughts, the spirits of those that had gone before and his God. An impenetrable room of one's own.

I would pop in to say hello and ask him what he was working on. He wanted to me to share in the magic of the space and taking raw, straight silver and molding it into beauty. He let me hold the soldering torch and melt silver bubbles, one after another. He had a scrap box with loose silver bits from designs that he never finished. I was allowed to paw through the box and pick out small bits of silver. I placed them on the fire-resistant board sitting on top of the black pebbles. He would light the torch with a handheld lighter. I'd hear a pop before the blue flame appeared. We held the torch together and watched as the fire consumed the silver, burning it to a bright red and crawling in on itself like a worm on the driveway the day after a summer storm. The process never got old. We made bubble after bubble just to watch the metal head and transform. How does something so strong and sturdy do that? He demonstrated life lessons in that studio like patience and creativity.

When we went to Queens to visit Grammie Angelica, Abigail and I spent most of the time in the yard just guessing where

Grandpa George had buried all the silver. We were told it was in the yard, in the basement walls, under the floorboards and many other creative hiding spaces. There was so much mystery behind where the treasure was buried and we couldn't get enough of it.

Grammie Angelica had the same black and white photos on her walls that my dad had in his photo book. Grandpa Sergio's studio had been turned into a dining room, but the display case in the wall still held some of his larger pieces. My dad would pull back the heavy, brocade curtain, unlock the door that had been built into the drywall and reveal a glass menagerie of jewels nestled on blush-colored fabric. I thought about telling my friends about the jewelry in the wall, but no one would have believed me. It would be like Samuel telling us at recess that he could bend a silver spoon. What were the chances?

17

Grammie Angelica lived alone after Grandpa passed. She wore floral house coats and gave us permission to feed her dog, Skippy, cheese slices. Her kitchen was decorated with sky blue tile that ran up to the top of the fridge and melded with orange and yellow flowered wallpaper. She made sauce with meat that was tied together with string and for dessert she would pull a box of Entenmann's off the top of the fridge. If I had my wish, it was raspberry danish. We were each cut a thin slice and I savored the bits of drizzled frosting like it was manna.

I know Grammie Angelica loved Abigail and me, but I'm not sure she liked us. I saw the way she looked at Abigail and my mom when they complained about the sheets not being clean or the rug in the family room having too much dog hair on it. I tried to distance myself from them and hung onto my dad when we were in her house so she wouldn't associate me with them. I was so embarrassed at their brazen attitudes of entitlement. I cut my verbiage from little to nothing when we were visiting. I wasn't quite sure how to act. I wanted her to know that I was different, that I was in on the preciousness of her home and her past, her legacy.

I loved going up to the attic with my Dad to explore all the old photos and boxes of memorabilia. It was full of weathered books and treasure. When Dad wasn't completing the list of items to fix that Grammie had written on the chalk board on the kitchen wall, he was in the attic. The stairs were steep, and I always worried that I would fall backwards down them and end up in a wheelchair too. My neck would surely snap.

I'm not sure what mom or Abigail did while we were exploring, but at night, after dinner was cleared, we would sit on the green couch covered with plastic and watch *Gilligan's Island*. I tried to look comfortable on the couch with its sharp corners and sticky surface. After the show, Abigail and I went to bed in the room off the kitchen with the two twin beds. There was a choice to be made. If I picked the bed near the window, I risked a stray bullet coming from the untamed city street outside, through the glass and barreling into my head. If I picked the bed by the closet, I risked a burglar hiding amongst Uncle Roberto's navy uniforms ready to murder me once the lights went out. Abigail chose the bed by the closet and I took the bullets. I wiggled my body as far down the mattress as I could, covering my head from the exposed window with a sheet.

Grandpa Sergio was the one who was worshipped, but I'm pretty sure Grammie was the hero. It was years before I heard Grammie Angelica's story of how she raised three kids and took the bus into the city for work every day. She was one of the best court stenographers in New York City at the time. Grandpa Sergio left the hospital paralyzed from the waist down and in a wheelchair. She said it him, "Well, I guess we better have kids" as if maybe she wanted more for herself. What that was I don't know. I do know that there was sadness in her, the same kind I saw in my dad. The only time I heard her soft laugh was when she would visit and I would sneak down to the basement to watch *General Hospital* with her.

"Your mom is not going to like you watching this," she said, but never made me leave.

We never talked while the show was on or about the storyline afterwards. During each love scene I sat perfectly still, taking it all in and trying not to move. When she went back to New York, I continued to make my way downstairs at three o'clock for the soap opera. In some ways this introduction to life outside of my Christian centered walls was better than any jewel.

I watched *General Hospital* for the next fifteen years, following each story and hanging on the delicious treat every day after school. The show became such a daily comfort for me that I refused to try out for any sports or activities fearing I would lose my Port Charles friends that I had made. I needed to know what would happen to Luke and Laura, Sunny and Stone. The familiar characters and love stories offered more comfort than I could glean from anything else in my house.

Grammie Angelica died several years later in her own wheelchair at a nursing home. When I said goodbye to her in her white casket, I looked at her face and body and was relieved. I felt like she finally could sleep. She was finally done. Goodnight, Sweetheart.

18

Death was very real during that time. We had gone to what felt like many funerals all with open caskets where my mom would reach in and touch the body. Was it cold? Stiff? I remember going to a great uncle's funeral and begging for a burger before we had to go to the reception. There were cold meats laid out on a table covered in a floral tablecloth. I assembled a sandwich with the slimy turkey parts, adding a pickle under the top piece of bread to make it resemble the warm burger that I really wanted. The TV was on in the room where the kids collected themselves. I took a few bites of my sandwich and felt nauseous. It was cold and wet like the ground, like a dead body in the soft earth.

My heart beat a little faster as I realized it was MTV. We didn't have cable at my house and if we did, we certainly wouldn't have been allowed to watch music videos. I heard the beat, the voices and watched the video of the band walking on the beach. I didn't know if the video was black and white or it was the actual TV, but it didn't matter. It was intoxicating. The song was everything and I wanted to go up to the screen and get as close to the boys and the sound as possible. They were the coolest people I had ever seen. I wanted to drink up every word. I wanted to memorize the song and their faces. I was euphoric. This wasn't evil or bad. This was music. This was MTV.

It was about this time with all the dying that my fears started to take permanent shape in my jaw, my head and my hardening heart. My mom used to tell me not to confess the negative. If I was admonished for talking about things that upset me or things that I feared. If I couldn't talk about things that were coming my way like a freight train at a murderous speed, then where would I put these feelings? I'd have to slip them under the covers of my bed at night hoping they didn't pop up in my dreams. And if I wasn't allowed to talk about what scared me, how would I handle these things when they in fact did creep up in my daily life. I wanted to talk about my fear of flying and small spaces and the tremors that ricocheted through my body when the phone rang. I wanted to work all this stuff out, but I had no idea where to start or what to do. I was willing to learn. I just needed help. Just help me and I will work to my bitter end to combat the fears.

What happens when fear is just allowed to sit and stew in the mess of a child's developing brain? Well, I think these slippery things become part of the structure in there. They become buildings in a city that is constantly being developed and before you know it, they are skyscrapers, dated buildings that are fixtures and would cost too much to take a wrecking ball to them and rebuild. So, they stand tall in a field of other important feelings and memories.

Each one of these became their own, rooted building. Fear of throwing up, fear of crowds, fear of small spaces, fear of conversation, fear of the ocean, fear of loneliness, fear of new people, fear of my dreams, fear of the wind, fear of flying, fear of earthquakes, fear of the phone ringing, fear of speaking on the phone, fear of falling down the stairs, fear of riding in the back, fear of rollercoasters, fear of asking for help, fear of needing help, fear of dying last and all the rest of them. Some were rational, but most irrational. It would have taken just a small, comforting hug, a tiny conversation to put these back on the shelf.

I can think of a memory, a trauma, that goes along with each one of these, enough to fill a whole diary for certain. And that's where I put them. I wrote them down. I put them in journals to try to get them out of my head. It didn't always work. They still found their way into my life, my dreams, and no medication or amount of therapy will ever be able to eradicate them all together.

19

I'm pretty sure we arrived at the church before everyone else. My dad was always early. Always. Very early. We waited in the cool morning air for an hour until more kids arrived and the bus driver let us on. We were to leave our duffle bags on the sidewalk to be stored underneath.

"Bye Hon," my mom said and hugged Abigail.

"I don't want to go," she said. "I don't want to go for a whole week. Can you pick me up?"

"No, but we'll pray for you."

I stood behind Abigail waiting for my turn. My mom hugged me and said, "You're going to have a great time."

I didn't answer. My stomach was doing flips. I looked around at the growing cluster of kids, ranging in ages ten to eighteen. Everyone looked so calm in their hoodies and flipflops like they had left home like this all the time. Some of the older kids even yawned.

I gave my dad a quick hug and climbed the steep steps of the bus, the driver's small fan blowing in my face as I passed his seat. The church had hired one of those commercial busses with the bathroom and TV screen. I was grateful that we were not caravanning with a bunch of minivans and parents driving us the three hours to Tennessee. There would have been nowhere for me to hide.

I wanted to find a window seat so I could wave to my parents. I made my way down the rubber-matted aisle, scooted my bum along the plastic seat and pressed my hands to the window. My eyes wildly searched the crowd of waiting parents. My mom was off to the side talking to Grace's dad. She was laughing. I tapped on the window trying to get her attention. There was so much noise as the older kids made their way to the back of the bus, hyped up and excited about being away from home for a full week. I slapped the glass with an open palm. I couldn't get her eyes to turn. I watched as the bus driver swung the last duffle bag from the curb into the underbelly of the bus. I knew my dad had probably already gone to get the car so he could be the first one out of the parking lot. They weren't looking for me to say goodbye. The bus's engine revved and I felt it rock.

"Can I sit here?"

It was Maddy. She had been going to our church long before I had, and her mom worked in the nursery. She felt familiar.

"Sure." I looked at her and then back out the window in time to see my mom walking to the side parking lot where my dad idled in the car. My stomach dropped and tears stung my eyes. I did not want to cry because I didn't think I would ever stop.

"Do you want a top or bottom bunk?"

Maddy was talking to me, but I couldn't understand what she was saying. I held my breath and tried to look ahead at the bus driver's face through his large rearview mirror. My stomach bubbled and I wanted to throw up.

"I want a top bunk. You should take a top bunk too. We can run to our cabin when they let us off the bus and get one next to each other."

"Ok." I still didn't know what she was fully saying but wanted to be friendly and assure her that I was a fun person, that I was worth investing in. Maybe I could just latch onto her and she could get me through the week.

No one had explained to me exactly what we did at Camp Horizon. It felt like I was being sent to jail, a place that was unfamiliar and I couldn't leave. My parents did not ask us if we wanted to go, but just signed us up. I didn't know who else was going to be there or what the camp even looked like, which would have helped me mentally prepare. I didn't know if I packed all the right things or what was going to be asked of me. Was I going to have to stand in front of all these kids and give my testimony? Was I going to have to perform one of those interpretive dances that they sometimes did at church? Would I be able to say no to these things or would I be too scared to say anything at all? I was at the mercy of the bus rocking my body with its movement towards the unknown and I wanted to cry. I knew Abigail was somewhere in the back of the bus and wondered if she was faring better than I. I wanted desperately for her to come check on me and comfort me, but I wouldn't see her until we arrived at camp.

"Do you want some trail mix?"

"What's trail mix?" Maddy pulled out a crinkled baggie with lumps of brown seeds and raisins.

I looked at that bag desperate to pick at the pumpkin seeds. It was the kindest gesture I had felt all morning.

"Thank you." I don't know if it was the seeds finding my empty belly or Maddy's kindness, but in that moment, I had a glimmer of hope. It lasted only moments as the bus started moving forward. I steeled my body. The motion sent me into a panic, my palms sweating and my eyes blurring. I tried to ground myself by looking out the window at the rough greenery lining the highway. We sped up and I thought I was going to throw up or faint or die. I prayed for the latter knowing I had no strength to fight through the dizzy feeling kidnapping my insides. I was never going to survive this bus trip, this movement.

I looked over at Maddy like a rabid animal and she smiled back at me. "You okay?"

"Yea. I guess I just don't like busses."

"It's a short trip. Let's play the license plate game."

I didn't want to play a game, but I loved her and her yellow-tinted teeth and smooth white skin. She placed the snack baggie between us, and the generous offering melted the edges of my panic.

Our reverie faded when we heard a voice coming from the front of the bus. I looked up and saw a large man or boy. A man-boy. I recognized him. Ben. He stood leaning on his left hip, his jeans two sizes too big, were rolled at the ankles revealing large, sparkling white tennis shoes. A belt held the pants in place along with a short-sleeved button-down plaid shirt. Green, red, green, red. Kind of like a Christmas tree. His belly hung over the ledge of the jeans and revealed the fact that he no longer fit into our demographic. He was probably thirty-something, balding just slightly at the corners of his forehead, letting the rest of his brown hair flop unruly to the sides. He had a bit of scruff along the jawline, not in a deliberate way like Bo and Luke Duke, but enough to make him look fully disheveled and possibly not quite integrated into adulthood to remember to buy new razors. I noticed a crumb of something at the corner of his mouth that stuck there while he was talking. I stared at it willing the brown speck to fall so I could try to take in what he was saying.

"Guys. Guys!"

The older kids in the back continued to laugh and talk loudly.

"Hey Guys! Guys, quiet down."

He had my full attention. I thought for a brief moment that maybe he was going to tell us that camp was cancelled due to the blanket of grey clouds ahead of us, and we could all get off the bus and go home.

"Guys, I just wanted to say a quick prayer before our week gets started. Dear Heavenly Father, thank you for this opportunity to fellowship with one another and worship you this week. We ask that you give us a blessed time at camp. Keep us all safe and touch our hearts as we learn to grow and love you more deeply. In Jesus name, Amen."

"Amen."

I reached for a raisin as Ben made his way to the back of the bus, passing Maddy and I without a gesture or a smile.

20

Maddy was as Godsend. She talked the entire time mostly about things that just required me to nod and smile. I studied her as she talked, hyper-focusing on her face and mouth. She had a line of rogue, dark hairs on her upper lip. Her hair was long, longer than her shoulders and the bits near her scalp were greasy and dotted with white flakes. She smelled like butterscotch. We finished the trail mix and she put the empty bag in her purple backpack with an iron on patch of a cross and a rainbow that read "Jesus Lives." Her sneakers looked flat and white like they were meant to be the name brand but were probably purchased for a much lower price at discount store.

I had no idea who else was on the bus. I refused to look around in case it made me sick and I was content to live in the bubble Maddy had made for us. The only people I could easily see were the girls in the seat across the aisle. Their hair was pulled back in tight ponytails secured with white scrunchies and each one held a Bible on their lap. They were laughing to one another and I couldn't help but wonder what it was that was so funny.

The bus pulled off the highway around eleven o'clock. We had been on the road for about three hours and I felt the immediate relief of the bus as it slowed from the highway and now moved through the backroads making its way to the camp. Ben stood up again.

"Ok, guys. We are just about there. The counselors will be standing off to the side of the bus holding a sheet of paper with their names on it and a list of campers. You should have been given the name of your counselor in your paperwork. Find your counselor. That person will then lead you to your cabin and your assigned room. You will have time to unpack before lunch. Then tonight we will meet in the chapel for worship.

We climbed out of the bus and like a hoard of bees and flew around one another searching for our counselors. I prayed that Maddy would be in my room. We moved together to the two female counselors holding pieces of paper that read "Erica." I looked up and down the first sheet until I saw my name, Christen. Maddy's name was farther down the list, but I didn't notice it. I only saw Beth's name. Beth was here.

I whipped my head around searching for the tall, skinny brunette amongst the other girls.

"Beth!" I exclaimed reaching out to touch her shoulder.

"Oh my gosh! I didn't know you were coming too!"

It was like the heavens had opened up and Beth came floating down with the glow of the sun behind her. Beth was my favorite friend. She lived in my neighborhood, had three sisters and two dogs. She lived like a beautiful, wild horse, running and jumping with blissful abandon. She rode horses in Great Falls and knew all the words to every Beach Boy song. Beth was the coolest girl I knew and when I was with her, I felt cool too. When we were younger, Beth would come over to my house and turn on the radio to FM. We would dance to music in my room and I would mimic her hips rocking back and forth until I learned the movement, arms in the air. We laughed and talked about boys that we liked in our classes. She had gone to Hope Valley, but her parents moved her and her sisters to the public school after first grade when a boy was paddled in her class. It was like she changed from wearing uniforms with me into this girl that knew all about Ricky Schroder and where to buy jelly sandals. I couldn't be envious because I was too busy soaking up all she had learned.

Beth taught me what Fun Dip, French kissing and *Dirty Dancing* were. She sang the Beach Boys and taught me all the words to the latest DJ Jazzy Jeff and Fresh Price song. We stayed up all night so I could learn the words. She was so patient and repeated every line until I learned the entire song and could repeat it back to her. I loved learning all the words to every song she was willing to teach me. She was my gateway to the outside world.

I felt like she was reaching for me, giving me her hand and pulling me up so I wouldn't fall into the canyon below. She was my lifeline into a world full of color and decorated with freedom and excitement. And unlike Maddy, Beth was normal. Not just church-normal.

My mom hated the person I became when I played with her. She had anger in her eyes when I walked Beth to the door, both of us still dancing and gleefully singing the words to the song I spent all night learning. I was confused by my mom's stern expression and didn't understand why she was not delighting in my play. When Beth left, I felt her gaze on me and I stopped dancing feeling a sense of shame at my movement.

But, I wanted more. I wanted to go over to her house every day and run between her sister's rooms and play loud music. Beth wanted to come to my house and shut the door to my bedroom and play with my things which she didn't have to share with her siblings. She loved my little pin frame, the one where you put your hand or an object flat into the pins and the image was left behind in the negative space.

"I didn't know you were coming." I said with excitement.

"My mom was late in signing us up. I looked around and saw her sisters grabbing for their bags near the bus. "Hold on, I need to get my bag. Go get us bunks!" She yelled over her shoulder not missing a beat.

She turned back to the bus and I saw that her hair was in a messy ponytail with pieces from each side hanging in her tanned face. She was so beautiful. I followed her with a newfound sense of confidence through the gaggle of kids to find my bag. I didn't want to be the last one in the room and not get a top bunk. I spotted my blue duffle bag and yanked it up from the pile of backpacks and bags piled on the dirt next to the bus. I dragged it back to the counselor where a collection of other girls stood. I saw Grace with the straight blonde hair, Emily, Tori, Alison and a girl with sad, dark eyes that I did not recognize from church, all gathered around.

"Let's move towards our cabin and we can introduce ourselves." Our counselor, Erica, was one of those beautiful blonde high schoolers that would never acknowledge you in the real world but stood with pride at being one of the chosen church counselors during camp week. She wore tight, white shorts and a red V-neck tee shirt that outlined her curves. Her hair was pulled back in an effortless bun and she smiled widely down at us as we gawked at the perfect dimple in her cheek.

We dragged our belongings, kicking up dried mud, to where Erica had stopped in front of one of the cabins. The sign above painted in white lettering read the name of ours, "Salvation." Each cabin was named with a Biblical reference – Grace, Mercy, Peace, and Faith.

"Hi. I'm Erica. I will be your counselor for this week so if you need anything you can ask me. We will go over some rules and the schedule. But before we do all that, let's go to our room and put our bags down."

I heartlessly forgot about Maddy and her trail mix as we all ran into our room scurrying to reach the bunkbeds. My eyes were focused on Beth as she unapologetically slid around the other girls to get to the front of the pack.

"Get the top! Get the top!" Beth threw her bag on the top bunk next to the window and I did the same with the adjacent. I thought my bunk was even a bit better because it was in the corner, in the middle where I was surrounded by the other girls. Grace was on the top next to mine and Gillian next to her. The sad looking girl with the black hair unloaded her things under Beth's bunk. It didn't look like she cared about being the only one on the bottom. I watched her look out the window and run her finger along the screen as if she could pop it open and escape into the woods beyond.

After circle time with Erica including introductions and prayer, we were given a schedule for the week and a map of the camp. We had swim time, art time, free time and a service every night. After we were all settled, we were dismissed to go to the cafeteria for lunch. I liked that the girls in our cabin all stayed together - walking together, bunking together and would sit and eat together. Beth was next to me and had already promised to show me how to make an anklet like hers out of embroidery string. We entered the cafeteria that was lined with screened windows and whirling box fans. The heat, the noise and the smell of fried chicken made me want to dive into the food line panicking that everything would be gone before I got there.

It felt like we were late as I looked around the room and saw that the rest of the camp was already seated and more than halfway through their meals. Kids were buzzing around the long tables like frenetic bees at a hive, their chatter and laughter exhausting all the air in the room. The older kids sat in the back performing for one another filtering out the alphas from the more conservative, home-schooled students. I looked for Abigail and saw her sitting amongst the other middle schoolers, next to Elizabeth Portner, Grace's sister.

My group looked like babies walking through the line timidly with our red plastic trays sticky from the group that had already eaten and moved on to quiet time. We were the youngest kids at camp and dreaded the critical eyes of the senior high youth group. I nodded my head yes to the woman behind the steaming service trays offering me fried chicken and grits. I had no idea what grits were but prayed they didn't leak from my tray as I balanced it all the way to a table that Grace had found. The rest of our cabin sat cluttered together on the bench pulled up to the table, relief in their eyes that they too did not drop their food in front of the crowd. It was so hot that I couldn't even imagine eating the chicken before me even though all I had eaten were the sweet raisons Maddy had offered me on the bus hours before. Sweat dripped down my temples and dotted my lip.

"I can't eat, it's way too hot."

"I have a ton of candy back at the cabin." Beth said. Of course she did.

"I hear we are having a campfire with s'mores after church

tonight."

"We are?" We all exclaimed in excitement, the promise filling us with new energy.

We finished picking at our lunch, none of us touching the pool of grits on our plates and left the now empty cafeteria letting the screen door swing shut behind Gillian with a bang. The camp felt old like the original part of Reston that was built in the woods that my parents would bring us to to feed the ducks. Most of the buildings were log cabins and seeped the same mildew smell into the air when you walked past them. The camp was surrounded by gigantic oak trees whose branches reached up to the sky and shadowed the camp in a dark cloud, keeping the sunlight from getting in. The air felt moist and cool like leaving our baby peach skin vulnerable to the elements. We huddled close to one another as if at any point we would see danger in the forest - snakes appearing on the weathered ground slithering towards us, flicking their tongues. The main camp was in the shape of a diamond the cabins on the left half and the community center, canteen, art building and pool on the opposite. The sharp points on either side of the shape were the entrance to the camp, the chapel at the opposite end.

We made our way back to our cabin for some quiet time per Erica's instruction each of us taking up space on our bunks, letting ourselves sink into the feeling of being away from home. Beth passed out Twizzlers to everyone and we chewed the cherry liquorish while trading information about ourselves.

"Christen, you need to sing. You have the best voice." It was Beth. I loved to sing and despite being shy, I always wanted to. It felt like something I was good at. Even at Hope, my first-grade teacher would call me up to the front of the class, turn me around so I didn't have to face the room, and have me sing song after song. I imagined the class looking at the back of my pleated skirt and hoped it was clean.

I sang the first verse from one of Whitney Houston's songs that I had somehow, somewhere learned that summer. I had all their attention. The girls were staring at me with awe on their

faces. It was the best feeling in the world. I tested their adoration by stopping.

"Keep going! Keep going!" They chanted. And when I got the
words wrong or forgot them Beth would remind me. Afterall,
Beth had taught me the song.

Dinner was at five o'clock and we all decided to shower, having collected puddles of sweat under our arms and necks. Beth
and I were the first in the shower and first dressed. We sat just
outside of our room and waited for the rest of the girls. We
walked in our cluster to dinner where they again served fried
chicken, but instead of the lumpy grits we were each given a
biscuit. I picked at the flaky crust, feeling my stomach growing
nervous for the evening service.

After cleaning off our trays we walked through the wooded
path until we reached the chapel. It was the farthest building
from the rest of camp and buried deep within a wooded area.
Inside there were pews where most of the kids had already filled
since again we were the last to arrive.

"Guys, sit back here." It was Erica, our counselor. "This is our
section." She was wearing the same red top but had changed
into white jeans decorated with a triangle patch on the back of
one of the pockets that read "Guess." I knew these were the jeans
that the popular kids wore because Abigail had been begging my
mom for a pair.

I didn't see the ridiculous felt banners or the loaves of bread
for communion. We started out with prayer and praise for the
evening, but I felt it in the air. I knew what was coming.

I had no idea if there were alter calls in other churches, but
I had learned over the years what they entailed. The piano
music would slow to long broken chords lulling the congregation into a time of contemplation and quiet reflection. John
Stuart would usually come to the tippity-top of the altar stairs
and float his angel arms out wide, eyes closed. And in a slow
hypnotic rhythm people would slide from their aisle and march
towards the front. And then it would happen. One by one, men
and women would fall backwards, caught by a waiting member

of the church who would lay them down on the red carpet like a corpse. There would be an entire line of dead-like people at the altar. I would hold my breath and look down to the ground when my mom scooted past me. I never looked up to see her fall.

Sure, enough after a short sermon about asking Jesus into our hearts – to ensure that everyone at camp was saved and would be going to Heaven – Ben asked for an altar call. It felt as if we were sitting ducks just waiting for our heads to be severed from our bodies for the church as a whole. But, we were children. Wasn't there an easier way to love God? To be close to Him? Or did we have to lay down our bodies in this death-like ritual?

"God wants your heart. He wants you with him for all of eternity." Ben prayed with closed eyes and arms opened to his sides, palms exposed like Jesus on the cross.

It was Maddy that went first. Then another older girl and one after that. A few boys. When there was a line of nine or ten standing side by side, Ben and the other ministers walked towards the kids. My heart started racing. I didn't know if I should run up and try to steal them away or join them. Ben touched the first girl's forehead, speaking in soft tongues, the language given to only a chosen few and only by way of being slain. The first girl fell straight as a pin backwards and into the arms of a counselor that laid her softly down.

The counselor that laid her on the wood floor, stepped over her body to the next child that Ben had already laid hands on. One by one they all fell backwards. They fell in a rhythm so that when the last kid was laid on the ground the first girl quietly made her way to her feet and back to her pew. I wondered if she had it now. The gift of tongues. It didn't happen every time, but you couldn't get the secret language until you went to the altar. More and more kids followed until just about the entire congregation had been touched by Ben's hand, including my sister. It was down to me, Beth and one other boy that sat on the far side of the building all alone. I had never seen him before, but I could see the sweat dripping from his sideburns, his knee nervously bouncing up and down.

I closed my eyes and crushed my fists into my stomach trying to make myself smaller. I watched the boy to see what he would do. He stared down at the ground. The fear that my counselor was going to ask me to go up to the altar was coursing through me. I bowed my head and closed my eyes pretending that I was in a deep mediative prayer. She wouldn't disturb me if I was lost in prayer, would she?

"In the name of the Holy Spirit, I ask that your rid this dear child of the evil spirit that has taken hold of him. I cast you out of him, Satan."

My eyes flung open to Ben's voice that now commanded the room. His palm was on a boy's head, fingers tips bearing down forcefully into his rug of hair.

"Out, Satan. I command you. Out of this boy."

The boy's head was bowed and his arms shaking. He wore a *Simpsons* t-shirt and I recognized him as one of the older kids from the cafeteria. His arms were flapping wildly as Ben widened his stance, grounding his feet. He was surrounded by three other counselors their eyes watching the boy closely. I felt the air slip from the room and a dark fog roll in.

"I'm going need the congregation to stand with me. Reach out your hands to our brother, Jason."

We stood and held our arms out in front of us, our fingertips stretched out as if we were touching Jason all the way from our seats.

"God Almighty, we lay hands on Jason. You say that if two or more are gathered in your name that you are with us. We know you are in this room. We know Jason is a child of God. Rid him of this demon."

The boy shook harder, I held my breath and he fell backwards. Ben continued, "Get behind me, Satan."

The room was buzzing as we all craned our necks to see Jason on the floor. Did anyone see the demon leave him? Was there blood? Was he still breathing? We still had our arms out-stretched and kept them there until Jason opened his eyes and returned to his feet, smiling bashfully.

Ben started clapping forcefully his large hands beating together in a drum like beat. We followed suit, filling the church in a thunderous roar. Jason smiled sheepishly as he made his way back to where his friends were sitting. They patted him on the back and hugged him one after the other. I looked around the room where girls were crying, wiping tears, and hugging one another. I pretend to wipe my own tears even though my eyes were dry as a bone.

21

We followed a similar schedule for the rest of the week. We would do a craft or go to the outdoor pool during the day and then at night singing and alter calls in the chapel. I grew more and more embarrassed refusing to respond to the altar call. Even Beth and the sweating boy caved mid-week, I was hoping I was small enough and quiet enough that no one noticed me. At this point everyone around me had either the gift of tongues or felt a supernatural peace. They would all go to Heaven. Each night when it was all over and we were walking back to our cabin, I wanted another shot. I wanted to be brave enough to try. I hated myself for being too scared and not just putting one foot in front of the other.

Some nights were more laid back than others. Each cabin was asked to write and perform a skit that held a lesson that would lead to discussion. The senior high performed one that night that acted out the struggle of a Christian boy trying to tell his friends about Christ. They made it funny and all the kids laughed. I laughed too, but also kept looking over at Ben wondering what was going to come after this bit. He had one of the counselors come up with his guitar and lead us in worship. We sang for an hour. We knew these songs from church. I saw kids raising their hands to the ceiling. Up, up, up. I tried to force my arms up in the air like them. I tried and tried. But, they were like lead. It didn't feel comfortable and I didn't know how to do it. I felt like I would just be faking it. And so, my hands stayed next to my sides and I hoped no one noticed.

"We are going to move into a time of deep prayer now. I want you all to search your hearts and when you are ready come to the front to experience God's blessing."

No. God, not again.

It was happening again. I didn't know how I was going to hide this time. Surely, someone was going to grab my hand and force me. Abigail was one of the first to go this time. I watched as she closed her eyes and seconds later fell backwards. I was so impressed that she could do it so easily. I wanted to know what it was like. I wanted someone to explain where they went when they fell. Did they really just, like, black out? Did they meet Jesus in that blackness? Were some of them faking it? Surely, some of them were faking. But, I knew speaking in tongues was real. My mom did it around the house. "Shannnnanannnanannn-nanannanna Gushanannanan." Everyone's language was a bit different and my mom's sounded like the beginning of a name repeated over and over and then turned guttural. It was a long, repetitious sound. If I only went up there I could have it too. But, again I failed at moving my body to the front and no one seemed to notice. I was so impossibly small that they probably didn't see me with everyone standing and singing. I watched as the boy from the night before went up easily this time.

Chapel time was so long each night that we missed the campfire and s'mores that we had heard rumor of. Instead, my cabin continued our performances of Whitney Houston and Michael Jackson songs, each of us getting a turn with the flashlight on their face like a spotlight. The girl under Beth's bunk still fiddled with the window and in the middle of the night I heard enough rattling that I was sure she found a way out.

It was finally Friday, the last day of camp. I had a little stash of crafts that I had made and planned on giving to my parents. I hammered leather key chains with crosses on them and bookmarks with Bible verses. We were told that there was going to be a talent show on the last night. Beth wanted me to sing. No way I told her. But, as the week went on I did consider playing a piece on the piano.

My parents didn't put Abigail or I on soccer teams or dance classes. I was afraid of basketballs hitting my head and hated sweating. I didn't own sports shorts and thought it would be too assuming to carry a water bottle. But, Gram had asked me if I wanted a piano. She asked me directly and I said yes. Grandpa had an antique piano shipped from New Hampshire down to Virginia. It was so old that the keys were made of yellowed ivory and there was a red velvet inlay. Several of the keys did not work unless pounded upon, but I didn't mind. I was in my second year of playing and was learning *The Entertainer*. I was so excited because it was a piece of music that I actually knew. Like, it was real and not just one of those practice pieces in the learning to play piano books. I signed my name to the list for the talent show. I was going to play *The Entertainer*.

My little cabin was excited for me and when the last night came, we all showed up early to the community center, that was really just a room with cement floors and walls and grabbed the front row. The piano had been moved to the front of the room, a few feet away from the folding chairs that were lined up for the audience. The show was filled with kids singing worship songs and some doing the interpretive dances that they learned at church. I had seen the dancers at church. They wore flowy skirts that flew behind them like wings as they tip toed around the stage and moved their hands up to the sky, towards God.

I followed the program that was printed on a yellow piece of paper. I was next. Erica announced my name, calling me Christian instead of Christen. I ignored the offence and approached the unfamiliar piano. The keys were white, really white. I didn't know where to put my hands and they started to shake before I even touched them. The room was quiet. My fingers stuttered and until I found the first note and then I played from muscle memory. I started and stopped in places and barely made it to the last measure. It felt like it was over before it began. I took my bow and sat back in my seat still shaking and absolutely mortified.

Before I had a chance for my body to settle back into my chair the large boy with the Simpson's t-shirt from the chapel and gotten up and made his way to the piano. I looked forward to the relief that would come with someone else putting their talent on display. Then I heard it. The D, D #, E, C, E, C, E, C. Oh no. Oh my GOD. He was playing *The Entertainer*. But, not just playing it. He was The Entertainer. He was fast and peppy, his body rocked and his hands glided. People started hooting and clapping even before it was over. He nailed the last cord with more strength than I had in my body. The clapping erupted before I could process what he had just done. I wanted to die. I wanted to run away and die. How could the large kid that didn't do the altar call the first day do this to me? Did he mean to hurt me or was he excited to play *The Entertainer* too. Before the tears had time to prick my eyes, I felt a tug at my sleeve. It was Jeff, the cutest, senior higher boy on the entire planet with his jet-black hair and blue eyes. He leaned over to me, "I liked yours better."

The tears started to fall. It was the nicest thing that anyone had ever said to me.

22

Every year my mom scheduled an appointment for me at Children's Hospital in DC. I had no idea until adulthood that it was because my parents were unsure if I was growing properly and if they should put me on growth hormones. I dreaded the experience more than anything else in my life. I knew I was getting inspected, but I wasn't sure why. They'd do a bunch of tests and take my blood, which scared me more than when the babysitter deliberately locked Abigail and I out of the house in the Virginia summer heat for two hours while she talked to her boyfriend on the phone.

No one had ever explained to me what the appointments were for, but I had one annually in the month of August. My mom's calendar, where she penciled in upcoming events, hung on the kitchen wall above the phone. "Baby Jesus" gifted her a wall calendar every Christmas and this one highlighted Titian's paintings. Woman with a Mirror was June's piece. My mom didn't like sensuousness of her demeanor, the smirk on her face, and so she put a sticker of a dancing red heart with cartoon-like arms and legs over the model's mouth, vandalizing the painting.

When no one was looking, I climbed onto the kitchen stool and flipped through the calendar to August. There, I saw my hospital appointment written in pencil (thank you, God Almighty). I took a pencil from the jar on the counter and erased the appointment. I spend the rest of the summer with a heightened sense of panic that my mom would discover that I had wiped out the appointment and would have my dad spank me for it. I'm not sure which was worse – the phlebotomist's needle or my dad chasing me around the kitchen, grabbing me at the waist, hand hitting my naked backside, my skirt flipped up onto my back.

My mom never found out that I had tampered with her calendar, but she did make another appointment. I figured they must have called to remind her. I knew that something must have been terribly wrong with me, my body, if we had to go so badly.

"Next Monday we have your appointment at Children's Hospital." She said one afternoon after school.

"No. No I can't. I can't!" I started crying uncontrollably and crashed to the floor. I crawled under the kitchen table in an irrational manner considering my age. I was ten and didn't want to go to the hospital and get a needle in my arm. My mom rolled her eyes and busied herself while I continued to cry on the floor waiting for her to meet me there. I cried to her every night until Monday's appointment, begging her not to make me go. The appointment had taken up so much of my energy that I found myself spending more and more time in my room on the floor buried between my bed and window where no one could see me. If they couldn't help me, I wanted them all to forget about me.

That morning I threw up once in the upstairs bathroom and once in the powder room. I knew my stomach was not going to hold. I grabbed a grocery bag, stuffed it in my pocket and wondered if it would hold all the vomit, all the fear, that would inevitably arise. I ruminated about the feeling of my insides coming back up my throat and seeing the contents of my stomach splashed all over the floor in front of my eyes and any witnesses. It would be both devastating and uncontrollable.

I sat as small as I could in the front seat of the station wagon. My mom sung along to Sandy Patty, holding the steering wheel with one hand and raising the other in praise to the Lord during the chorus.

After circling the parking garage, my mom getting more frustrated with each level, we found a spot large enough to fit the car on the very last level. She threw the car into park and flipped down the visor revealing a tiny mirror.

"Hand me my purse."

I passed her the purse that was tucked out of the way near my feet and watched silently as she dug through it, retrieving a Mary Kay lip pencil that had been whittled down to a two-inch knub. She carefully outlined her lips like a coloring page that had not been filled in. She pulled out a comb and brushed the back of her hair looking sideways at her profile until she was satisfied.

"Ok, let's go."

I moved like a slinky from the car to the elevator, one step behind her. We rose from the pit of the shadowed garage up to the main level of the hospital, its waiting room dotted with tiny, plastic red and orange children's chairs and blue tables. There were Dr. Seuss books stacked on an abandoned coffee table and a bin of used toys, a little piano and some wooden puzzles in a corner. The information desk was across from the gift shop that I remember from last year's visit. I gazed longingly through the glass windows at the bright pens and notebooks and little stuffed animals that sat on the shelves as my mom checked us in.

We walked to another set of elevators that carried us up the tower, deeper into the confines of the building. I smelled bleach and rubber and saw shades of mint green in the hallways. We sat in another, smaller waiting room that was painted with bright colors and filled with more children's books. I looked at them out of my periphery, embarrassed to grab for one in case my mom thought I was too old for Daffy Duck. Instead, I chewed the inside of my right cheek until it bled, the salty taste filling my mouth and administering temporary relief from my fear.

We were called back into an examination room where a nurse measured me, weighed me and Velcroed my arm tightly, pumping air into the sleeve until I was left without feeling in my hand for several seconds. She was close enough to me, fiddling with my body parts, that I smelled a hint of lavender soap on her hands. I dared to look her in her eyes hoping she would make a connection apart from my mother who sat in chair just low enough that her and I could have shared a few private words. I was a good girl and obeyed her like my life depended on it, opening and shutting my mouth like a goldfish waiting to be fed, lending the innards of my ears for investigation.

She flung her stethoscope around her neck, a tiny grey koala bear pinching the tube, and walked out of the room without a word to either of us. We waited in silence for the doctor. I sat alone on the examination table, the thin paper crinkling loudly and ripping underneath my thighs. The prints around that room hung in cheap, black frames, their colors having given up fading with the pressure of the sunlight that poured through the exam room window, Monet's *Water Lilies* now coated in a faded, blue filter.

The doctor entered the room with a large smile directed towards my mom. They seemed to talk in the air just above me where I couldn't understand the language or connect with either of their eyes. She held out papers with printed charts, numbers and wavy diagrams. I waited distracted by Monet's blue bridge, hoping that their chatter would cause them to forget about the blood test that was to come. I found my shoulders relaxing downwards with the minutes that ticked by, that when my mom gestured to her chest, grabbed her boobs, and lifted them up and down I was mortified.

"Hear that, Chris? You are going to have big ones." She puffed out her cheeks and made the movement with her hands on her chest once again. Then laughed. I looked at her as if she was telling me that I was going to grow horns out of my head. It was as if she had just found out that I was going to morph into a disgusting teenager with a chest so enormous and bulbous that I wouldn't be able walk through a doorway. I immediately thought of the short, overweight blonde eighth grader at my school. Her hair was frizzed out to the sides and her belly fell over her uniform skirt. Her unruly chest bulged rivaling her yellowed teeth bound by metal braces for a monstrous look.

I wanted to hide under the exam table. I wanted to run into the street screaming. I wanted my mom to hug me and tell me that I wouldn't look like a small person with Dolly Parton-sized boobs that everyone would laugh at. I wanted her to tell me that it was going to be fine and nothing to worry about. I wanted her to tell me that I was perfect the way I was. Instead I just felt like she had sloppily blurted out that I was going to be an ugly ogre and there wasn't a damn thing I could do about it.

I missed the rest of the conversation as I tried to figure out a way that I could secretly cut my two developing breasts from my body. And if I couldn't do that then I would find a way to drown myself in the bathtub or walk into oncoming traffic. I refused to grow up knowing I was going to be this unsightly.

"So, we'll see you all next year."

Did I hear her right? We were dismissed? I perked up at the sound of the conversation reaching an end.

"Bloodwork right through there."

Oh God, oh God, oh God. Please Heavenly Father, let this floor swallow me up whole so that I won't have my blood taken, throw up on the floor in front of all the nurses and grow up to have big boobs.

My mom and I were led into the small, hallway-like room where a chair was set up with a padded arm rest. There was a woman moving around in the space like she lived in there, a cave with vials of blood and no windows. She sifted through file folders until she reached mine.

"Christian?"

I didn't have the voice to correct her and say, "It's Christen."

I walked into the tiny space, leaving my mom at the door. I looked back at her and wasn't sure what felt more cold, my mom or the room with linoleum floor.

"I don't feel good."

I grabbed my stomach and pulled at the bag in my pocket. I shook it out, sat down and threw up.

"Wow!" said the young phlebotomist. "I've never seen that before."

She was referring to the bag I had brought with me and I stopped vomiting to register this new mortification. Carrying a bag with me just became as embarrassing as the mess that came out of me.

My mom stood by the door and laughed awkwardly along with the nurse. They were having a moment of connection at my expense. I was now mortified, sick and angry. I felt betrayed by my mother who didn't move towards me but stood still. She was embarrassed by me. I ignored them and looked over my knees to the tiled floor below, perfectly clean.

23

Once upon a time Mrs. Brayburn convinced the principal that we should watch a movie filled with God's redemption and grace. And so, one day before Christmas break, the fourth graders and fifth graders gathered excitedly in our classroom where a television had been wheeled into the room.

My friends and I were giddy and looked at each other with excitement at the idea of watching a movie at school. Mrs. Brayburn turned off the lights and we all pulled our desks closer to the television. The movie started out with a beautiful, young girl with long brown hair. She was so happy and so pretty.

The girl was in high school and they showed her in a track and field uniform running with all the energy and vibrancy in the world. She had lots of friends at school and a very close family. The movie showed the girl with the long brown hair living a happy life.

One day, she got in her car. She was going to meet her friends at the mall. A truck came out of nowhere and slammed into her car. They showed her little red car get crunched in like a soda can and trap her behind the steering wheel blood oozing from her head and face.

The girl with the big smile was removed from the smashed car by paramedics and taken by ambulance to the hospital where she was in a coma for six months. Girl's family came to her bedside every day. Girl had tubes coming out of every part of her body. The doctors didn't think the girl would live, but Girl woke up from her coma and screamed and screamed because she couldn't walk. Girl cried and screamed every day and went to physical therapy and took lots of medicine. Girl eventually walked but could never run again.

Add this to the list of fears, please. The movie and the girl and the coma and the paralyzing.

24

I remember when Jesus came to our house. Or I thought it was Jesus until I got a really icky feeling in my stomach that it was just a man acting like Jesus. By the way my mom was behaving, I'm not sure that she thought it was an act.

"When does he get here, Hon?" asked my dad.

"Uh, about four o'clock."

He was actually one of the missionaries from church and was in town for Christmas. My mom had invited him over for what she called a light dinner and prayer.

I had heard his name before from my mother and her church friend, Monica. I think even Beth's mom knew who he was from church. I had no idea who he was or what he did, but by the way my mom was moving around the house, I sensed his appointment meant something to her. My mom was scurrying around arranging and rearranging the living room. She bought new pillows for the couches, blue drinking glasses and a candle.

"Henry! Henry!" She yelled upstairs. "They are here!"

My dad had gone upstairs to lie down. I followed him down the stairs and looked out the front window to see Jesus walking down my driveway. But, it wasn't Jesus, it was the tallest man I had ever seen with long hair brushed to the side and a full beard. He was wearing a short sleeved, button down shirt that exposed a puff of dark chest hair. His pants were loose and on his feet were open-toed sandals that I had only seen on pictures of Jesus.

My mom opened the door before they knocked. I watched her hug Monica quickly and then turn to the man. They exchanged a few words and then he held out his arms as if on the cross and wrapped them all the way around her in a tight embrace.

I saw the giddy smile on my mom's face, thinking that if her cheeks grew any bigger or pinker, they would explode like a pinata. He held her small hand with his own very, large, tanned hand decorated with several silver rings and the three of them walked towards the door.

I scampered backwards into the kitchen where my dad was leaning against the counter.

"Henry? Henry!"

My dad put his glass of water down on the table and went to the front door to greet the guests.

"Hi Henry." It was Monica. She walked up and gave my dad a big hug. I crept out of the kitchen and slid along the hallway wall so I wouldn't be fully seen.

"I like your cross." My dad smiled.

Monica was wearing a silver cross with a garnet in the middle that my dad had made. She also had a knot ring on one of her ring fingers and an onyx in a braided bezel that was made by Grandpa George.

"Do you know, I never take it off." She responded then turned to the man she had brought with her.

"Henry, this is Elijah." Monica put her arm around my dad and ushered him towards the man that was a giant compared to my dad. I have no idea if his name was really Elijah, but it sounds about right.

"Henry." He said in a smooth, quiet voice. "I've heard so much about you."

"Well, hi. You've come a long way." My dad said with a smile and a laugh at his own joke.

"Well, I'm staying with Monica, but yes, I've been in Honduras for over a year now."

"Isn't that something."

"Elijah, come on in." My mom invited him into the living room, its blue couches with embroidered flowers saved for special company. "Can I help you with your bag?"

My curiosity got the best of me and I entered the room. We had never had a missionary in our home before.

"Elijah, this is Christen, our youngest." She said looking into his eyes. "Where is your sister?"

"Hi." I said.

Elijah held out his enormous arms and walked towards me. My face came to his chest and I squeezed my eyes shut in case I landed in his chest.

"It's a pleasure to meet you." His voice was like butter.

"Where is your sister?" My mom asked again.

"I'll go get her."

I took the opportunity to run upstairs and take in a deep breath. "Abigail? Abigail, mom wants you downstairs."

I knocked on her door. She was in bed reading with an oversized t-shirt on. I brought my nervous energy into the room and expected her to match it.

"Are you coming?"

"I'll come in a minute."

"Mom wants you now."

She looked up at me with a straight face, "I'll COME in a minute."

I wanted her to sit next to me on the couch in the living room. I didn't know what to do with myself around Elijah. He was so large and hairy and carried himself like he was an angel from heaven. I didn't know if I could stomach watching my mom and Monica fawn over him. I didn't know if that was normal. I felt scared and a part of me wanted to run back to my room and close the door and the other part wanted to rush back downstairs so I didn't miss anything.

I was also hungry, and my mom had put out a several appetizers on the dining room table. That afternoon I watched as she boiled the eggs, peeling and cutting them in half. She scooped out the solid, yellow yolk and mixed it with mayonnaise, salt and pepper and then returned the mousse back to the egg white carriage. There was a special, crystal dish she used for deviled eggs. It was circular with a dozen etched beds for each egg half. Once the eggs were laid in the dish, she took a pinch of paprika and sprinkled it on the creamed egg. My mouth watered watching this delicate exercise. I stayed to watch her make the lemon-lime Jell-O in the bunt pan, begging her not to put the maraschino cherries in it.

I ran down the hall to my room and looked at myself in the mirror. I picked up my brush and pulled it through my long hair to the very ends, smoothing it down the other hand. I had put on a dress not knowing what to expect but knowing that our guest was unlike any other.

I walked past Abigail's room hoping I would hear movement. There was silence beyond the door. I went down the stairs hearing the familiar pop and steam of the coffee machine. It smelled so good. My mom loved coffee more than most things and when I smelled it brewing, I knew all was okay.

I could hear their voices joined together in singing a song I knew from church. I thought it was so weird to hear the words and the melody without a band in the background. Did it feel as odd to them as it did to me? I somehow doubt it.

Their eyes were closed as they finished the song. I crept back into the room and sat on a dining chair next to the loveseat where my dad sat. There was silence as we all waited on Elijah.

"Ashala humana rhumana bahala. Ashala humana rhumana bahala." He repeated over and over. He was speaking in tongues and my mom and Monica's, eyes closed, listened with reverence. I looked out from my bowed head to see his serious face. My dad's head was also bowed, his hands clasped together. Abigail had come down in shorts and the t-shirt she had on in bed and sat on a chair next to me. We all sat patiently waiting for something to happen.

Without missing a beat, Elijah opened his eyes. He brought his leather bag up to his knee, pulled out a pink, hand-stitched pouch and out of the pouch a small glass vile. My eyes opened wide. There was liquid in it. He unscrewed the top and turned to my mom who was sitting close to him.

"Ashala humana rhumana bahala. Ashala humana rhumana bahala." He recited, delicately touching my mom's forehead, moving her bangs to the side. Her eyes were still closed, but I could see her eagerness in accepting whatever he had to give.

He drew the sign of the cross on her forehead, pressing the vertical stroke with his large thumb. His lips didn't stop moving as he continued in tongues, his wide bronzed lips purring the words. He turned to his left where Monica was sitting. She was primed with a straight back and ready to receive just as my mom was. He pressed into her forehead.

Elijah stood up and walked over to my dad whose eyes were still closed. I could see where this was heading and before the large man bent his body over my own small one, I jumped to my feet and tip-toed out of the fancy room, circling the downstairs and finding my way to the relief of the stairs. I ran up to my room and closed the door.

A few minutes later, I heard more quiet singing. I could even make out Abigail's voice. I was shocked that she was participating.

I put my head down on my pillow and looked out the window. I saw some little kids riding bikes on the sidewalk. Mr. Patel, our Indian neighbor, was in his driveway washing his silver Mercedes. He dipped the yellow sponge in and out of the bubbles until he was satisfied. Then he took the hose near the garage and aimed the water at the car. The bubbles and dirt ran down the sides and from the roof to the hood to the asphalt. He let the water rinse the car until it ran clean. He picked up a white rag and gently wiped the vehicle, moving in small circles, taking great care to wipe every spot until it was clean.

25

I think I would have let the white walls of my room absorb me if it weren't for my cat. She was a holy thing. Unlike my sister's cat, that I admit I took a bit of delight in terrifying, Pokey held all of life's secrets in her little grey and white puff of a body. Grey and white and grey and white. It's the reason I need cats around me all the time now. My mid-life crisis. No, my mid-life-I am forty-something-and-I-now-I-can-get-what-I-need-for-my-damn-self.

Cat lady and I don't mind.

They each have a million past lives in their eyes and if you are really connected to their ethereal souls, they will know what you need. When I find myself in times of trouble, a cat will come to me, sit on my chest and face to face we will solve all the problems. Breathing in and out together. Usually that's all it takes for me to fall into an alternative space, one that exists all alone, but parallel to the cold physical house around me.

I was so little and so was she. Pokey found her way to the end of my bed each night, running into my room as if the clock were going to strike midnight and she'd turn back into the Dahli Lama. I treated her like she was magic because she was. She was my only safe keeping in the entire house and I am forever grateful for her. She and that very room with the three windows saved me like a lifeboat adrift in a rocky sea. We didn't know when we were going to reach the promised land, but we were there together.

It was Pokey that taught me about surrender and trust and unconditional love. We couldn't save ourselves in the outside world, but we could tuck ourselves away and preserve what we were born from. Like fossils.

She knew what it was like to be owned and I hated that for her. I wanted her to feel extra love because she would never feel what her ancestors experienced out in the wild as a house cat from the pet store. I wanted to make up for all that. And what she gave me in return was a home, my face pressed against her soft belly when the tears started to fall down my face.

We both knew what it was like to be misplaced and have no recourse. Death would release us from this and I couldn't help but think about that and all that the cat and my copy of Emily Dickinson's complete poems taught me. The real truth was that Emily Dickinson was dead and Pokey would die before I would, most likely, but I had a second act and needed to fill up and preserve and save all of me for when I was released out into the wild. I just hoped I was prepared enough to make it past the neighborhood unharmed.

When I found my husband, he knew I had cat-tendencies and when we adopted the little brown and black striped tiger cat from the shelter, he got a close up view of all the traits we shared. I think it was Pokey that helped keep who I was intact. The curious, the soft, the whole-hearted, and the fun. All those things that my family had no idea I had in my soft, little body.

26

I woke up to my parent's alarm clock every day, which wasn't an alarm at all, but a radio station set to 99.7. It went from one evangelical preacher to the next from five o'clock a.m. to ten o'clock, changed over to a few hours to worship music and then capped off the afternoon with Dr. James Dobson and *Focus on the Family*.

"And God said to His people…"

It was Pastor Buck Taylor and he was not just preaching, he was yelling. Yelling at five-thirty a.m. into the dead silence of the upstairs where we were all sleeping. The alarm clock radio was a 5x5 square with one speaker in the side but carried the sound deep into my REM and startled me awake every morning.

He repeated himself and yelled louder. He said the name God like *Gawwwwd* and he paused at various intervals for dramatic affect. I jumped out of bed to the sound of Pastor Buck for the next seven years.

While my parents stirred, I threw my sheets back, panicked by the emphatic preaching. I was the first one up and out of bed. I showered the night before so all I had to do was brush my teeth and hair and put on the outfit that I had laid out for my first day of sixth grade. I was going to public school and had left Mrs. Lynch and Hope Valley behind me.

I matched my peach turtleneck with the peach skin on the painted, wooden handmade doll earrings that I bought at the church fair that summer. My hair fell in long blonde waves past my shoulders and unbeknownst to me was my superpower that year along with the status of being the new girl.

There were a few new girls that year, one of which was my

neighbor, Sadie, who lived across the street. She was transferring from the local Catholic elementary school, St. Luke's. I met Sadie at the top of her driveway, and we walked to the bus stop every morning. I was grateful that I wasn't the only new student on the bus and in my class. Sadie was quiet like me until the summer of seventh grade when I noticed a shift as if she decided she was going to be the sarcastic, funny girl in school. It worked for her. She was sarcastic and funny and made lots of friends.

I didn't know what I was walking into that year, but knew I needed to own a pair of jeans, learn what a blow job was and pretend that I had at least gotten to second base with a boy. I fixed the jean problem first.

The kitchen was usually pitch black because I was the first one up. I went down to the dark kitchen and flipped the switch for the overhead light. I looked up and saw the small, black bugs that had been caught within the frosted glass shades of the ceiling fan. I moved through the kitchen quietly, making myself a piece of buttered toast and sipping just enough water to get it down.

My parents were still in bed as was my sister who was starting high school. Abigail didn't want to go our local public school. She said she didn't like the kids.

I didn't realize how much I would miss out on by not having my sister at my high school. I didn't realize that I would miss someone older looking out for me, driving me to school and paving the way through tricky social situations like how to drink a beer without having to taste it and how to get into a club downtown while underage. We would live down the hall from each other for the next four years and would be more distant than ever before.

I nibbled my toast, looking at the microwave clock and feeling the nerves start to play in my body. I went to the powder room, pulled up the toilet seat and puked up soggy bits of wheat bread. After wiping my mouth, I unzipped the front pouch of my new L.L. Bean backpack and pulled out the little laminated card:

Take this card and hold it dear.

When you read it know He is near.

I sat in the living room reading the little card over and over as the sky turned from black to blue. It was about six-thirty and time to leave. Sadie and I had agreed to meet at six forty-five at the top of her driveway and like my dad, I was always early.

I opened the door and felt the cool, clean air on my face. I took a deep breath. I was relieved I didn't have anyone to say goodbye to. It made everything less worrisome. I closed the door behind me with a click.

Sadie and I walked the ten minutes to the bus stop at the corner where there was a spread of elementary school kids. The older ones were huddled together with their brightly colored backpacks. The smaller kids ran up and down the driveway of the house in front of the stop sign. The two of us stood there awkwardly looking towards the kids that were our age. There was a girl with long blonde hair like mine and deep brown eyes. She was standing next to a boy that I had never seen in the neighborhood. Sadie knew him, though.

"Hi William." She said.

"Hey."

William wore a patrol belt. It was neon yellow and I knew this meant he patrolled the bus, but was not sure what that really meant. We didn't have patrols at Hope and I didn't know that it was a sixth grade honor to be one. He got to stand on the bus and was the first one off, making sure everyone was safe.

I pretended to be busy looking for the bus. I heard its squealing breaks and knew it was close. When it pulled up, I walked up to the doors.

"Kindergarteners first!" William yelled at me as I flinched and stepped backwards. I had no idea what the bus rules were and would not make that mistake twice. The smaller kids climbed into the bus as William stood by the side of the door.

When the little kids were all safely aboard it was our turn. I followed Sadie up the steep steps timidly this time. When I got to the top I stared into the deep length of the bus. It was so long I could hardly see what was happening in the way back. I wanted to sit up front so I could look out the window, but the seats near the driver were occupied by all the younger kids including a small child that lay sleeping in the front seat that was the bus driver's daughter.

Sadie walked straight to the back of the bus as if she knew what she was doing. She found an empty seat and sat on the aisle.

"Can I sit with you?" I asked uncomfortably.

I assumed we were both being thrown into this fire together.

"There's another empty seat over there."

She pointed to a seat a little farther up from the back seats where all the sixth graders were sitting. It was empty. I slid in next to the window as the bus pulled away. William walked to the back of the bus crawling down the aisle with his hands touching every seat.

He sat down in the very last seat near another boy. I got lost in the rhythm of the ride, anxiously watching groups of kids board with each stop. We had a total of four more stops before the bus turned into the school, Forestville, our neighborhood school. The one that I would have gone to if I had not been at Hope for the last five years.

The bus pulled into the half circle drop off area in front. The kids around me jumped up, ready to run down the bus stairs. Teachers waited outside directing the younger children into the school.

When I climbed cautiously off the bus, I must have looked lost because one of the female teachers asked me who my teacher was.

"Mrs. Whitehill." I said having walked up to a friendly looking woman. The rest of the older kids flew through the front doors. I felt a push of cool air on my face and a new rush of adrenaline coarse through my body.

"Okay, you are going to go into the lobby, make a right and go down the hall until you see the purple wall. That is the sixth-grade area. Make a left and Mrs. Whitehill's classroom is straight ahead of you, I believe. If you can't find it there should be some patrols in the hallways to help."

Patrols also helped find classrooms.

I smelled the school before entering the double doors. It smelled like new carpet and library books. There were posters hanging on the walls and smiling people in the hallways. It felt happy. I passed a red section where kindergarteners gathered like a hill of ants then made my way through a rainbow of halls – yellow, orange, green, blue and then purple.

I walked through the entrance to where the sixth-grade pod opened up into a great, big room with a pit in the middle and two steps that went down to a flat center like a mini atrium. Four classrooms outlined the area.

I walked straight ahead until I saw a tall woman with thick, bouncy blonde hair and high heels. She looked at me with wide eyes.

"Hello. Are you in my class? I'm Mrs. Whitehall."

"Yes," I said gripping the straps of my backpack with my sweaty hands.

"And what is your name?" She asked with a bright smile.

"Christen." I tried to mirror her smile back to her.

"Welcome. Head on in and find the desk with your name on it."

The classroom was even brighter than the hallways. The walls were painted a buttery yellow and were covered in what looked like hundreds of posters. There were alphabet cards that wrapped around the top of the walls, each letter with an image. "A" with an apple next to it, "B" a ball. Another series of posters were lined below with printed addition and subtraction, each one with a friendly character like a smiley little worm with glasses. The ABC pictures looked really babyish to me and I was confused as to why we had math answers on the wall. Wouldn't it be cheating to look up and see the answer?

There were enormous white boards behind the teacher's desk and on the opposing wall, contrasting the dull green chalk boards that I was used to at Hope. I saw the markers on a ledge that she would use.

The desks were set up in a large square. Each desk was flat on top with a cubby beneath and stood on four legs. I walked around the room looking for my name, expecting to see it spelled wrong. People always spelled my name wrong and said it wrong. I was Christen with a "K" or I was "Christian" or "Christine" or "Christina". I was never brave enough to correct anyone and sometimes I was known by a completely different name.

Sadie was way ahead of me and had already found her space. I felt a nervous energy fill my stomach as I searched for my name. More kids entered the classroom and began unloading their backpacks. I still couldn't find my desk and started to panic. What if there was no desk for me?

When I felt just about ready to cry and pee on myself at the same time, I saw it.

"CHRISTEN" written out in beautiful, bold letters. I pulled out the plastic blue chair sat down and began unpacking. Two boys sat on either side of me and joined me in pulling out the notebooks and pencils that we were required to bring.

"Hi Class. Feel free to organize your desk and then please place your lunch, if you brought from home, in the cubbies in the hallway. I made my own lunch the night before. I made a peanut butter and jelly sandwich and carefully wrapped five Ritz crackers in plastic wrap. I would have to find a water fountain if I wanted anything to drink.

"Hi." Said the boy next to me when I had made my way back to my desk. I looked over at him. He was small with brown hair, freckles and a huge smile.

"Hi," I said quietly.

"Is this your first day?"

"Yes."

"Did you just move here?"

"No, I just went to a different school." I looked down uncomfortably and played with my pencil case.

"Where do you live?"

"A neighborhood off Georgetown Pike. Just a few minutes from here."

He had a lot of questions, but I was relieved that I had found someone friendly to talk to me and take my mind off of looking at the rest of the faces around the room. There were too many kids staring back at me.

His name was Harry and he was too small to be intimidating. I was glad my seat was next to his.

"Okay, Class. We are going to go around the room and introduce ourselves. Please share your favorite memory of summer. I will go first." She cleared her throat and swung her thick bob left and right, patting the sides down like an unruly pillow. Her hair was so big that some strands didn't comply.

"My name is Nora Whitehall. My favorite memory from my summer was going to the beach with my niece and nephew. Now your turn," she said to the girl sitting at the corner desk.

"My name is Jenny and I loved going to the beach with my family and playing in the waves."

Just about every student said that their favorite memory was of the beach. When Sadie's turn came, Ms. Whitehall told the class that she was a new student.

"Sadie and Christen are new to Woodlawn. Please make them feel welcome." She bobbed her head at Sadie who told the class that she loved going to the beach this summer.

My turn was coming up and I felt my hands sweat and eyes blur. *Let's go around the room* was the worst thing you could say to me and possibly any introvert. I wish I could become invisible every time I heard an authority figure speak the words, *Let's go around the room.*

I dreaded having all the classes' eyes on me. I didn't want to say I had fun at the beach like they all did. In fact, I couldn't because we had not gone to the beach. I could have lied, but I worried about my face growing into an unstoppable shade of deep red.

Harry was speaking before I knew it, "I'm Harry and I got a new dog."

I could have kissed this sweet boy with the freckled face next to me for offering up something new he did that summer. Thank you, Harry. Thank you forever and ever.

"Hi. I'm Christen. My favorite memory was going up to New Hampshire and spending time with my grandma."

That was a good one. Everyone could relate to grandparents and New Hampshire was kind of different. It wasn't California or New York, but still far enough away from Virginia to be a bit interesting. The spotlight quickly moved from me to the boy on my right named Nick. He spoke softly about his beach trip and I could imagine us being friends.

We spent the morning passing paper and cracking open new textbooks and before I realized how much time had passed, it was lunch. We were asked to line up at the door and to my relief we were not required to line up by size. Halleluiah. This was going to be a good year. I followed closely behind Harry as we moved in a snake like line to the cafeteria. I smelled pizza before we even made it through the cafeteria doors. And even though I had packed my lunch, the idea that pizza was being served at school made me cover the huge smile that had grown on my face.

Some of the boys that I recognized from my bus clambered to the back of the cafeteria where they grabbed trays and slide them along a counter where the warm food was being served. They moved like they had been buying lunch for years – and they had. It was like there was a restaurant in the school and one in which kids could order themselves. I could not believe that a place like this existed.

All the sixth-grade classes had moved into the cafeteria and the chatter was loud. I looked around at the round tables and walked over to where I saw a few empty seats next to a pretty, brunette girl. She was sitting with Jenny, from my class, and Sadie.

"Hi. Do you want to sit with us?" The girl with the bright

smile asked.

She was adorable and I instantly could imagine us being friends. Her name was Brooke and her smile was even bigger than Harry's. I loved her immediately.

I watched as the table filled with other happy, chatty girls. They all pulled out their Capri Suns, cups of pudding, packaged chips and various sandwiches. I tried not to stare at the bag of Cheetos the girl across from me had just ripped open. After each twisted chip left her fingers coated in orange dust, she put her thumb in her mouth sucking it clean.

"You guys are all invited to come and swim at my house before we close the pool. Maybe Saturday?"

Brooke had just invited the entire table over to her house where she had a pool. We all said "Yes!" in unison. A few moments after the amazing feeling of my first invitation to a new girls' pool, I thought about the old bathing suit that I had stuffed in my bottom drawer. I immediately felt a flood of shame at thinking about the pink one-piece.

"Ok, guys." Said a teacher that I did not recognize, her voice streaming through a white megaphone. "Throw away your trash and line up by class at the doors for recess."

Recess. I followed a pack of sixth graders out to the black top and without thinking about what the other cafeteria girls were going to gravitate towards, I ran out into the wide, green field. The grass, the sky and then the Spider.

The Spider was a metal jungle gym spread out like the insect with six metal rods for legs. I gleefully ran to the enormous structure and climbed up to the top. It was the best feeling I had had all morning. I walked all around the top, balancing on the metal bars. In the back of my mind I thought everyone would have rushed to the legs of the Spider, thinking it was the best piece of equipment on the playground.

After about fifteen minutes, I realized that no one was interested in the Spider like I was. I was keeping a look out for the other sixth graders to join me when I realized they were not as enamored as I was probably because they had played on it for the past five years.

I gave myself five more minutes then climbed off, running up the grassy hill to where the other girls were. I saw Sadie playing Brooke, Jenny and a few other girls and asked if I could join. Four Square was definitively not as fun as the Spider in the green grass.

I tried to take in all the activity around me. There was a tall pole with a ball attached by a string that some boys were playing with, swings, a huge basketball court and black top, and two huge playgrounds spread out in the field. The kids clearly knew the lay of the land and had a sense of freedom. I could never imagine getting used pizza at school and now this.

Twenty minutes few by quickly and before I realized it, a teacher standing by the back doors blew a whistle that signaled recess was over. We were sweaty and happy. How different it was to be in shorts and not my uniform skirt that I had to worry about flipping up.

We entered Ms. Whitehall's classroom and I felt the air conditioning kiss my hot face and body. We were asked to sit in a circle on the carpet while the teacher read to us from *The Phantom Tollbooth*. I don't remember ever being read to by a teacher and certainly not a whole book. At Hope we were expected to read a novel within a night on our own. Were we really just meant to sit here and listen? Not answer a sheet of questions about the book or write an essay at the end of it? Just listen? I felt like this was something that Kindergarteners did. I certainly didn't require a teacher to read to me. Did the others?

I took a seat next to Harry. We all listened for the full hour as Ms. Whitehall enunciated each piece of dialogue like we were toddlers and she needed to keep our attention. I was so confused by how delicate she was treating us.

We were instructed to go back to our seats and as I sat down Harry turned to me, "Justin wants to know if you'll go out with him."

Go. Out. With. Him.

Go out with him?

Go out with him. Go out with him. I tried it on in my head. I was quick enough to know that Harry was asking me if I would be Justin's girlfriend.

"Who is Justin?"

Harry pointed his finger underneath the desk towards a boy that I remember seeing at the back of my bus that morning. He was tall, super skinny and had hair parted to the side that looked a little greasy. I knew nothing about Justin, but more than that, he had no idea why I was asked to *go out* with someone that I had never met. I was so confused.

Did he think I was pretty? Did he like my hair? My clothes? Did he want to go out with the new girl? Did he know anything about me? I sat there distracted by all these questions and more as the science teacher came in to go over this week's lesson.

What did going out even mean? Was he going to call me? Hold my hand? Kiss me? What was expected of me if I said yes? But, I would never say yes. The embarrassment rose at the mere idea of this boy calling my house and my mom answering the phone gave me my decision. I could not have a boy call my house or, God forbid come into my house.

When the science teacher was done explaining what we would be studying the next few weeks, and we were transitioning subjects, I leaned over and whispered to Harry.

"Tell him I said no, and I hate him."

I was hoping that this would be enough to get Justin off my back, call me or ride his bike to my house – all of which were fears that I was now contemplating. What if he rode his bike to my house? What if he knocked on my door? What if my mom answered or Abigail?

I needed to be as mean as possible and ensure that he wouldn't come around me. I was terrified of him for reasons that had nothing to do with going out with him. I was terrified that my family would find out that this boy liked me.

I knew my reaction was too strong the moment I said it. I hated him? How could I hate him? But I couldn't risk him liking me out loud. It felt like all too much and I wanted the whole thing to go away.

27

"I'm a Christian." I responded to William who had asked me where I was the night before, Halloween night.

"I'm a Christian too." He said. "But, I still go trick or treating.

I spend the previous night on the floor squished between my bed and my window, the lights off and the shades open so I could see the groups of kids in their costumes come down the driveway to collect candy. I wanted so badly to be in one of the clumps of kids, my new friends from the neighborhood, carrying large sacks of candy. I wanted to dress up like Madonna or a Backstreet Boy – singers I was introduced to since being at Forestville. I was still trying to catch up on all the things that I had missed while at Hope the last five years. My learning curve was steep, but I was determined to know everything the others knew.

Michael Jackson had a creepy video out called *Thriller*, MTV was a station on cable with music videos. We didn't have cable at my house and I craved every moment I was allowed to sit in front of Sadie's TV and absorb it. French kissing was kissing with your tongue and girls were not giving blow jobs, they were just talking about giving blow jobs, which I now knew what they were. Jeans were a big deal and every girl had their favorite pair. We went to the mall on the weekends and bought CDs. My first "secular" cd was Mariah Cary. I knew every song and referenced them whenever possible. Girls and boys had started going out and breaking up all around me. Although I now had a crush on a boy and thought about him all the time, I was still deathly afraid of him knowing or coming anywhere near me.

Halloween night was the first time that I found myself conflicted by what I was learning at Woodlawn and what God expected from me. We were still going to church every Sunday and were taught that I was called by God to be different, to do different, to talk differently. I was asked to minister to friends about Jesus and ask them to let Him into their hearts. I was supposed to invite them to church and pray for them.

In previous years, we had always gone to church on Halloween. The church would host an evening of games, candy and ended with worship music and prayer. They called it the Halleluiah Party and if we brought a non-believer, we would get extra candy. I always wore the same costume that my mom had made for me in first grade, an angel. The sheet was big enough that it still fit me. I'd panic the night before and peel through boxes in the basement trying to find the cardboard wings.

At the end of the night, during the final prayer, Ben asked if anyone would like to pray and invite Jesus into their hearts. He asked us to keep our eyes closed so we couldn't see around the room, but he counted. He sure counted. The next Sunday he would tell us the number of kids that had prayed Jesus into their hearts, congratulating us and himself.

Abigail had told my mom that she was going a friend's house near her school. I guess because of that we never talked about going to the Halleluiah Party that year and I never asked to go trick or treating knowing my mom thought it was an opportunity for Satan to wreak havoc. It wasn't just about not being allowed to go, though. I was also afraid that God was going to be mad at me if I went and let Satan have a foothold.

My mom hated Halloween. She hated the skeletons and spider webs and thought it was a "dark" holiday. I didn't think I would have the feeling of missing out until night fell and I could hear all the laughing and cheering outside my window. I now had friends close by and couldn't help but think of them all having a great time collecting candy and being set loose around the neighborhood.

But, I was a Christian and Christians didn't celebrate dark holidays. The feeling I had of being left out turned into a type of

defiance when I walked to the bus stop the next morning and responded to William's questioning.

When we got to school, and Mrs. Whitehill asked us to go
around the room and tell the class what we dressed up. I wanted
to melt. I was an angel.

28

Somewhere after Hope and into the fall at my new school, I stopped throwing up.

I forgot about getting up early to make sure I had time to clean myself up after purging the contents of my stomach. I forgot about holding in my belly tight. I forgot about the plastic grocery bags and the feeling of being trapped. I avoided the powder room all together and the haunting memories I had created in that space. It didn't exist for me anymore.

I made new friends, I bought new clothes, I listened to new music and I talked for hours on the phone. I felt like I could breathe. The kids in the neighborhood would all meet at the pond after school or ride bikes in the rain. We'd find ourselves at the gully and goof around or at Sadie's house where we'd watch hours of music videos.

I went to my first boy-girl party and was more intrigued by the gigantic bowls of chips that Brooke's mom had laid out for us on the basement ping pong table than any of the boys there. I had put Hope out of my mind completely and turned my focus to how to paint my nails, use a curling iron and insert a tampon.

My mom was always somewhere in the kitchen making notes, my dad tinkered, and Abigail had started dying her hair and wearing black lipstick. I flew down the stairs and out the door feeling a new sense of freedom. My world was opening up and the sun was breaking through the clouds. It was a new and beautiful time. I thought the bad was behind me and life was going to turn out happy.

Then Dove happened.

Her death came out of nowhere. It was fast and violent, and

my family kept it a secret until they couldn't. I broke all over again. This time swiftly and permanently.

29

Dove came to Hope in the spring of third grade. She was gorgeous with her long, blonde hair and honeyed eyes. I looked at her across the room, as all the girls and boys did, and said to myself, "I want her to be my best friend." By the end of the year we were inseparable.

Dove's house was like a magical oasis. She lived on Lake Anna with a floating dock and a small boat. Her mom bought Barbie cereal, made chicken nuggets for dinner and her living room had the largest couch I've ever seen. It was a brown, suede sectional with the middle filled in with additional ottomans so it was like one big, cozy island. We watched tons of movies with large bowls of popcorn that Dove's mom would fill with M&Ms in the bottom, so every bite was perfectly salty and sweet. Once we discovered the movie Overboard, we watched it every single time I went for an overnight, which was almost every other weekend. I wanted it to be every weekend, every weeknight.

Her brother Dylan was much older and in college. He had a waterbed in his room that we jumped on, laughing uncontrollably as we tried to stay still through the waves. Her dog was named Sammy and her mother was the most beautiful woman I had ever seen. She smiled with her eyes and talked softly with pink lips.

She would say things like "Dove, why don't you girls make cupcakes? I just bought a box of Duncan Hines with strawberry frosting." Or "Dove, why don't you girls try on that new nail polish I bought you."

She was always doing little things like this for Dove and would include me in the treat. I saw delight in her mother's eyes even when she looked at me. She liked me. Could she ever love me? Like a daughter? She told me that I looked just like Olivia Newton John. I didn't know what to do with this information beside hide my bursting smile and say thank you. Her mom's name was Susan just like my mom's. Dove's Susan let us take long walks along the lake and search for smooth rocks near their dock.

I slept in Dove's big bed with her and Susan would come in and tuck us in. She'd go to Dove's side of the bed, kiss her and tell her "sweet dreams". Then she's come to my side of the bed with a soft giggle, kiss me and say, "sweet dreams." And they were. They were the sweetest dreams I ever had.

The next morning, Susan would have breakfast laid out on the table. It reminded me of the way Gram had breakfast table set up. There were two plates set out with placemats underneath, a fork, a spoon and a large glass of orange juice. There was always cut fruit, at least two boxes of cereal to choose from and Susan would still offer to make us eggs.

"Christen, do you want eggs, Sweetheart?"

Just hearing her say my name made me want to hug her and never let go. I never wanted to leave.

"I'm fine but thank you so much." I wanted to thank her with the sweetest voice I had so she knew how much I appreciated and loved her. She floated through the kitchen in a soft, pink bathrobe like a cloud, humming to herself, available if we needed her.

"Who died?" I asked as a joke. My mom whipped her head around and stared at me. I had just hung up the phone and had to get ready for my piano recital. My grandparents had come down from New Hampshire for a visit and to see me perform. They were still paying for my lessons.

I jumped off the counter and scurried to my room to get dressed. I put on the sundress that I had bought while at the mall with my friends. It was yellow with pink flowers. I also purchased wedge sandals that made me two inches taller. I felt good. I played Bach, accepted the flowers from my grandparents and got to choose whatever I wanted, my dad offered, off the menu at the Silver Diner. It was a good day.

We all got up early Sunday for church. I watched my mom introduce her parents proudly to her friends and acquaintances as we walked in. I sat next to Gram during the service and held her hand. They were taking us out to brunch at Clyde's in Reston Town Center, a special treat. I had already thought about what I was going to order – eggs benedict.

"Chris, why don't you drive with me?" My mom said after church as we approached the parking lot.

"I want to go with Gram."

"Dad's going to drive them over and reserve a table. You come with me." Something felt off. My mom looked at my Dad and my Dad looked to the ground.

"I'll go with you guys," Abigail said.

We walked to my mom's burnt-red minivan that they bought last year. Abigail let me have shot gun and before we had left the church parking lot my mom was talking.

"Chris." Her voice trembled and then shook. I was growing scared. "Hon. Dove was in an accident."

I looked at her and then looked to the floor of the car.

"Is she ok?"

My mom didn't answer. She cried harder letting her mouth droop downwards. I didn't know what she was trying to say.

"No, Hon."

"What do you mean?"

"She died." Her voice squeaked out the words as she covered her mouth from her own sobs, leaving one hand on the steering wheel.

I couldn't lift my eyes and imagined the street below the car moving by quickly. I stopped breathing.

"She's not even sad. I at least was crying." Abigail said from the back, staring at my bowed head.

I was beyond responding to my sister but would not forget the comment. I was desperate to cry. I wanted to ask a million questions. But, I swallowed them along with all my emotion not trusting the response I would get from my mother or sister. I wanted to keep everything I felt inside until I landed safely in my room. I sat stiffly, paralyzed and managed to ask one more question before retreating to the recess of my brain.

"How did she die?" I said quietly.

"There was a car accident." My mom said relieved to unload the details she had been holding on to. "There was an accident on Friday."

My brain did another hiccup. She had known for two days that Dove was dead and no one had told me. My Dad knew. My sister knew. My Gram and Grandpa knew. I was in this car so they could tell me. I made a joke on the counter yesterday before my recital. We were going to go out for brunch, and I was going to order eggs benedict. It was going to be a good day.

Friday?

"A truck hit Susan's car. Dove and three of her friend's died. Susan is in the hospital."

I pursed my lips and tightened my neck trying to shut it all down. I stared out the window and tightened my face. I wanted my room.

"Do you still want to go to brunch?"

"I want to go home." I said it quietly, but assertively. "I want to go home."

"Ok."

She drove home.

I ran upstairs, pulling myself inward until I reached my door, locking it behind me and finding the bed. I crawled under the covers and squeezed my eyes shut. The pain was too great to process. The headache that arrived was never going to leave. I was never going to be okay. I didn't know what to do with my body. I didn't know where everyone was in the house, but it had been three hours since I had seen anyone. I wanted someone to come and find me and talk slowly to me. I wanted someone to talk slowly and tell me everything.

I opened the door and looked down the hall. I heard quiet voices downstairs and crept to the stairwell. I walked halfway down the stairs.

"Mom?" I was vulnerable and didn't want to be, but I needed her. "Mom?"

"Hold on." She said to the room. "Yeah, Chris?" She walked over to the stair wiping her hands on a dish cloth. She had been cooking.

"Do you have the article?"

Abigail had said that there was an article in the *Post* and I thought this would be easier than to expose myself to talk to my mom.

"Uh, yea."

I felt like I had inconvenienced her. Like, I had asked for something when she was already too busy. I was right not to trust her with what was happening in my mind and body.

I heard her walk to the kitchen and then back to where I was on the stairs. A part of me still wanted her to tell me that she would come upstairs with me, rub my back, and explain everything. Instead she handed the newspaper to me without a word and walked back into the kitchen.

I took the paper and ran up into my room and locked the door. I sat underneath the window on the floor and read about how a mac truck had hit Susan's car on Rt. 7 and Lewisville Road. She was turning left and did not see the truck until it hit her. The other fourteen-year olds in the back seat died immediately. Dove was in the front passenger seat and was thrown from the car into the street and was medevacked to Fairfax Hospital where she was declared dead. Susan had survived and was in the ICU.

My heart. My head. My body. The pain was white hot. I needed someone to talk to. I needed to tell someone. I decided to walk over to Sadie's. I knocked on her door, holding the newspaper. She said she was very sorry, but it wasn't enough. It was nowhere near enough. Heaven was not enough. I left unsatiated and went back to my room until the sun went down.

I was alone for what felt like days. It had been almost seven hours. I didn't know what I needed. I didn't know what anyone downstairs could offer me. But, my stomach was unrelenting and crying out in hunger pains. I smelled pasta.

I walked down the stairs and into the kitchen. My grandparents were still there. I went over to the counter where my sister handed me a bowl of bleeding spaghetti. I took it into the family room and sat on the couch. My grandfather was sitting on a chair watching the little, black and white television.

He said nothing to me. I awkwardly asked him if he had heard what happened. He looked over at me with bullet blue eyes that were brighter than my mom's and bright red cheeks, purple blood vessels ruptured near his nostrils.

"Do you think you know death?" He pursed his lips and stared down into my face. "You know nothing about death."

I looked away, tears filling my eyes. I couldn't stomach the angry man in front of me and his lack of empathy. I put my fork unused back into the bowl, brought it to the kitchen and placed it on the table.

I walked back up the stairs quietly so as not to be noticed and closed and locked my door.

30

I lay in bed from until morning falling in and out of sleep - waking in the night crying into my pillow and then tearfully exhausted falling back into sleep. I didn't want to get up. I didn't know how to get up. The pain and confusion had pulled and twirled inside of me until I felt a huge knot. The roots grabbed onto the mess of pain that was already there and expanded inside of my stomach. It was alive and growing. It was every question I had and everything I ever had to say and all the anger that I couldn't express that I had shoved down my throat and stuck there. It was a place where I felt would never receive release. It would solidify before it saw the light of day, before I let it seep out through therapy and tears and anger. I would chip away at it for the rest of my life like I was a miner at a quarry working by myself from sunup to sundown, releasing only rubble from the dark mass. I felt it when I slept, when the nausea crept up and tried to come up and out my throat. I'd swallow it with glugs of Pepto until it receded into its cave.

That next morning Gram came to my door. I opened it and allowed her to sit on my bed. She told me how sorry she was. I let her see me cry.

My mom came to the door.

"Well, what do you think about going?"

"I don't know."

My parents were supposed to drive me down to Brevard Music Center in South Carolina the next day. I had auditioned and gotten into the July session. It was four weeks of intensive piano performance and theory. I was looking forward to escaping and now I couldn't imagine leaving. I desperately wanted to ask my mom when the funeral service was, but, a deep fear kept me from showing her what I needed. It was too sad and too much. I didn't know how to talk about it, and she didn't offer a listening ear.

"Chris, I think it sounds like a wonderful opportunity," Gram said.

I looked into her eyes. She grabbed my shoulders and held me. I let the tears flow until my face ached. She looked into me with intentionality. She was trying to convey something that only her and I could understand through our eye contact.

"I think it may be really good for you to get away. What do you think?" She tilted her head and refused to break her stare.

"Maybe."

"Chris, I think you should go." My mom was standing, and I could feel her agitated energy. She went into the hallway, collected a large duffle bag and placed it on my bedspread.

"Let's go." She pressed.

I felt like it was the wrong thing to do. I felt like it would be shoving down more of my sadness, but I also knew that the well was dry here. There was no one that was going to feed me and nurse me back from death. I swallowed.

"Ok." I said.

I stood up and tried to pack, but my hands were shaking too much. I couldn't think straight and didn't know what to put in the bag. My mom took over, folding underwear and shorts.

"You'll need a few long-sleeved shirts as well because it will probably get cold at night."

I moved around the room and aimlessly flicked through the hangers in my closet. I grabbed a plain, blue sweatshirt and put it on the bed. I couldn't do anymore. I wanted everyone out of my room, even Gram. I didn't want to pack, and I didn't want to talk about packing. I sat down on my red beanbag chair and let them move around the room. When they were done, I let them leave without saying anything.

I made it downstairs to say goodbye to my grandparents. Dad was taking them to Dulles. I hugged them both goodbye. Gram hugged me and looked deep into my eyes once again, telling me she loved me. I stayed downstairs until dinner was ready and ate a huge plate of buttered noodles.

"We are leaving at four a.m., girls."

My stomach flipped thinking about leaving home for a full month. But I was so tired, and my eyes were so sore that I let myself fall asleep easily. At three-thirty in the morning I heard Paster Buck Taylor and climbed out of bed.

31

The next fall I started high school and it was a beautiful distraction. Herndon High, Herndon Hornets. Class of 1996. I established a core group of the best girlfriends anyone could have. They were like snowflakes, each one unique in their own way and complimented my personality like a sweet winter snowfall, a white blanket coating all the sharp edges and bringing me much-need relief.

We shopped at thrift stores, listened to the Indigo Girls and the Beatles, made mix tapes and wore our hair in braids. We were liked by everyone but refused to fit ourselves into the confines of the other groups of kids around us. We were smart and thoughtful and wanted to do dreamy things with our lives like become writers and musicians. We were in love with Holden Caufield and read e.e. cummings before bed.

I was constantly out of my house puttering around town with the girls, grabbing coffee and seeking out used bookstores. If I wasn't out with my friends, I was home in my room behind a locked door.

I tried to never cross paths with my mom. I'd run from my room out the door to Nina's refurbished convertible or Molly's hand-me-down brown station wagon she named Buddy. We would go to Nina's house where her mother would teach us how to make baklava and stuffed grape leaves while we talked about her life in Paris. We were eating hummus before hummus came in six different flavors. We ate Nutella before Costco sold it. And we went to little Indian restaurants, ordering all the vegetarian dishes we could afford.

We fell in love with boys that drove vintage Saabs and skateboarded. We took hikes at Great Falls Park and ate caprese sandwiches at the little market on the way home. Our favorite movies were anything with *Audrey Hepburn*. We painted our toenails white and quoted Jane Austin. We loved *Anne of Green Gables.*

And we were just good.

I dreamed of living in London after college and writing. I finally knew who I was becoming in high school and that was a writer. I published several short stores and won local competition. I worked on our school literally magazine, *The Scribe*, and published more pieces than any other student in the school. I won the yearly writing contest every year. I was a writer.

I bought books with my allowance - poetry, fiction, and a healthy stack of meditation and self-help books. I knew what I wanted to learn about and the kind of person I wanted to be. I was the writer who could recite Williams Carols Williams. I was going to go to a liberal arts college and sit under a tree and learn to play the guitar.

Molly got us all jobs Wolf Trap National Park for the Performing Arts. I worked backstage and met famous people like Tony Bennett and Art Garfunkel, the entire cast of River Dance and served the National Symphony Orchestra their grilled cheese sandwiches.

Nicole worked as an usher and Molly was at the concession. We met up after work and sat on the grass of the outdoor amphitheater, catching the remainder of the shows. When the Indigo Girls came, we bought front row tickets every summer and tried to get Amy and Emily to notice us, notice that we knew every word.

During my junior year, I decided I wanted more. We made friends with older boy that smoked weed and dropped acid on the weekends. They all smoked, expect Ryan because he didn't want the BMW he bought himself smelling like smoke. Robbie was already a recovering alcoholic and I let myself bum cigarettes when we stayed out late.

I researched different kinds hallucinogenic drugs, settling on peyote, which I read about in the Doors of Perception. And if *Riders on the Storm* was written during a trip then what wonderful things could come from my own? Did I dare find out? And how would I score peyote anyhow?

The fear of experimenting in this way overshadowed my curiosity. I had no idea what my parents would do if they found out or if I needed help. Would they send me away? Would my mom refuse to look at me? Would she give up on me completely?

Abigail was somewhere far away probably doing similar things. Where my mom seemed to look right past me as if I was invisible, she was equally hyper focused on my sister. Abigail was dying her hair every week, ultimately dying it a total of thirty-two times or so she said. She kept each Clairol box on display on a shelf in her room. She wore black fishnet tights and lipstick, snuck out of the house, shortened her uniform skirt. Every week I overheard her telling my parents that she had detention after school. But, she still made the honor roll, she still maintained straight As and my parents adored her, maybe more so, for her antics.

Abigail provided the levity my parents craved. I observed her pulling and pushing boundaries, but my parents seemed to find such humor in her. They loved her for it. Abigail was unabashed about her development and interests. She invited my parents to go to Dupont Circle to shop for clothes and out to dinner with her friends. Everything was out in the open. My parents were included in all of it. If I had to guess, my mom was even living out some of her missed experiences through Abigail.

I rotated the opposite way. I didn't want to include my parents in my friend circle or my ideas and thoughts. I knew they wouldn't understand me because I had tried to no avail. At that point my anger was at a simmer, being tempered by my independence and friend groups. I didn't trust my parents with who I was becoming. I learned long ago not to trust them. I was learning to put up boundaries to protect myself and both parties seemed to sign off to this unwritten arrangement. I won't require anything of you if you don't ask anything of me.

If they had knocked on my door, asked to talk and catch up over a cup of tea, I would have felt a warm sense of gratitude and love. I would have cherished the interest on their faces. But, as I was discovering, they were both lost somewhere underneath their surfaces, turning and spinning with their own memories and feelings; too distracted to notice me.

32

My family still went to church together when we were in high school. Even if Abigail and I arrived home at curfew, we were still expected to wake up for the nine o'clock service. We skipped our showers and pulled on tee shirts and dozed in the car. We would both crawl into church with tired eyes and foggy heads, only half paying attention to John Stuart Mills' message. When we returned home, we both crawled right back in bed.

While Abigail was safe and tucked in at her private school, I was receiving an education that went beyond any textbook. Herndon High would later be linked to gangs and violence. I kind of liked it that way. It felt like real life.

Maybe I couldn't be book smart and make straight As, but I could certainly be street smart. I could anticipate threat and keep myself safe. It was home for four years. All the kids knew which hallways to detour through if we saw groups of kids fighting, sparing in the middle of a circle of rowdy spectators, blood spattered on the lockers left for the janitorial staff to clean up after school. There was little supervision and kids of every color got away with most everything. I recall more than once a teacher being threatened and leaving her classroom in tears.

It felt like white kids were the minority at my school. I'm not sure if that was true or not, but I watched as the arrogant, white boys yield to the stronger, more dominant black boys that walked tall in their starter jackets. When the white guys started mingling with the black and brown kids, they learned quickly that their position was at the bottom of the totem pole. No so for girls and especially small, blonde girls like me. I got more attention from many beautiful black guys than I had from anyone else in my life during that time. I felt wanted, protected. Some called me shorty and it had nothing to do with my height.

The first boy that I ever called my best friend a tall, lanky black guy named Tyler. We talked every day on the phone after school. For hours. I fell asleep to his breathing on the other end of the phone most nights. At school we'd see each other in the hallway, and he'd lay an arm around my shoulder.

We walked tall through the hallway. He liked my blonde hair and small stature. I liked how he made me feel.

I had my girlfriends and he had a few boys that he hung out with, but there was a space that was just for us on the phone after a long day. We needed each other. I depended on him like I would have depended on an older sister. I counted on his time. He was sweet to my girlfriends and joked around with all of us at lunch when he would make his way to our table, but I was his favorite.

The following year, Tyler made the football team and the basketball team and we talked less and less. While at home I was being pushed more and more.

"Why don't you wear your hair down?" My mom literally grimaced at me in what looked like disgust.

I thought back to the times that she would touch my hair when I as little and comment, "Your hair is fine, but you have a lot of it." She said it all the time until it carved a loop in my brain. I pulled my hair up, trying my best to hide it inside buns and clips, incorporating it into my look.

I was confused and didn't know what she wanted from me. I felt like she was repulsed by me and I didn't know how to make myself presentable to her.

"She didn't even spell nightingale right."

The words haunted me.

The wound had not healed and the damage was irreversible. There was such disdain in her voice. It felt like a confession.

That she was finally admitting that she wanted nothing to do with my interests and exploration. I took the message and buried it with all the other messages she had offered throughout the years.

This. This right here would be one of those memories that would stick like tar around my insides, too hard to clean out. No therapy good enough or long enough to wash away.

33

I played *The White Album* from a tape in the car.

"This not the Beatles."

"Yes, it is," I said.

"Ugh." My mother let out that guttural sound she made when she was disgusted and frustrated at the same time. A sound a wild animal would make, loud enough to startle someone. She hated my music.

I never played *The White Album* for her after that.

I found such relief in music. I discovered Joni Mitchell and Crosby Stills and Nash, Cat Stevens, Paul Simon and my favorite song, *America*. I still get goose bumps up my arms when I listen to the lyrics, a story about two young people sitting on a bus in search of freedom, a new land to make their own. They are lost, but they know there is something more out there for them.

I was a teenager in the 90s and equally identified with the grunge, alternative movement, the misfits like Nirvana, the Cranberries, Smashing Pumpkins. These bands were an antidote to pop culture and music at the time. If you were into these bands, you were also alternative. You were not the boring cheerleaders or soccer players that stayed in their vanilla lane. Music was a gateway, like it is for most teenagers, to a sense of identity. It is important.

I bought tickets to WHFS Festival every year at RFK Stadium and took the Metro in with a bunch of drunk friends. I remember being the only one sober one, but also refused to spend money on food. I'd get home sweaty, sun-burned and puking. I was able to hide the noises from my parents by running the water in the bathroom and flushing the toilet. I let my mom think whatever she wanted while my head spun from the nausea of not eating.

34

I slowly removed myself from the framework of my family. They expected me for dinner and for church, but other than that, I was not around. I found my own way with my friends, music and my books. I spent time thinking about what the future would look like. I was still young enough to think that I could be a writer.

I wanted to be good at something that my parents would deem worthy or at least invest in the idea and help me achieve my professional goal. Writing was what I was good at. It's the only thing that teachers noticed about me. It was one of the main characteristics my friends identified me with. I was the writer in the group. Nicole wrote a song to one of my poems and played it on the guitar, but I couldn't help but think that I was on borrowed time. There was no real profession where I was going to be paid to write poems and short stories.

I resigned myself to consider journalism even though I was still painfully shy and fearful that there I would not be able to chase someone for an interview. I made myself work on the student newspaper. I hated it.

I started having nightmares that I would never make it out of Herndon and joked that I would still be working at the Wolf Trap canteen when I was thirty. At the bare minimum I knew I needed to make enough money after college to get a job and move out of my parent's house. But the expectation of making money did not seem like enough when I heard Abigail talking about environmental engineering and grad school. No one had these conversations with me.

The nightmares came later when every night I dreamed that

I couldn't escape. I had to stay there, in the house, in my room, because I had no money and no one to save me.

I needed to find solace from my growing anxiety before I started getting physically sick again. There was one place on the planet that had comfort in abundance – Gram's. That spring break, I flew by myself up to Gram's house in New Hampshire. My uncle picked me up from the airport and I stared out the window at the tall pine trees lining the winding roads and taking me to what felt like home. The air was still cool and felt cleaner and less stuffy than in DC. A thrill went through me as we pulled up the driveway to my grandparents' house tucked into a little cove of trees.

She was waiting outside for me, holding a bundle of freshly cut daffodils in her hands.

I jumped out of the car and let my body surrender into her delicate arms. She hugged me so tightly I could feel her arms shake, "You're here."

"I'm here."

She pulled me apart from her chest to look me in the eyes.

"I can't believe you came all this way just to see me."

I couldn't express to her what being in her arms meant to me. She would never understand. There was no place like the safety of Gram's home for me.

"I needed to see you. I'm so excited to be here."

"My goodness. Look at you. You are such a beautiful young lady. Are you hungry?"

"A bit."

"How was the flight?" She asked as she grabbed me by my waist and guided me into her home. We walked through the breezeway, my uncle close behind with my suitcase.

"I'm just going to put this here." He said.

"Thank you so much for getting me from the airport, Uncle Steve."

"No problem, Sweetheart. Now don't you girls get into too much trouble, okay?"

I gave him a hug and thanked him again before turning into

Gram's warm kitchen. I smelled apple crisp immediately and saw the kitchen completely set up for guests. There was a table-cloth with little flowers dotted over it, pink placemats, forks, spoons, knives, glasses full of juice and plates ready for serving.

"Gram, you shouldn't have gone to all this trouble."

"Oh, don't be silly. It's no trouble. I can't believe you are here." She gave me another hug and we stayed like that for several minutes, each of us soaking up one another's presence. I felt like I was healing right then and there, absorbing all her energy and love.

"Grandpa's in the bedroom lying down if you want to go say hi. I'm just going to pull the chicken pot pie from the oven."

"It smells amazing."

I immediately wanted to go into the guestroom, put on my sweatpants and take off my shoes. I wanted to soak in the spirit of her and her home. But, before changing, I went into Grandpa's bedroom.

"Big Bird! Is that you?"

"Hi Grandpa."

"Get over here."

I went over to where he was laid out on his bed, the top half slightly raised and a quilt covering his legs. The television in the corner was on and he was watching golf. I heard the whisper of the commentators as I leaned over the bed to hug him. He wrapped his Popeye arms around me and squeezed me so hard I squeaked involuntarily, "Ok. That hurts." He didn't let go and kept me in his grip just a few more moments.

"Great to see you, Kid."

"Now, you go help your Grandmother."

"I will. Do you need anything?"

"Nope, I'm good." His focus was back on the television and I took my leave. Uncle Steve had wheeled my bag into the guestroom down the hall. I walked in and saw the queen-sized bed draped in my favorite butterfly patched quilt. The smell of Gram was everywhere. The dresser held pictures of all of the grandkids throughout the years and I took my time looking through them. I unfastened my hair that had been pulled in a ponytail and unzipped my sweater. I kicked my shoes off to the side of the bed and let me feet sink into the plush carpet. The adjoining bathroom was decorated with peach accessories - layered fresh peach towels on the towel bar, a cake of peach soap and a little bowl of potpourri. I leaned down and sniffed in the scent that was Gram.

I was overwhelmed with an intense relief that I was here in her house, in her company. She was a greater presence to me than anyone in my life, then God Himself. I had no doubt of how she felt about me. We talked weekly on the phone and she listened when I told her what was happening at home. She was a secret-keeper. She was love itself. She was apple pie and a warm blanket and Christmas. She was magic and nothing else was like being here with her. There was no other place I'd rather be.

As much as I felt her goodness, I was also aware that there was a sleeping dragon in house and one that I had better tip-toe around very carefully. He was just in the other room and I prayed that golf was going to be on the television for the rest of the week.

35

He pulled his hand back like a sling shot, his arm shaking and his face trembling. I closed my eyes waiting for contact and when I opened them his hand was still in the air, his blue eyes piercing into me like a million swords. What had just happened?

I looked from his eyes to his blood-thirsty mouth to his hand realizing he had every intention of hitting me across the face. What had stopped him?

"Don't you dare." He growled at me. "Don't you dare."

I tried to process what had happened and what I had just said to make him turn from sitting across from me as we watched TV to him wanting to hit me. I became impossibly still, paralyzed, afraid to move – a fawn sensing danger and stilling her body and breath as if dead until the threat was removed. But, he didn't move. Not his gaze, not his hand. And I didn't move for fear of him grabbing me with his enormous arms.

It felt like we sat like this for hours, days, but I'm sure it was only seconds before tears started filling my eyes, too heavy to keep in place no matter how I willed them to.

"You're not going to cry, are you?"

I begged my tears to reabsorb so I could stand up and leave the room. I was also confused. I thought all adults knew that saying "God" was not okay unless referring to the God in the Bible. My mom scolded people all the time for saying the Lord's name in vein. What had I done wrong?

There was a part of me that did want to put him in his place; to let him know that I saw him for the monster he was. I know my mom was working on changing him. She had books about witnessing to your parents and prayed for him in the living room.

I guess on some level I thought he'd turn and say to me, "Oops, you're right." I thought we both knew the rule. But, we both didn't know this rule. Or maybe we, in fact, followed different rules. Maybe what I was taught was not how other people thought – not how the world thought.

I was set to leave the following day after a beautiful week with Gram and felt as though I had narrowly escaped his ire. I overheard him call me a nerd to Gram a few nights before as we gathered our purses to drive over to Swanzey for an outdoor band performance in the town square.

"You know she's just a nerd." He said it with a bent "e" sound revealing his New England accent. I willed my ears not to hear it and waited for Gram's response, terrified that she would agree.

"She is not. She loves her music. Now stop it."

This little woman fought back until the monster receded to his bedroom, his cave. I was afraid of him hurting her in defense of me. I sighed in relief that the conversation had not escalated.

Now, I was in front of the beast myself deciding what my next move was going to be. I wanted to pretend that we were not sitting across from one another and that I had just kept my mouth closed. If I had known the true danger of my tongue, I would have cut it off to save me from the fear of his abuse.

I stood up.

I put one foot in front of the other and walked my heavy-laden feet out of the family room and into the guestroom. I shut the door and fell onto the bed, wrapping myself as tightly as possible in the butterflies. I let myself sob quietly into their rainbow wings and feel the soft cotton between my fingers. I fell asleep that way until dinner time.

Gram's puttering in the kitchen woke me up just as the sun was setting behind the deep wood in the backyard, the pine trees so stately and proud against the purple sky. I made my way to the bathroom to wash my face. Mascara had bled down my cheeks and my lips were puffed. I splashed water on my face and practiced smiling in the mirror. When I felt like I could get away with looking unscathed, I left the room to go help Gram.

She was shuffling around the kitchen. I thought I smelled meatloaf and saw a mountain of mashed potatoes in a crystal bowl, golden rolls and glistening string beans already on the table.

"Hi Gram. What can I do to help?"

"Not a thing, Dear. I'm just –

She looked over at me. "What happened? What's wrong?"

A tear escaped as she recognized the pain in my face. She saw me even when I tried to hide my sadness.

"Tell me what happened." She pulled out one of the wood chairs for herself and another one for me. She patted it, inviting me to sit across from her. Her eyes looked deep into mine and it was as if there was nothing else in the world that was more important than my troubled face. I opened my mouth to tell her everything when a sob escaped. Her eyebrows furrowed in anger and knowing, "What did he do?"

She stood up with a fierceness I had not seen before.

"Sit down, sit down. It's okay, Gram. It was my fault. I said something that I shouldn't have."

She pulled me up to stand and gathered me into her chest, letting me cry and just feel held. I didn't want to tell her; I didn't want to cause trouble for her. It wasn't worth it. It wasn't worth him spitting fire at her too.

"Let me just help you finish dinner."

She looked at me for another full beat and said, "Ok." We both knew that her comfort meant more to me than another altercation. We let him sleep and she served the meatloaf.

I blew out the tapered candle she lit just for her and I and pulled up the placemats to wash. I was leaving in the morning.

"Thank you for dinner. That was amazing. I want to write down a few of your recipes before leaving."

"Oh, I'll do that for you after dessert."

I washed the dishes, letting the warm water run over my hands. She worked behind me, putting all the serving dishes in their places and drying the silver forks we had used and tucked them into bed in the drawer.

I woke up early the next morning to Gram laying a hand on my shoulder, "Time to get up, Sweetheart."

I showered and gathered my things. Gram had set the table with two place settings, including an English muffin and a half a grapefruit. She had sprinkled sugar on mine.

"You know how much I love you, don't you?" We were in the driveway saying goodbye. My face was in her hands and her eyes inches from my own. I saw the little shadow her glasses created at the corner of her eyes and a sparkle of a tear.

I nodded, "I love you, Gram."

There was always a feeling in the air that we may be saying goodbye forever; that she could be taken away before I was to see her again.

I boarded the plane, settling into my seat near the window. "Just pretend you are in a hotel. Look at the other people." I could hear Gram's words in my head as I gripped the arm rests. I looked out of the airplane window down to the patchwork of land below us. I thought about what happened with my grandfather and let the shame course through me. I should have known better. I should have kept my mouth shut. I didn't even realize what I was saying. One minute I was watering the flowers on the windowsill and the next minute I opened my mouth to correct him, "It's not right to say God's name in vain."

He was talking to Gram who was in the kitchen at the time and said "God, Martha."

It was his tone that stung my ears and his red face that made me speak. I don't think I hated what he said, but I hated him. His eyes matched my mom's, his straight lipped expression was hers. The difference was I could hate him out in the open with no loitering compassion. With my mom, the inconsistency is what made me feel like I was on a Ferris wheel. I never knew what I was going to get – love or shame. I wish it were always the latter, then I could have moved on sooner. I could have left and not felt guilty about not turning back in the hopes of a smile.

36

I was desperate for a boyfriend by junior year. Not the boys that pulled up their chairs next to my girlfriends at lunch or even picked me up in the hallway saying I was the cutest thing they'd ever seen. Not the ones that invited me over after school for a hook up or kissed my neck at football games. I wanted someone to write me love notes and listen to me sing, pick me wildflowers and touch my hair softly. I knew this type of gentleness would save me.

I was so primed for love and touch that when I was almost raped, part of me wanted it. To be touched fully would mean that I wasn't disgusting.

I felt so special driving around with him. He always picked me up, played Tribe Called Quest, bought me dinner at China King, and went to Seth's to hang out. That day we were at Starbucks. I thought I was gaining weight and decided not to eat even though I picked my clothes by raking the hangers forwards looking for the smallest size they made. Sometimes even the zeros didn't fit.

He picked me up and swung me around in circles. Over and over. Boys liked to pick me up and I craved their touch. I let them all pick me up.

"Oh God. Put me down. Put me down!" I yelled frantically. He spun me a few more times before adhering to my request. He put my feet down on the concrete, but my head did not stop moving. It was literally moving in circles. I found a concrete planter and threw up into the mulch. The acid crawled up my esophagus and into my mouth refusing to stop. I threw up again.

"I need to go home." I told him. He pulled the car up and my friends and I climbed in. It was growing into night. I didn't want to get into the car. I wasn't going to stop throwing up any time soon.

He drove as if nothing was wrong and my friends chatted in the back. I asked him to stop on the parkway, opened the door and threw up from the side of the car. I wiped my mouth and tried to steady my head with my two hands. We bumped through Reston when I asked him to stop again. It was near a patch of forest without a curb to drive up on. I didn't care, I climbed out of the car and stumbled up into the woods, moving through the trees and crunching the leaves under my feet. I wanted to find some privacy and get it all out. There was no food in my stomach, but the dry-heaving and saliva wouldn't stop until my head would stop. I got onto the ground and faced upwards to the sky. I held my head still and tried to breath.

He came out of nowhere. I don't know where he parked the car. Maybe it was still in the street with the hazards on. I was so relieved that he had come to check on me - that he was going to help me and take me seriously. He bent down on to the leaves. I was waiting for him to pet my hair and move the sticky parts from my brow. Instead, I felt his knee swing around me so that he had one large thigh on either side of my hips. He laid his body down on top of mine. I was caught between feeling the acid on my breath and the closeness of his body. I didn't know what he was doing until he used his words.

"I could rape you right now."

His face was so close to mine that he brushed his nose against my mouth. I waited, wondering what he was going to do next. I pulled my lips in hoping he would not smell my breath. I willed my stomach not to grumble with bile. I waited. I waited. I waited.

"Christen?! Chris?" It was Jessica. I could hear her feet crunching the leaves. She was close. He quickly climbed off of me. I felt a feeling of disappointment that it didn't just happen. That he didn't just do it.

I called my mom from Jessica's house that was on the other side of the wood. She came through the door, walking past my friends to where I was sitting with my head in my hands. I wondered if she was going to take me to the hospital. I looked up at her. She was boiling with anger.

"Where are your parents, Jessica?" She looked at her and then at the other kids littered around the room. They were all silent, watching the scene play out.

"Where is your mother?" She asked again.

"They are sleeping. Christen wasn't feeling good."

"I can see that."

I followed her out the door. She didn't say a word to me in the car. I was in trouble. I was sick, there were leaves in my hair, a boy almost raped me, and I needed her to say something to make me feel better. She didn't.

She parked the car in the driveway and walked in ahead of me, leaving me to make my way up the stairs and into the hallway bathroom where I sat myself on the cool tile in front of the toilet. It felt so smooth under my fingers and I was grateful for it. I thought my mom must be getting me some water and crackers until I heard her whisper something to my dad in their bed. All the lights were off and I stayed on the bathroom floor. My legs were shaking as my stomach erupted again. Her silence was deafening.

37

When I wasn't worrying about finding attention or dodging teachers that wanted to call on me during class, I was ruminating about my freckles and my hair. I would go for about six months worry that my hair wasn't thick like Abigail's. I heard my mother's words in my ears, "Your hair is fine, but you have a lot of it."

I stopped putting my hair in pigtails after she said it to me for the first time in Kindergarten. I didn't want her touching my hair. I grew it long. It was blonde and wavy like the pictures I had seen of Stevie Nicks.

Once in a while I let her trim it. I'd sit on the stool in the kitchen and she'd repeat the same message, "Your hair is fine, but you have a lot of it."

I cut it in sixth grade to my chin. The hairdresser asked if I was sure I wanted it short. I thought if I tried to keep it short, it would then be beautiful to my mother. I would be beautiful. I repeated my mom's words to the stylist, "My hair is fine, but I have a lot of it." I was embarrassed that this poor woman had to cut it when she probably had ten other clients that day with beautiful, thick hair.

I wanted to be a hippie in high school – the fashion, the music, the rebellious nature and the and the freedom were so alluring. *My hair like Jesus wore it, halleluiah I adore it. Halleluiah Mary loved her son, why don't my mother love me?* I grew my hair out again. I braided it in two braids on either side. I put it in low buns. I braided the wisps on the sides and clipped them together around the back to look like Princess Buttercup. My friends started to do their hair in the same manner, and it made us feel intentionally different. Birkenstocks, braids and any wooden heel we could get our hands on.

When the seasons changed, I switched from ruminating about my hair to my freckles. I had freckles all over my body like my mom, my red-headed Scottish grandfather. There was no pride in this though. I heard my mother scoff at all the freckles on her own arms, moving her hand up and down them as if to erase the markings. Mostly, I worried about the freckles on my face. The ones I couldn't do anything about.

My mother asked me into her room and asked to look at my face up close. She pulled a lamp over and grabbed my face in her two hands like a specimen. She got close, so close that I could feel her warm breath on my cheek. She rubbed her fingers over my face as I waited for her conclusion. I searched her eyes trying to decipher if what she saw was acceptable. If I was going to be allowed back out into the world. If what I had to show was permittable and not repulsive.

I stood there vey still waiting for the verdict and dared to pray that she was going to discover that I was beautiful.

"Well, you have a mole there. Right there on your upper lip."

My stomach crashed to the floor into a million pieces. Too many to ever pick up. I had failed the inspection. She turned off the lamp and turned away from me. I walked out of her room devastated.

I went into my room, locked the door and stood in front of my dresser mirror. I tried to see my face through my mom's eyes. I brought over the little lamp from my desk and ran my fingertips along my skin. The tears started falling as I looked at my face in the mirror. She was right. I was disgusting.

38

Rachel told me her news over the phone as I sat on our living room couch just steps away from my mom at the dining table. She must have known already.

"I'm pregnant."

"Wait, what?" I asked.

"I'm pregnant. I got pregnant."

I started crying not knowing what else to do.

"How? What happened."

Rachel was one of my closest friends that had also grown up in the evangelical church and knew what it meant to have sex before you were married. It was the equivalent of pulling out a gun and shooting yourself. We were given purity rings by our fathers as a symbol of our commitment to God and our abstinence. We were taught that premarital sex was evil, the greatest sin imaginable. We were taught that saving ourselves for one man only, our husbands was what God wanted from us. The church had declared it a sin, citing it in the Bible.

Christian kids around the world heard the message loud and clear, we were meant to deny any natural physical desires as they were a temptation from Satan. It was a path to the destruction of our very spirits and would crush our relationship with God and therefore put our entrance into Heaven in jeopardy. The fear of losing everything kept church-going girls locked in an alternative world where we had to pretend that our vaginas did not exit, that the friends that were having sex around us were sinning and we were to keep our bodies holy and for one person for the rest of our lives.

"John. I had sex with John."

I didn't understand. "Did you use protection?"

"No, I didn't think about it. We just did it."

"How many times?"

I was trying to understand. Rachel had sex. Rachel was pregnant.

"I don't know. I love him. I love him so much. I'm six weeks along and living at his house."

"You are living with him?" If having sex was the number one sin that would send a girl to hell, then living with a man was the second. Third would be abortion.

"I have to. My parents kicked me out."

She was struggling to get the words out. I heard tears and snot and dry heaving on the other end of the phone. I lowered my voice so my mom wouldn't hear.

"What are you going to do?"

"I don't know. I don't like it here. He left me home all day today and yesterday. There's no food in the house. He doesn't have a job."

"Rach, what do you want me to do? I will do anything. You can't stay alone in his place with no one helping you."

Holy Jesus Christ Almighty.

I wanted to tell her she could move here, move into my room. I wanted to scoop her up and save her.

My mom glanced over at me, her eyes bullets. I responded to her gaze with understanding. She knew what I was just finding out. Our mothers were friends and knew each other from Hope, where Rachel had also spent a few years before her mother pulled her out when a student in Rachel's class was tied to his chair with a rope and his teacher duct-taped his mouth closed.

"Why can't you go home?" I whispered into the phone, connected to the wall by a spiral cord and limiting my privacy.

"My mom won't let me. She changed the locks on the doors and put my stuff on the front stoop. She's going to emancipate me."

I didn't even know what this word meant. "She's what?"

"She's going to disown me."

I lost my breath. The weight of her news felt like the sky had fallen in. I thought about what this meant for my friend and her baby. I thought about me. I thought about how if this could happen to Rachel then it could also happen to me. My mind ran to an image of the both of us on the street, sitting on grates that blew heat from the ground and begging for money. I soothed myself from the terror of the image by telling myself that I would have an abortion if that ever happened to me. I would keep it a secret, use my savings and my parents would never know.

I talked and cried with Rachel for another thirty minutes. There was a new hole in my stomach for her. I didn't know how to fix this. It was a mess and my best friend was living with a guy that wasn't even around. She was going to have a baby. How was she going to have a baby at seventeen? I wanted to ask her if she was going to keep it. What were her choices? Would she, could she abort it? Could she give it away just so she could get back into her house, into her room and finish high school?

I hung up the phone and tip-toed up to my room. I didn't want to discuss any of this with my mom who was still lingering in the adjacent dining room. I told Abigail I didn't feel well and wasn't coming down for dinner. I was too shaken. I was also trying to figure out a plan to save my friend. I stared out my window and swore that I would find a way to raise money for her. I'd write her letters every day. I'd fly to Denver to be there during the birth and I'd help raise the baby. I even allowed myself to imagine my parents letting her live with us. I had to help save her, her baby and myself at the same time.

I snuck downstairs that evening to seek out my mother. In all my planning a fear had emerged from my belly and I needed an answer to a very important question. If I became pregnant like Rachel what would my own mom do?

"Mom?"

She was standing in the dark kitchen with a little lamp lighting up the piece of counter she used as a desk.

"Uh huh." She didn't look up. I was grateful not to see her eyes on me.

"You know about Rachel."

"Yes, I heard"

She looked at me without saying a word. There was so much I wanted to talk to her about. I wanted to know if she would help me help Rachel. I wanted to hear her say that our family was going to take care of her and sweep her up into a warm embrace like Jesus with the wayward lamb. I waited and grew more uncomfortable. I was suddenly afraid that she was going to take out her feelings about Rachel on me. I felt like I had only room for one question. A very important one that shot to the heart of what I was feeling.

"Mom, if I got pregnant would you do what Rachel's mom did?"

"If you got pregnant, Christen, I would disown you." She looked at me hard and then dropped her eyes back onto the papers before her.

39

My mom was glass. Sometimes strong enough to keep out the wind and sometimes delicate enough to shatter. When I wasn't feeling tortured by her lack of empathy, I felt sad for her. I knew she was broken, and I wanted desperately to fix her. I wanted to make her feel loved. I wanted to heal the pain I saw behind her eyes.

I wish she had tried for me. I wish she faced her pain head on, worked through it and built up her own toolbox so she could love me, see me.

That didn't happen.

And so, when I was stronger and older, I built a big, strong damn to hold back the waters that would annihilate me.

I volleyed between meeting her needs and meeting my own. There wasn't room for the both of us. And if I was who she wanted me to be, I was sacrificing what I wanted for myself. It was me or my relationship with my mom. When I was living in her house, I had to choose her. I needed food and shelter and clothes on my back.

When I left, I saved myself.

PART TWO

1

"I go home all the time if you ever want a ride," he offered. "I'm really close to my family."

"I'm really close to my family too. I only have one sister though!" We both laughed. He was one of six. I could not imagine what it would be like to have that many people in one family. He had two sisters that had graduated college and three younger brothers still at home. He made it sound like they were a team, unbreakable even with distance between them.

"I can't believe you know Beth too. What a small world."

"I dated Beth!"

We laughed again at our undeniable synchronicity.

"Do you think we ever met?" I asked. "I hung out with her all the time when she lived in my neighborhood."

"I don't think I met her until middle school. I can't remember." He looked up at the *Abby Road* poster I had mounted above my bed. Paul, John, George, and Ringo.

"I remember going to a middle school dance with Beth. I was terrified because I didn't know anyone."

"No way. I was probably at that dance."

"Oh my gosh. Too funny. All I remember was a ton of white, blonde girls grinding with boys on the cafeteria floor."

He let out a deep belly laugh, his warm smile revealing straight teeth and his eyes crinkling at the corners. "That sounds about right. I'm sure most of those girls were good friends of mine."

Sam, my roommate came in with her backpack slung over one shoulder. "What's up, Guys?" She asked casually.

Brent and I had been talking for over an hour. "I guess I better get to bed. Early day tomorrow."

We had been at school for only a week and I had become fast friends with all of Sam's friends. Our group consisted of several boys, including Brent, living right below us in our dorn and a few girls just down the hall. Living with my friends was the best feeling in the world. I'd roll out of bed, pull on a hoodie and walk down to the boy's suite where we'd all gather to walk to breakfast. On the weekends we were inseparable, hopping from party to party and when we had all been studying in our rooms for too long, we'd call Papa Johns and split a few pizzas.

"Are you sure you don't mind coming with me?" He turned around one last time at the doorway.

"Nope. As long as I don't have to look."

"Promise," he said slapping the door frame. "Night, Guys."

Sam shut the door behind him. "Uh, where are you going with Brent Bensten?" She asked skeptically.

"The foot doctor."

We both laughed.

"It's so random, but he asked me for a ride. I think he's getting a toenail pulled off and won't be able to drive home."

"Uh, ok." She made an overly exaggerated look with her eyes. "Have fun with that."

"It's totally weird. I know." I told her.

What I didn't tell her was that during that one conversation with him, I knew he was the man I was going to marry.

2

It started with chicken fingers.

I was happy. Brent had come and I gave myself permission to order off the main menu. No substitutions. No hold the meat. I wanted the meat. I wanted the soft, chewy strips of white meat under the salty, crumbly fried breaded bits.

I uncloaked myself. I let the façade fall and acknowledged my hunger. I abandoned the nine years of vegetarianism like the prison it had become, a part of an identity that kept me from trusting myself, trusting my choices.

I wanted to color outside of the lines.

I wanted pleasure.

I wanted bags of Cheetos, bagels with double chive cream cheese and Big Macs. I ate buffalo wings, licking the burnt-red sauce from my fingertips and double dipped the bone-flesh into the bitter blue cheese dressing. Footlong turkey and cheese subs with everything, eggrolls with the chicken and broccoli dinner portion and cheesecake for dessert. Chocolate chip cookies, sugar cookies, lemon cookies, pasta with butter or red sauce. A mountain of parmesan mounted on top.

Pizza all weekend in our dorm rooms. The kind that came with the small container of garlic sauce, crinkled fries soft from a layer of yellow cheese. Soft, sweet donuts, mac and cheese, meatballs, tacos, nachos, queso for lunch, egg and cheese croissants, salty potato chips and onion dip. Pads of butter on crusty bread.

I ate all this and more and nothing bad happened to me. I let myself soak up the pleasure of eating whatever I wanted, whenever I wanted.

Freedom.

3

Brent became my ride or die in college. I wasn't sure if he was just the most upstanding person I had ever met or if he actually thought I was special. We become fast friends and before I knew it, he was driving me to all my classes and paying for my groceries. We walked to parties together and waited for each other's classes to end so we could walk to the dining hall. He came with me to the library when I wanted to study just to keep me company. When I was super tired, he would even push me up the hill from our dorm by my backpack as I leaned into him. I let him hold me up. We studied in my dorm room and took breaks to go to 7-11 for coffee with hazelnut creamer and Cheetos. We had coupled off without being a couple.

The safety I felt by being Brent's focus made me feel seen for the first time in my life. I had never experienced this kind of attention before. I was the center of someone else's world. It was intentional. It was caring in way that said, I thought about you before I thought about me. I want you to be happy. I want to see you smile.

I studied in London my junior year because I promised myself I would. But, the lonely feelings that I grew up with found me on the cold, city streets. I was alone in the world again, fending for myself. Brent was at home where the sun was, and I needed to get back there. I just didn't want to go back to my childhood room. I was afraid I would get stuck there.

"Maybe I should just stay here." I said with the same heaviness I felt.

"What? You can't stay there. You have to finish school."

"I could finish at Kingston. I would just need to get student housing."

"I thought you didn't like Kingston. Didn't you say no one there likes Americans?"

"True. I don't love it, but I only have one more year left and then I could try to find a job at a newspaper here."

"Stop. You already have an internship lined up at *The Reston Times*. Don't you start in a few weeks?"

"Yea, but I don't know. I don't know if I want to go back home. I don't know. I just don't know what I'm going to do after graduation. I do know I'll need a job and a place to live though. My parents already told me that they'd make me pay rent if I came home. I mean, what if I can't find a job? What if no one will hire an English major?"

"Well, you can always stay with me."

"Ha. Yeah, right. Like my parents will go for that and what about your parents?"

"My parents wouldn't care at all. Listen, when you come home, we can spend all summer trying to figure it out."

"Yea, but you'll be working." Brent was the only one I knew that had accepted a real job before graduating. He was going to be working for Morgan Stanley where he had interned for several years. He knew what his future was going to look like. "I don't know when we'll even get to see each other."

"Don't be crazy. We'll see each other just like at school."

He said it, but I didn't believe him. I was scared. So much was going to change. The four beautiful years I had lived far from home was going to disappear and I was going to have to sustain myself by myself.

I was terribly lonely in London, but it was so far away from my home in Virginia that I felt like maybe I could start a life without anything holding me back. I could try all the things that I wasn't able to try back home. I could even shed the weight of being a vegetarian, part of my persona that followed me around, once a badge of honor and now just a rule that I had to abide by. I could die my hair pink and take the Chunnel to Paris and date French men. I could drink copious amounts of wine. I could smoke cigarettes and get that nose ring I wanted.

When I returned from London my senior year, so did my panic attacks. We were getting closer to graduation and I wasn't sure what my life was going to look like. I didn't want to leave my college town. I didn't want to leave my friends and the safe little nest I made there. I didn't know what my choices were as an English major and wouldn't know until I tried to get a job. I didn't realize that at the time that going home, back to my room, was not a real option for me. But, my body knew and it rejected every step I took closer to that reality.

I couldn't make it through a full class senior year without feeling trapped and desperate. I started waking up hours before class and turning on cartoons to calm myself. I sat on my floor counting my breaths and watching *Little Bear*. When my resources ran out, I became desperate. I stopped going to class and socializing. I found myself hiding in my room again.

At the end of middle school, I asked my mom to find me a therapist. I had been hiding under my bed, refusing to go on field trips with my class or out on Saturdays with the family. I didn't want to leave my room and I knew I was at the point where I needed professional help. She said Jane Montgomery from church was a counselor and could help me. My mom and she were friends and when Jane asked me to invite my mother in to have a session together, our time was spent with my mother trying to skate around my accusations of not feeling heard. It started and ended with the two of them talking over my head. My mother drove me home that night in silence. I never went back to Jane.

When I tried to find my own therapist in high school, the counselor asked to speak to my mother and get permission as I was underage.

"What are you trying to do here?" My mother snatched the phone from me. "Hello?" She said seething with anger. "Why are you talking to my daughter? What do you want?"

I pressed my palms together in a symbol of prayer and mouthed to my mother, "Please, please be nice."

"Uh, huh. Well, I'm not comfortable with it," and she hung up the phone.

I walked back up to my room embarrassed and defeated. I was also terrified of my mom's ire at my having reached out to a therapist for help. But, my anxiety was reaching its fingers into other areas of my life and I was afraid that soon I would lose the ability to function. I needed help. I tried again.

This time I made an appointment without telling my mother until after I met the therapist. Brent helped me with my insurance questions and drove me to Vienna, an hour from school, every Thursday at one o'clock for my appointment. He said he didn't mind, and spent the time catching up on homework as he waited for me in his car outside the building. I was floored that someone would want to do this for me. That I was worth waiting for.

He continued to wait for me until senior year when I ended my relationship with the boy I had been seeing and turned towards the boy that was in front of me, helping to smooth out the wrinkles from the past and the road before me. I had spent the past three years wondering if he was going to tire of me and my complicated emotional baggage, but the more time we spent together the more bonded we became.

This was someone who wasn't going to leave. This was someone who saw me and met me where I was. He pursued me and asked nothing in return. It was a stronger love than I had ever felt, and I laid down my fear. We went from best friends to married two years later.

4

The next few years were bliss. We bought a 1950s house in North Arlington and spent every weekend and every spare dime at the hardware store buying what we need to renovate our home. We were both in love with the idea of space as a place of beauty and respite. Brent came from a family of builders and he knew how to do the labor. I knew how to create an environment. Ying and yang. We were in sink and worked together, learning and growing and leaning into one another with trust and love. I found someone that could help me take down the walls I had put up around me and it was there in that space that we lived. We set up house.

My mom didn't understand any of it. Why did we buy an old home that was falling apart? Why were working so hard on this project? Why didn't we rent a new apartment and go to the movies on the weekend?

She couldn't understand why we chose to spend our time tiling the kitchen, refinishing the wood floors and building out the basement. It was so far from what she would have done. But, it was our happy place. We thought, dreamed and explored design. We were in our own DIY heaven. We were DIY before there was DIY, making our own furniture and excitedly planning future projects. We were building a castle on a hill with whatever materials we could afford at the time.

The amount of pride we had in our home was an understatement. We were babies, getting married at twenty-four and renovating a house from scratch. Our dream was to one day design and build a house for ourselves. We spent years dreaming of the day we could afford to do so.

"You have built the sweetest love nest, Christen." Gram said to me on our weekly call. "I just love you two so much."

Gram supported us when we had very few friends and family that understood our dream. We knew what we wanted and had no hesitations about going after our united goal. There was so much noise around us, disagreeable faces and criticism, but we did our best to shut the door to all that and stay safe in our nest.

After I graduated, I took a job downtown, blocks away from the White House as a marketing coordinator at a design firm. I loved my job, I loved how the office was full of architects and interior designers. I loved working with the women in the marketing team and walking around DC on my lunch break. I had no idea life could be so sweet. I felt independent. I had my own money, my own home and my life partner. Everything was beautiful.

Until it wasn't.

The dynamic at work started shifting as two of my bosses left and the rumors were flying about layoffs. My anxiety came creeping in like a snake, winding its way around my throat slowly choking me.

I began to get panic attacks in meetings and on the metro, anywhere I felt trapped. I thought about what it would feel like to just step out onto the tracks of the Orange Line right before the train sped into the station. Things were getting bad again and I didn't see a way out. I needed to find relief from the debilitating anxiety that had me in its grip and was growing. I felt like there was nothing that was going to solve this problem. I was lost in the recess of my mind with no way out.

I cried every night. I was desperate.

Every day I stepped into my office I felt a wave of panic coursed through me. I thought someone was going to ask something of me that I couldn't do, I thought I was going to be laid off at any moment like half the design staff had been over was the summer, I was worried that I would make a mistake and be punished like a child. It was irrational, but so real at the same time. I was just sitting there waiting for someone or something take me out, destroy me. I realized later that the past was coming to haunt me. I was being triggered.

At the end of the day, I knew Brent and I couldn't afford to keep the house with one paycheck. I couldn't just quit despite my debilitating anxiety. I was trapped. So, I went back to therapy.

I was twenty-six and she was the third therapist I had seen. Her office was tidy with plants lining the air conditioning vent, blowing slightly when the air clicked on. It was an older building, the elevator creaking up to the fourth floor every Tuesday when I made my way to her office.

She had two leather chairs sitting opposite one another. I was used to a therapist in a chair and I in a couch and this felt different. A good different like we were equals. It gave me the courage to speak up on our first session.

"I'm a pretty quiet person and I've found that it makes me nervous when there is a lot of silence. I don't like not knowing what you are thinking, so if you could respond to the things that I say, that would be really helpful."

"Good to know," she replied.

I thought I had explained enough to let her know that what I didn't want was her staring at me in silence. It felt like a trick and I didn't like it. I wanted feedback not eyes staring back at me.

"Tell me a little about yourself."

I went through my history of anxiety starting with the throwing up every day in elementary school all the way to college when I had to take my tests in the hallway so I didn't throw up in the classroom.

The therapist didn't seem jarred or concerned. She just asked more questions.

"Do you have siblings?"

"Yes. One older sister."

"So, you were supposed to be a boy." She said plainly.

I was taken aback. I had never, ever, ever thought of it that way. I stopped breathing. I wanted to hide my face in my hands. She was insinuating a major rupture in my family, in my mother's life, by me turning out to be a girl.

I had analyzed my entire childhood and young adulthood up until that point, but that little fact never registered. Could she be right? Is that what my parents felt? When I was born did they look at my privates and look at one another with disappointment? Is that why is felt like they had less to give me or that I was in the way or they had no interest in listening to me?

Could be. Very likely could be this.

I broke up with the therapist a few sessions later. Not because she had casually speculated that the reason I didn't feel empathy from my parents was because I was supposed to be a boy, but because she did that quiet staring thing. I didn't need another woman in my life with a critical eye on me.

5

Brent and I went back to my childhood church as a newly married couple. I had grown in the years I was away, but I was not yet able to allow myself to question the conservative views I was raised with. They still had a hold on me and I was fearful enough not to question them.

"We have to go to church every Sunday and raise our kids as Christians."

Despite how my church had terrified me, I still believed it was the one true church, no exceptions. I was taught to believe this and like a victim of Stockholm Syndrome, I did. All other denominations were fine, they just weren't right.

> *Jesus answered, "I am the way and the truth and the life. No one comes to the Father except through me."*

-John 14:6

This meant that only those that accepted Jesus into their hearts were going to Heaven and all the others, even the recyclers and doctors and animal shelter volunteers were going to Hell. Just because you are a nice human did not mean you were going to Heaven.

We had been groomed to answer non-believers' questions about other religions, so when I started questioning my own belief system in college while taking a religious studies class, I let myself look for answers that were beyond what I was taught.

"How do you know Christianity is the one and only religion?"

I asked the female head clergy member at the little Episcopal church I had discovered near school.

"Well, you don't. You are often born into a religion and you follow that path and see where it takes you."

I left her office confused at the lack of conviction in her answer.

"But, isn't there only one way into Heaven?" I pushed.

"I don't know."

This woman, this female rector, gave me incomplete answers. Part of me wanted to explore more of what she was saying and part of me wanted to file our meeting way back in the library of my mind never to be opened again. I didn't like the idea that the sweet Hindu family that gave me candy every time they came home from a trip was going to be damned to the flaming pit of hell. They were so nice. And what about the indigenous tribes I learned about in anthropology – the ones that were so far away from white society in the Amazon that they may never heard the message of Jesus? John Stuart Mills or Pastor Ben never had a good answer for that one. So, they were either going to Hell too or some brave missionary would eventually find their tribe before it was too late. Unborn babies? Well, God was going to let them into Heaven because they didn't yet have a chance yet to sin. God wouldn't send a baby to Hell, would He?

I was taught we served a selfish God. He wanted all of us and it wasn't a bad thing. I was taught that if I had the cure for cancer, didn't I want to share it for everyone to be healed?

I was taught that Jesus was going to return to earth, dig up all the dead bodies and take us to Heaven and all those that didn't believe in Jesus were going to the Hell.

I was taught that the *Bible* was the Word of God and everything in it was beyond cultural and historical interpretation and was to be followed as a manual.

I was taught that the only church I had ever belonged to knew what was right and what was wrong.

Brent agreed to attend. He had little choice if he wanted to be with me and if he wanted to get into Heaven.

"Brent, you are going to have to take this seriously. You are going to have to ask Jesus into your heart. I'm not going to be able to save you. I'm not going to get to Heaven and turn around and say, 'God, he's here with me.'" I pointed my thumb behind me at Brent in my parody.

He laughed. "I got it, Chris." He responded way too casually for my liking.

"I mean it. The man is supposed to lead the family in a Godly way. I'm going to need you to pray with me and we have to find a small group."

I needed Brent to abide by the same rules. I was desperate for him to live with me under the umbrella, the safety, of my church even if the speaking in tongues, the dancing in the aisle, and the hand raising didn't make sense. If we didn't understand it then maybe we were the ones that were limited. His acquiescence was a matter of life and death.

We came back from our honeymoon and the following Sunday and attended church. We sat next to my parents as they clapped and sang along with the same old songs.

I loved the songs and although I never dared to let myself clap, even now as an adult, I did close my eyes, and hoped still that my mom didn't rub my back with pride. I urged Brent to clap and pushed his arms apart every time I saw him cross them or slouch in his chair. When he jiggled his leg too much that the vibration hit the edge of my chair, I quickly slapped his leg back into submission. We could not take this lightly.

We sat in the same seats on the left section that we had during my childhood. The same people sat around us, but everyone had aged. There were gaps around the room where I used to see the same faces that were no longer there. Jenny's parents moved to a Baptist church when she went off to New York to study. Emily and her dad had moved to a different state. Bridget's dad and mom were still in the back row of the middle section. He was as cool as ever with his cowboy boots and relaxed jeans. John Stuart Mills was still the head rector and had officiated our wedding that year. I felt a new connection with him and hoped that after seeing me wed, he would acknowledge me at communion and even speak my name.

There was very little about my church that had changed. There was a new man playing the piano and they had added a few guitars, but the monk-man still held the cross at the beginning of the procession, the same songs were played and we sat in the same, hard plastic chairs. My mom still took moments throughout the service to stare at me, which still made me feel like my space was being invaded. I found myself doing what I did when I was smaller by holding my breath until she looked back at the altar.

My parents wanted to go to brunch with us after the service every week and we often did because of the pull I felt from my mother's eyes. I would rather sit for another two-hour service than have her disappointed in me.

"Do you guys have time for a quick breakfast?" My mom would ask after every service.

I didn't look at Brent because I knew he wanted to get back home to enjoy his Sunday before starting the work week. I didn't know how to say no. I didn't know how to disappoint my mom or explain that we needed alone time. She would not understand.

"Sure." I would say with cheer in my voice.

I wanted to please them and be what they wanted. I wanted them to see that my husband could also be a good Christian and love them like parents. I wanted Brent to slide into the unwritten rules of our family by shaking my dad's hand and standing up to hug my mom.

I wanted my mom's approval at all costs. I wanted her to see that I was an adult with a husband and a real job and look how well my life had turned out. I searched her face for admiration and pride when she looked over at us at the bagel shop. What I found was an uncomfortable look passed back and forth between her and my dad. I tried to correct the energy in the room as I always did.

"What else do you have going on today?" I asked with a bright smile, kicking Brent under the table. He had crossed his arms and slid down in his seat.

I was trying to knit our new foursome together like a conductor, but it wasn't working, and I was growing exhausted by my efforts.

"Oh, not much, Hon. I will probably tinker." My Dad replied.

My mom pursed her lips and I asked if her coffee was good. My mom hated bad coffee.

"It's ok." Like a light switch she turned off and offered nothing more to hang a conversation on.

I looked back at Brent who was now gazing out the window.

"Well, we better get going." I didn't wait for a response before turning in my seat to grab my purse. I was officially full of my everything bagel with extra chive cream cheese and resentment at my mother and Brent who refused to play by the rules.

I got in the car and pursed my own lips, closing my eyes in exhaustion.

6

I returned to my hometown, back to the things of my childhood like the mall I grew up shopping in, the bookstore that I skipped school to go to with my friend Joy so we could read books in the fiction aisle and drink lattes. I was back at the same church and back with my parents. But, I wanted all these things to look at me differently.

"There's Christen!" I wanted these places and people to say, "Doesn't she look amazing? All grown up!"

What I really wanted was my mom to see that I had made it. I wanted to feel her smile on me.

I let her into my new world hoping to connect in a new and fruitful way. I let her into the details of my new life so she would feel welcome and this would please her and then I would feel her love.

"I don't think any married couple should be buying new furniture. Dad and I never had new furniture."

I was excited to show her the olive-green velvet chairs that I had saved up for. Brent bought me one for my birthday and I bought the other.

I loved furniture more than I loved clothes or shoes. If I had birthday money to spend, I always chose a little lamp or a blanket or a trinket for the console table. I poured over design magazines just waiting for the day that I could have enough money to buy larger pieces of furniture for our home. I spent my free time puttering around the house, arranging and rearranging, creating beauty and a place for rest. It was a language my mom didn't understand and even more confusing for me was the resentment in her voice.

"Oh, they were on sale." I was quick to rebut.

"No, they weren't." Brent said. I looked at him with anger in my eyes wanting him to keep quiet so I could smooth out the rupture.

When she left, after coffee and homemade lemon bread that I had made that morning, I felt the same kind of exhaustion I felt every time I was in her company. I worked so hard for her warmth and never seemed to get it.

I wanted her to come into my little family room and say, "Oh! They are GORGEOUS!" and sit on one of them. "Look at you! You have such a wonderful eye. You have always had good taste. I remember when you used to move your furniture around your room every weekend. You had the best room in the house, Christen!"

That's what I wanted to hear.

I began to feel like I was baring my neck to her, waiting for approval, but feeling like I had only disappointed her. I was inviting her in, and she was saying, nope, I don't like any of this. I was trying all the ways I knew how to fuse us and still maintain who I was trying to create in myself.

It was not working. The things I liked, she did not like and the things she wanted to make me a part of were so far from who I was.

"No, I can't go to the women's retreat." "No, I can't go dress shopping at Anne Taylor." "No, I can't meet your women's prayer group for dinner at the Cheesecake Factory."

I was equally frustrated at her not knowing me as a separate person from her as I was sad that I could not find a way to make her happy with me.

I found myself saying no to too many things. I felt like I was walking a thin line, a calm before the storm where she erupted at me. The push and pull were becoming too much, and I found myself wanting to hide behind the locked front door of my home.

7

Brent and I had our first baby in 2006. Greta Belle came to me in a dream. I saw a young mom following a toddler on the sidewalk in front of my house. The baby was pushing a little, pink stroller and stalled when she heard her mother, "Careful, Greta."

I never knew if it was a dream or I actually saw Greta, but we in our third year of fertility treatments and I was desperate for signs and miracles.

I screamed when they pulled her from my belly in early October 2006.

"Ahhhh!" Pure joy bellowed out of me in an uncontrolled way.

"Oh my God." Brent said next to me as the nurses cleaned her off. There was a person in my body and I had pushed her out of me, my first duty as mother, and now she was on my bare chest. Skin to skin.

They whisked her away to weigh and dress her and when the brought her back, she was this warm, perfect bundle in one of those heavenly hospital blue and pink baby towels.

"Oh my God," Brent said. "I can't believe she's here."

The doctor continued to stitch me up. I was in a dazed bliss as Greta purred in my arms. Nothing would ever be the same again and I didn't want it to be. This was all I wanted.

"How could anyone not love a baby?" I said to myself.

My heart burst with joy. I was never going to release my new baby from my arms. My parents came over the night we were released from the hospital. We had taken my mom up on her offer to make us dinner that night, but something was wrong. Her face was stern, her mouth a line. I tried to ignore the urge to turn towards her and ask, "Are you okay?"

I attempted to only thank her once for the salmon dinner instead of repeatedly in an anxious pattern as I normally would. It didn't work. She said, "You're welcome" with pursed lips as she wrapped the fish in foil, putting half in my fridge and saving a half to bring home. She was not happy. I couldn't correct it now. I didn't want to. I wanted only my pink baby.

I eased my way onto the couch, trying not to tear the stitches the doctor had to make for my third-degree tears. I resentfully sat down in the family room as with guests even though I just wanted to crawl in bed and find sleep with my new baby.

"I can hold her if you want." My mom said from her chair across the room.

"No, thanks." I pulled Greta closer to my chest.

"Well, some new mothers would want to take a break," she said tartly.

"Not me." I wanted to yell in her face. "I will never want to take a break."

A cold war started that night. I was ready for battle. God bless the woman that tries to put a wedge between a new mother and her cub. I had waited my entire life for this moment. Baby Greta gave me a reason and permission to fight when I couldn't fight for myself or my marriage or my new life, but Greta, ah, she was like holy water poured out over me and christening every motherly instinct and feeling that turned to fire that night. I would never let her down. I would never give up on her and no one, not even my own mother, would destroy our bond as hard as I saw her eyes challenging me that first night.

Greta had come. I put on my best armer. And when she would cry, starving for food, I'd jump up, hold her in my arms and feed her from my own body.

8

The garden that I had started long ago, sowing, seeding and tending to was growing and blossoming in colors that I never thought were possible. It was as if a cloud had moved across the sky, revealing that the life-giving sun was there all along. It shone on me and my new family creating a warmth in my belly. A feeling of fullness and contentment that I had never experienced before. We were growing upwards like a vine reaching its fingers towards the glow, the fire that would heal us.

Brent and I laughed and playfully pushed each other out of the way to get to the baby's room when we heard her cry. We both wanted to see her first and grab her for an endless snuggle. We wanted her baby eyes to see our wide, loving eyes and know that she was everything.

Life had changed and we welcomed all of it. We wanted to tuck into our little family and just love one another as tightly as possible. Nothing else mattered. And I felt welcome in the world as a new person, a born-again woman and mother.

With my growth came a shift that ricocheted throughout my extended family. We stopped going to church because we didn't want to bring our newborn, we declined family dinners and left early on holidays. It was Brent, Christen and Greta against the world.

The push back was immediate.

My mom stopped by whenever she was in Arlington, unannounced. The dog would bark jarring Baby Greta and I snoozing together on my bed. I watched her breath as she puffed out her rosebud lips with each exhale.

"Hellllooo. Chris?"

The voice yanked me out of my reverie. I jumped up in distress, pulled on my yoga pants and looked into the mirror, throwing my hair back into a messy bun. I wanted to just be and not worry about my appearance, but the deep dark secret was that I still wanted my mom to think I was acceptable.

"I bet you are ready to get your body back," she said.

I let those words sear into me as I sat in my kitchen nine months pregnant wishing she would just ask to touch my belly and lavish me with excitement and pride.

"You here?" She called into the house again.

"Yea, I'm back here."

"Greta is in her bassinet."

"Oh good. Then you and I can catch up."

She didn't want to hold the baby and let her hand be wrapped by Greta's holy, pink little fingers. She wanted to talk over a coffee in the kitchen while all I wanted to do was sleep and hold my baby. Did she not know this? Didn't she know I was exhausted? Why didn't she offer to fold laundry or pick up the house like all the other grandmother's I knew? I looked at my mom confused and torn. Then I went to make the coffee.

My anger started percolating months earlier when my mom told me that she may not make it to the birth. "I may have my exam that day, Hon. And you don't even want us in the room with you guys."

Was she mad that we said no one in the room? Did she care? Was her personal agenda more important than the birth of her first grandbaby? I could not comprehend this. I could not stuff this one down with all the other bullshit she had fed me, gaslighted me.

She was getting her master's in order to become a counselor. A Christian counselor. I was proud of her, I supported her. I threw the damn graduation party and made all those little appetizers by hand. Smoked salmon on a perfect slice of cucumber with a sprig of dill, little crab balls, caprese skewers, bacon wrapped figs, pink cocktails, the cake.

"Wait, you may not be there for the birth?"

"I don't know, Hon. If you have the baby the day of my exam, I may just meet her afterwards."

I had pictured my parents out in the waiting room, Brent bursting through the doors exclaiming that their first grandchild had been born and mom and baby we perfect. I had watched the scene a million times on *A Baby Story* awaiting my turn.

"It's probably not going to coincide, but, oh well, if it does it does."

I didn't understand. Surely, this was a big enough event that she was going to drop everything to be there, right? That's what grandmothers did. Right?

I didn't cry. I burned.

"Do you not want to be there for the birth of your first grandchild?"

"It's not like we won't meet her."

I couldn't believe what I was hearing. It had to be a dream. I imagined this was to be the moment that I was going to feel all the warmth and love that she had been bottling up, saving for when it mattered most. I was finally going to feel a waterfall of acceptance and love wash over me. She was going to hold my baby and put her arm around me and say, "I am so proud of you. Look at her."

I could not imagine ever getting over her lack of interest or care. It erased any doubt that what I had been feeling about her and my childhood was legitimate. I had not made it up. Everything that happened actually happened. It was not a dream. It was real and I was now an adult and respond to these injustices with clarity. It was a rock bottom moment when I registered that not even a baby, my baby, was going to change her.

I cried like I had been shot, the shock and bloody mess too much to wipe away. I sobbed and shook until Brent came through the door and wrapped me in a blanket, "Shhh. Shhh."

My mom's arms never embraced me in the encompassing hug of pure adoration that I was waiting for. I really thought the baby would bring her affection like a gift waiting under the

Christmas tree for me to open. I wanted to feel my mom's heart beating close against me and see her joy. I had waited so long. The gravity of the moment was an earthquake. There was nothing big enough, exciting enough, earth-shattering enough to claim the love I desperately wanted from my mom.

I volleyed between anger and grief. It was the most magical time in my life and yet Greta's birth shifted nothing in my mother. However, something had shifted in my own body, waking up all the broken and buried bits and pieces. It was time for my resurrection.

The lava in me was rising to the surface. The dormant volcano was preparing itself for release and when it was time, it would pour forth and yield weeping and gnashing of teeth.

9

"Mom, what are you doing here?"

She used her key and walked in through the front door. It was only yesterday that I had gathered enough courage to ask her to call before popping in because of the baby's napping schedule.

"We were in the area. I didn't want to miss seeing you." She responded.

"I really need you to call next time." I stood at the front door not moving aside as I normally would, offering her a cup of coffee. The earth was shaking beneath me, mounting in strength and its heavy movement made my eyes blur.

She looked at me first with severe lips and a second later I watched her eyes fill with tears.

"Oh, I'm sorry, Hon. Dad and I just wanted to visit." She pointed to my dad who was standing on the sidewalk by the car, waiting for the all-clear to approach.

I stopped breathing, but pressed forward knowing this was the first step to freedom. "I really can't have you just pop in anymore. It doesn't work for us."

"Hon. You are not being nice."

Her eyes went from tearing to searing in moments. Her. Lips. Pursed.

"I'm not trying to be mean. It's just hard for us as new parents. Can you understand that?" Surely, she could understand that. She was a new mom once.

"Ok, but you are being hurtful right now." She switched her weight onto her other hip and crinkled her face as if I had just slapped her.

Red hot lava was rocking up into my throat, burning.

"See, things were different for you. Your parents didn't live close by. They lived nine hours away." I raised my voice as Brent came to the door.

I was trying to rationalize with her and get her to empathize with how I was feeling and how I was not intentionally trying to make her feel badly. I waited for her to register what I was saying.

"This is not the way your treat your mother." She snapped, eyes blazing as she walked back to the car.

And then it happened.

The volcano burst, magma spewing in thick, ugly spirts through every seen and unseen crack. The eruption was fast and loud, noise banging in my head and my heart beating uncontrollably in my chest.

I ran after her screaming.

"We don't want you stopping by unannounced. This is our house. I am married! I have a baby!"

It was the first moment as a mom that I had air under my wings. My body lifted off the ground and I was flying.

"You can't just come to my house like this." I screamed growing bigger and morphing into a storm cloud, raining sulfur on Godforsaken land. It was Sodom and Gomorrah.

I continued to scream, running after her until she opened the passenger side of the car and pulled it shut behind her. I looked at her through the car window and felt Brent's arm on my back.

"Ok, Chris. She got the message." He said calmly. "Let's go inside.

I didn't turn to see the car leave. I didn't hear Brent ask me if I was okay or if I wanted to sit down. I only heard the blood throbbing in my head and ears as I moved to close and lock the front door.

10

My anger simmered and by nightfall I was in a storm of panic and shame. How could I have screamed at my mom like that? She looked so frightened and upset. She was so sad. I wanted to take it all back. She needed me to be strong and steady. I was meant to be available, a tower of fortitude when she felt lost. She wasn't going to be able to handle my ire. I showed her thunder yesterday. How could I let that happen? I knew I was stronger than she was with more resources. She was just a broken child living out the life of a child of an emotionally abusive and alcoholic father. My job was to protect her, right?

Before I had a chance to compose an apology email, much safer than a phone conversation, I heard a knock on the door the following day. She was at the door. Brent was at work and Greta was taking her morning nap.

"Hi. Come on in." I warmly invited her into the kitchen and poured her a cup of coffee with cream and sugar, my hands shaking as I pulled the items from the fridge.

"I want you to know that I forgive you." She looked at me under her eyebrows. Did I feel big and explosive like the day before, a natural disaster? No. I felt relief. I was relieved that she was forgiving me. The guilt I had felt the night before was too heavy and I didn't know how to put it down. My mom was only trying to be friendly, right? She didn't do anything that harmful. I was filled with self-doubt as I scrounged the cabinet, finding a box of shortbread cookies to lay out on the table. My body folded in on itself as I sat across from her. I felt ashamed that I had carried on in such an unrecognizable way. I scared her. I scared myself.

But, then again, why had she come back to my house a day later? And why was she telling me that I was forgiven when I hadn't asked for forgiveness?

I tried to balance the two feelings in my head. This was my opportunity to clarify why I was angry and push through a hard conversation to get to the other side with mutual respect and understanding. Instead, I poured us another coffee.

"Let me go wake up Greta so you can say hi. She's starting to smile."

"Oh, yes. Go get her."

I scurried into the bedroom, looking over the bassinet at the sleeping baby. I lifted her up and unswaddled her, letting the cool air from the room reach her feet. I pet her pink cheeks and kissed her head trying to urge her out of sleep.

"She did not want to wake up." I said holding her like a precious jewel, offering her to my mom. "I have been trying to get her into a little sleep routine."

"Oh, Ok. Let me sit down." She took one more bit of her cookie.

"Did you need something?"

"Uh, yea, a napkin."

"We don't have any. You can just use a dish towel. Here, I'll get you one."

I pulled a towel from one of the kitchen drawers while balancing Greta in my other arm. I watched as my mom turned on the kitchen sink, pump the foaming hand soap into her hands and humming to herself. I stood behind her waiting with Greta in my arms, a precious gift.

"Ok. Let me go sit on the couch."

I placed Greta delicately in her arms and put a clean burp cloth on her shoulder.

"You aren't still swaddling her, are you?"

"Yes."

"Hon. She needs to move."

"I've read a ton of books on sleep and swaddling. It's important that a baby feels like they are still safe and secure in the womb. It also calms them down and helps them sleep."

I felt my blood pressure rise having to defend my parenting.

"Babies don't need to be swaddled. Do they, now, do they?" She whispered to Greta.

I sat down next to them on the couch. "I'm going to be feeding her soon then I'll have an hour before she goes down for her second nap."

"Another nap? She just woke up. You just woke up, now didn't you, Greta?"

I shut my mouth and pushed the growing frustration down. I thought about the day before and how the anger that had come up felt like freedom. I was shot out of a cannon at full strength after biding my time at the battle line, waiting to destroy the enemy. No one had ever given me permission to be angry before and I didn't know how to use the emotion. It was untamed and felt like a weapon that was too heavy for me to wield, but one that I needed in my arsenal.

"Well, I better go." She passed Greta back to me and I walked her to the door.

"Thank you for coming." I said reaching out to hug her.

My fury retreated back into its cave like a lion after feeding time. I was so afraid of my mother's ire and felt equally responsible for her happiness. In this moment it was easier to strive for harmony after the rupture of yesterday.

However, she did come with an olive branch. She did not come to apologize. She came to forgive me. I imagined shd had heard this in a sermon – forgive those that hurt you even if they don't ask for or deserve forgiveness. But, what about truth and connection and my feelings, my boundaries? I wasn't brave enough to have the conversation, the many conversations, we needed to have in order to establish clarity and understanding. I didn't know what lay beyond words and how her and I would survive once my truth was exposed. I imagined it would all crush her, sending her into a deep emotional hell and hadn't she already dealt with so much in her life? Maybe the least I could do was let her be whatever she wanted to be with me. I couldn't be the one to kill her. Would I kill her speaking my truth? Would she fall to the ground if I told her how I felt and how she continued to hurt me?

I pressed the feelings, the truth back down into my gut, my organs where they could eventually wreak havoc in the shadowy spaces. I knew the anger wouldn't stay put forever even if I wanted it to. I knew it was only a matter of time before I would need to pick up my weapon again. The war had barely begun. But, as for now, I rocked Greta in my arms as she rubbed her tired eyes.

11

Abigail said it first. "Mom's Borderline Personality."

I anxiously looked up the definition of Borderline as if discovering a major clue. I read several books by therapists on the disorder, highlighting passages that related to everything I had experienced. I felt like I highlighted entire books. This very well could be an explanation to everything.

Maybe the sky was opening up, the clouds parting revealing the glow of the sun like an answer to a question I had but could never articulate.

Maybe this was why my mother hated me, alienated me, emotionally punished me, pulled me and pushed me to my breaking point. Maybe this was why she placed me like one of her dolls in a corner and collected me, wiping off the dust from my face, when she wanted to play with me. Maybe this is why she never saved me. Maybe this is why my father couldn't save me. Maybe this is why I couldn't stretch out into the world, letting my curiosity and instinct guide me. Maybe this is why my family was always alone; was always other. Maybe this is why she hated everything she did not understand – including me. Black and white thinking. Yes.

I wanted desperately to believe that she was suffering with an ailment that she couldn't control. If this was true, then maybe it wasn't me after all. Maybe I wasn't disgusting or unlovable or unacceptable. Maybe I wasn't stupid or ungrateful or too sensitive or too moody.

If my mom was sick, then maybe I was healthy. If mom was diseased, then I could still love her.

I could hold her in a separate storage container on a shelf and say to myself, "She doesn't mean to hurt me. She can't help it." *

It was during this time that I wished upon a star that we had video footage of my early childhood. I ruminated and felt like I held each memory just under a thinly veiled surface, like a little scrap of evidence and proof of my legitimacy from about age five until adulthood. I really did not know if she left me crying in the crib alone or passed me off to neighbors or simply left me unattended on the floor.

Fiona, my second baby, had come into my life like a glorious summer day and I wanted to live in her radiating aura. She was everything beautiful in the world and allowed me to be a mother of two baby girls that would encourage me to grown into the world, her infectious energy intoxicating. These children were all mine, and I was going to love them in an uncompromised, unconditional way that involved all Heaven and earth, and nothing was going to stop me from tearing out my whole heart and giving it to them. These beacons of light would show me the way and I would follow.

However, my mom's words were clanging around inside my head and were growing stronger, feeding off my joy, interrupting my pleasure with doubt and haunting me with whispers that I did not deserve this feast before me. I was starving at a banquet. It felt like the better my life was getting, the more I heard her punishing voice and felt the heaviness of the guilt at not letting her be a part of it in the way she wanted.

*Childhood lived with a borderline mother results in an unspeakable tragedy. Few of the child's developmental needs are met because the mother cannot be a parent. – Christine Ann Lawson, PhD

My mother's undiagnosed disorder did not quiet the demons in my head. I wasn't sure if it was Satan or God speaking to me telling me that I was a very, bad girl and left me with debilitating anxiety and depression. Was God scolding me? I felt tormented, feeling like I was hurting my mom, my parents, by growing up, having children, a home, a community. I felt their disappointment at my lack of availability. I felt like they thought I was leaving them behind. Maybe I was. But, wasn't this the natural order of things? Shouldn't I put my husband and children before my mother's needs?

I doubted myself.

I knew what I needed to sooth my anxiety. I wanted her permission. I was waiting for her permission to be happy in a life apart from her, a life that I chose.

I knew that my little family was safe and cozy. I knew I was a good mother. I knew that I was in a successful and healthy marriage. I felt blessed. But, I still could not shake the years and years of conditioning and belief that only my mother knew the right way to live and be in the world. She was still coming at me with bullet eyes and wanted to move in on all our memories and if she couldn't then I was bad, and I had strayed from God. She wanted in on Sunday mornings and brunches, farmers' markets, Mother's Day and preschool performances. And I tried. I tried for so long.

Brent learned to hug her and called her Mrs. Williams as she requested. And when she walked into our home I continued to yield to my mother's expectations and played the good girl. I died every time I put myself on the shelf that she had created for me. I grew resentful with how she insisted on making memories with my little family that filled her cup and left mine bone dry.

I knew deep down that this was not working. I felt the red, furry bubble and twist inside my stomach. The anger was coming up my throat like reflux then was replaced with guilt that left me collapsed in a fetal position in my bed. Anger, collapse. Anger, collapse. It was a cycle that was taking me out to sea. I needed anti-depressants and therapy before I lost myself.

12

Dr. Evergreen moved slowly and with intentionality letting me unfold like a secret, all my parts organically making themselves known as we worked. I grew to trust her, and she became what I needed most, a steady witness.

Reid, my last baby, came into our world like magic. The happiest baby on the block. And with his arrival the knowledge that I didn't want to miss out on anymore of the banquet before me. I was ready for medication and a commitment to therapy. I knew I had a long road ahead of me and now was the time to unpack all of the built-up trauma that was affecting my new, precious life.

Trauma.

I cried out loud, shaking and shivering, putting my face in my hands when she said the word, pulling my pain out from the shadows, naming it and acknowledging my experience. She labeled my wounds with the biggest, strongest word I knew – a word that matched my experience. I wanted to take her home with me, link arms and have her walk-through life with me, interacting with my family and friends and any place my scars were wreaking havoc in my life. I would hold her out to the world and say, "Here. Here is my witness. She believes me. She understands. Just ask her. I'm not lying. I'm not exaggerating. I'm not just able to 'let it go' or move on. Real things happened and I have real scars and open, bleeding sores."

Trauma.

"Trauma?" I asked hesitantly, praying and hoping that it was everything this word meant - barns burnt to the ground, earthquakes, tsunamis, drowned babies, trafficked girls, 911, war, all of it.

"Well, what would you call it?" She asked me.

"Trauma. Yes." I grasped the word and put it on me like the hot seething brand that it was.

She had given me a gift by allowing me to label my experiences. For so many years I had wondered if I was making up the pain I felt. A voice in my head tried to convince me that I had a fine childhood. There was no divorce or molestation. But, what about the winter storm I existed in, the wind whipping around my hair and blinding me, burying me, confusing me in the deep snow until I completely lost my way. The barren terrain. The lack of resources and safety. Abominable fear.

I had to find a path out even if it meant chopping off my own hand that continued to reach out to my mom expecting normalcy and empathy.

I needed to untwist the chaos in my head and heart.

I cried every week on Thursday morning for eleven years. On week two Dr. Evergreen gave me a book to read. *Will I Ever Be Good Enough? Healing the Daughters of Narcissistic Mothers* by Dr. Karyl McBride. We dug deep into the frozen earth and waded in the midnight swamp, the muck, all of it - not letting any stone go unturned. I drank in our weekly meetings like fresh water, releasing the pain through tears and breathing in the new air. Christen was being resurrected limb by limb.

Dr. Evergreen spent the next many years hearing every single memory that was perfectly preserved, waiting for its safe release. I circled back over them - over and over again - until she knew every detail. I kept these memories close, refusing to release them because I needed them for so long. I needed to hold onto them so I could prove to the world why I was in such pain. I needed to be seen and legitimized. I needed to be authenticated. I needed to be healed.

"Whoever you are getting advice from in your life is Evil." My mom said to me one evening when I told her that, no, we would not be able to meet them for dinner in Ashburn.

"The kids go to bed at seven-thirty."

"Oh, Hon." I could hear her exasperation. "Really? You can put them to bed later."

"We can't take them thirty minutes away to a restaurant. Fiona and Reid will never stay still and it's past their bedtime."

It took every ounce of me to push back. I was still terrified of her and the backlash of my new boundaries.

When she tried to call me two days later, I didn't answer the phone. I texted her and asked her to stop calling. I told her I didn't want her calling four times a day and that I would get back to her when I could. I told her I had three children under four that needed me more than her. I continued to try to find her empathy. I tried to explain and rationalize my experience as a mother, but frustration led to anger, unleashing and pouring out of my open vocal cords, "Stop calling! Even if you don't understand, just stop calling!"

"You are so mean!" She snapped at me.

"I am doing my best. I'm trying to set up healthy boundaries."

"What about our grandkids! Are you not going to let us see them? Hon, how am I supposed to get in touch with you if you won't answer your phone?"

"Wait until I call you back!"

"But, what if I want to plan something that day?"

"Chances are we can't do anything the day of. Greta has preschool and the Littles have a nap schedule."

"What, so we are never going to see them?"

"You can see them, but we need to plan it. The kids and I have a schedule right now." I was pounding the keyboard as I emailed her, crying and feeling the anger run down my arms. I stopped breathing. I was outside of my window of tolerance. "Why can't you understand? I am doing my best. I am a young mom with three babies just trying to do my best! Don't you remember having young kids and trying to do everything?"

I tried to connect mother to mother. I was digging and digging and digging until I realized I was just flinging dry dirt. There was no soft earth, no restorative, life-giving soil below and my body was so tired.

13

We moved together in one straight line, side by side like in Taylor Swift's *Bad Blood* video. We looked like glowing, Heavenly bodies in white pristine pant suits and stood tall. The doors to the courtroom opened to us on cue and we swept through the room born ready. We were adults, we were women, and we were ready to try this case. The police investigation was complete, all the evidence had been submitted, and the witnesses were called. We were prosecuting the offender and going to trial.

Behind the courthouse was a vast desert, stretching into infinity. Sand and sky. The dust blew through our loose hair as we stood in a line looking at the defendant and the rows and rows of rusted, broken furniture and abandoned belongings my parents had collected through time and stored in the damp, dark basement. The pieces were placed in neat rows so the jury could see the evidence clearly. Everything they owned was there, everything that they had saved and collected throughout their seventy years, painfully preserved in plastic storage boxes. It was all there and all in order.

I was not alone. I was in a line, a procession of women warriors, ready for battle. The reckoning was here. They were defeated and we would win. We didn't want the spread of material possessions; we were after something much bigger. We wanted freedom. Like the Israelites escaping and wandering through the desert, all we asked for was our birthright, our freedom.

The verdict came quickly. Guilty as charged.

Before the guards could take her away, my mother ran into one of the rows of boxes. She knelt in front of a stack of records and feverishly flipped through them, searching for something.

"*Blackbird!*" She exclaimed hysterically. "I can't find *Blackbird.*"

I walked up the row of objects and calmly stood over her, my long shadow cascading over her head. "That's because you never owned *Blackbird.*"

"I did! I did! Where is it?"

"No, *Blackbird* is on *The White Album.* You don't own *The White Album.*"

She looked down at the pile of records and realized that I was right. I was right all along. I stooped down next to her as she wept in her hands, realizing her mistake. I felt sad for her and sang softly,

"Blackbird singing in the dead of night.
Take these broken wings and learn to fly.
All your life.
You were only waiting for this moment to arise."

I reached my hand out and touched her hair like a child.

14

Dreams like this came fast and steady, creeping into my sleep like movie reels. They were not always so redemptive. Most of the time they involved my mom finding new ways to chase me, pin me down and cut open my flesh. Many times the dreams were of me yelling in her face while she just smiled unwavering until I wanted to shake her. Others involved me desperately needing to get home and going round and round on a highway driving a car that was falling apart piece by piece until I couldn't drive anymore. I couldn't get back to safety and I couldn't escape.

My dreams pillaged my sleep until I went on new medication to stop them from retraumatizing me by morning. I found myself telling Dr. Evergreen a new one every session. We would analyze what my conscience was trying to iron out and they always seemed to make sense.

My mom chopped off my fingers one by one with her gardening shears, she forced communion down my throat before strangling me and she was always chasing me. Dr. Evergreen asked me to find a way to fight back. How could I fight back a monster?

"What would you do to her if you could?"

"Yell at her."

"What would you want to do?"

"Yell at her and kick her until she listened to me!"

"That's all?"

"Yes." I was trembling with fear and anger. I didn't know the right answer.

"Say it. Say what you would do." She pressed.

"Kill her."

Apparently, in therapy you are allowed to say that you want to kill your mother and in fact, it's encouraged. I scared myself by saying it allowed. I didn't want to kill her as much as I wanted to defend myself and if she attacked me, then yes, I would kill her. It was my power and fortitude that Dr. Evergreen was trying to get me to harness.

I began trying to fight back and save myself in my dreams and as we reprocessed my traumatic memories. I found a way to hit her and escape, press my fingers into her eyes so she couldn't hurt me. She always wanted me dead and all I wanted was my freedom. I had to kill her in order to save my life, own my life.

15

It was a miracle I had made it this far and not ended up strung out in a ditch under the highway. I had a home, a husband and three babies to love on. We were all bonded and hopelessly in love with one another. Each one of my babies were magically different and equally enchanting, like fairies. I felt blessed. We had done it. We had built this family, this fortress, that would never break. And when we had secured our party of five, we designed and built a home on a lively street with other growing families and life was sweet.

I had the community I dreamed of around me. I knew my mail carrier by name, I ran into the same moms from playgroup at the grocery and our pediatrician was just up the street. The children ran barefoot on the sidewalk next to the great, brown dog they liked to decorate with plastic jewelry. We were tucked into our little village with everything we needed. And we were thriving, blessed by God, a house on a hill. We only wanted to be orbited by love and goodwill. I started to feel entitled to peace.

However, the rupture with my parents crept in as my children grew, as holidays approached. I tried to share time with my parents, but my mom found ways to express her disapproval. She would physically move into my space, press her breasts up against my shoulder and tilt her face into mine.

"Hon, do you think it's wise to read books like that when you have little children?"

I was telling her about the book I was reading – *The Kite Runner*.

"I just don't think it's wise to consume material like this when you have kids in the house. I don't want it upsetting you."

I was angry. I had tried to connect with her on a book and she turned it into a weapon to use against me. In that moment I had a choice to make. I wanted to calmly say that she didn't need to worry about such things because I was an adult now. I could choose my reading material. I could parent my children. Didn't she notice how charming they were? The anger was throbbing in my face and since I still didn't know how to control what spewed out of me, I swallowed it. I smiled back to keep the peace and let myself get rolled over.

I walked her out to her car, a baby on a hip and two following behind me.

"Careful! Don't run in the street. This is a really busy street, Chris."

"Yup. It can be."

"I just don't know how safe I feel with you living on it with these kids."

"I know. It's not ideal."

She climbed into her car and I thanked her for coming over.

"You're welcome. Bye, everyone." She waved at the kids as she unlocked the Club, a long steering lock for her car. I laughed to myself imagining Brent seeing that she had put it on during the daylight as if we lived in a dangerous neighborhood where cars were stolen off the streets.

I put the kids down for a nap and let myself cry as I walked to my bedroom, closed the shades and climb into bed. For the next few days, I would mother my children with a heaviness like weighted chains around my body. I returned to my bed when I could and when the weekend came, I closed and locked the door, letting myself fall into collapse.

Our cold war continued for the next ten years, volleying between my submission or avoidance and her disdain. There were times when the weight of my relationship with her was so heavy that I put it down and went without talking to her for a time because I couldn't bear her punishment. I would find relief in the space I had created and thinking I was healed, I would try again. And again. And again.

In my head I heard my dad's refrain, "Life is so short."

16

"Hi Readers. It's Christen from *Blue Egg Brown Nest*. I am going to show you how to use Annie Sloan Chalk Paint. I have this beautiful vintage chest of drawers here that I found at a local estate sale. I took the hardware off and am planning on painting it Annie Sloan's French Linen. I love the neutral colors best because they will work in most rooms."

I turned towards the chest and picked up a can of Annie Sloan Chalk Paint.

"The best part about this paint is that you don't have to prep your piece. You don't have to strip it or sand it, you just have to paint."

I faced the video camera that I had poised on a small bistro table in the driveway and shook the can. I was thirty years old and was healing, working with my hands and creating beauty. The process of painting was life-giving.

"You want to make sure you shake the can or stir it before you paint so it's all mixed properly. Sometimes water can get trapped on the surface so you want to make sure it's really stirred."

I opened the can with a paint can opener.

"Isn't that beautiful?"

This was my first tutorial video on YouTube. I had no idea what I was doing, but loved the idea of teaching what I had learned to the readers I had established from my blog. I had been painting and refinishing furniture for about a year and knew what I was doing. People were starting to paint their old pieces because of what I was teaching them on my site. I wrote every day on Blue Egg Brown Nest and found myself connecting with my readership beyond paint.

I was transparent about who I was. I was ready to trust a public who was connecting with me over the process of taking something old and transforming it. I was riding the wave of what was then called "upcycling" and it was more popular than any DIY movement. I took precious pieces out of storage rooms and basements, encouraging people to paint them and transform them into coveted pieces that people wanted to display out in the open in their family rooms and dining rooms. My readers came from all over the world, emailing me asking for help and suggestions. They were painting entire sets of dining room furniture, king-sized beds, side tables, kitchen cabinets and more. They were praising my name for introducing them to the possibility of what old pieces in their homes could be like. An article in *Southern Home Magazine* crowned me the "Princess of Paint." I wore the title as I talked about paint, but what I really found myself doing was falling in love with people all over the country and world and they were falling in love with me.

I was transparent with my life too, sharing my family and kids in all my writing. I was a mom of three children and a creative person. I wanted to be both and show people that moms could have a creative identity outside of shuffling kids to preschool and changing diapers. I heard from women who were new moms all the way to seniors that wanted to meet me and share in the experience. I felt bonded to a community that I had created, and I felt beloved.

My readers knew Brent as Dear Husband and they saw daily pictures of my kids trying to help mommy paint. I told them when I had a bad review and they defended me. I rejoiced with them when I was published in a magazine or sold a piece to a good home. And when I made my first tutorial, an overwhelming amount of people watched it, over two million hits on YouTube and YouTube followers and my Facebook members increased to almost 30,000.

The best part was that I was still me, just doing my life and building a business. I made many more videos in the driveway, the kids always running around in the background in the sprinkler, coloring with chalk or making a lemonade stand. I shot the videos from a camera propped up by my diaper bag and when the Littles were in diapers and Fiona kept yelling for me in the background, I had to pause what I was teaching and laugh, throwing up my hands at the camera and say, "This is my life." And the love that came back to me from my candidness felt like the love of a family with its arms wide open. They wanted all of me and I wanted them just as fiercely.

It was only four months prior that we were in the midst of building our house on the same street we had lived in when we were married. It was the second home we had built together. Brent and I always knew we were going to knock down our home and build a new one. We moved into an older home with the goal of building and were itching to do so, even after all our renovations. At this time, no one was building in our area like we were and certainly no one in their late 20s. But, Brent and I never quite fit into the lines of what was normal. We envisioned more for ourselves and it was in this likeness and shared love of creating that we moved together in expansion of space, family and ourselves.

Our intention was set, and we were clear in our hopes of building homes until we were able to build one that would house our family. So, when our neighbors across the street offered to sell us their home without an agent, we took the risk and moved. We designed and built on our former lot. We watched from across the street as the basement that Brent had framed with his own hands was ripped from the ground by a monster excavator, the yellow walls being pulled like dandelions from the ground. We spent the next years pouring over plans and walking the house that was growing across the street. It was a house on a hill and taking shape before our eyes. Our babies, Fiona on a hip, came with us as we received the white kitchen cabinets and the five men it took to install the black, honed granite countertop. And in the summer of 2016, at the moment that the housing bubble was being burst, we sold the first home we had built right before the Recession. We watched from across the street as the SOLD sign was posted.

It was heartbreaking to see the home we had built sold to another family, but we knew this home was not ours. We did not have the funds to afford the home at the time and we would have to be patient. We would have to wait and dream, but in dreaming, we designed the house that we would build on the lot were living on. We were also establishing ourselves as designers and builders and it felt like a great success to see a finished product and all the work that went into the building process. It felt like Brent and I had been leading up to this point and we were walking through this pivotal time in our lives. We were building homes and building our family.

17

Brent walked in the door at almost ten o'clock. The Bachelor was over and I had been waiting by the window to see the headlights from his car on the street outside. I waited until I heard him at the door before walking out of the bedroom. Greta and Fiona had been asleep for hours and I made sure to avoid the creek in the middle wood board in the hallway. I hear his key in the lock first and scurried to the door.

"Hi." His hands were filled with a Costco box and three containers of Enfamil.

"Hi."

"I didn't think you'd be up."

"You are going to need to go back to Costco for more formula." I said sheepishly.

"What, I just got three containers. We'll be fine for a while."

I pulled out the pregnancy stick that boasted a pink plus sign and held it out to him like a badge of honor. "No, we are going to need more formula."

Brent just about dropped the load he was carrying, "What? What?" He wrapped his arms around me and then pulled my shoulders from him to look me in the face.

"I don't understand."

"I'm pregnant. I took this tonight. I wanted to wait until you got home."

His hands flew up to his face, his mouth opened in shock, "What?"

We both were in total and shock and disbelief. We faced impossible infertility treatments, including the darkest moments of our lives trying to get pregnant with Greta. We forged through more treatments and shots and meds and doctors to get to our sweet Fiona and now, without doing anything but living life and loving on our new family, we were having another baby. A miracle baby. It felt like the Heavens had opened up and were raining down all the love that was in store for us. Our family was here. We were walking on clouds. We held each other tightly and cried.

When we were ready to knock down our neighbor's home that we had purchased, we knew what we wanted and we knew how to build a home. The process was exciting for both of us – Brent because he loved building and me because there was nothing I loved more than playing at home design. I poured over interior design magazines and *Pinterest* and toured homes in our area. On Saturdays, we piled the girls in the car and drove all over Northern Virginia scouting out homes and pointing to designs that we liked. I created a huge notebook with pictures, ideas, fabric samples and pamphlets. In the past few years since building and selling our first home, our town had become a hot spot for building. The area was dotted with smaller homes on small lots, but it was also ten minutes outside of DC and had become a coveted area with some of the best public schools in the country. There were families that wanted to move into the area, but the ramblers were almost too tiny to fit a family of more than five. There were developers coming into the neighborhoods and buying up lots, competing with individuals that wanted to live in the area. Our area was in high demand and we felt validated with our decision as twenty-four-year-olds to move into an older home and bide our time. To everything there is a season and we were now reaping our fertile reward.

I wanted an English Cottage. Period. I wanted my Cotswold, Charlotte Bronte, moors of England, Elizabethan, horse-drawn carriage, enormous fireplace, book-reading home. Cozy. I wanted the cozy from all my Jane Austen books. I wanted a house made of grey stone with ivy growing up every side and crawling between every edge. I wanted a high-pitched roof, gas lanterns, hedgerows, a long drive, maybe a moat and lots and lots of ivy.

Unfortunately, an exterior made of stone was not in the budget and ivy was like letting termites loose in a house made of only wood. But, our architect helped me come up with little, cozy spots throughout the home where one could stop and read a poem or two – if they were not a busy mom of three children under four-years-old. I wanted a cubby under the stairway like Harry Potter's room and a slate roof so when it rained, we could hear the settling rhythmic pitter-patter. I imagined a secret garden out back with a place to grow vegetables and a gate with a secret lock with access to a maze made up of cut boxwoods. Our lot would not allow for these things either, but I found my cozy in the fixtures and furniture, including gas lanterns over the barn-like garage doors.

We had no budget for furniture and as I was designing each space from the kitchen table at my in-laws' home, I realized I didn't want to put in any pieces that I didn't absolutely love. This was our chance to create a new space with adult furniture and not pieces that we built with a staple gun and left-over fabric.

I scoured Craigslist looking for kitchen tables and chairs to no avail. Most of the furniture being sold was worn and dated and would not work in my new space. However, in the back of my head I thought about the demi-lune I had bought from Luckett's General Store, a vintage shop out near Leesburg. My mother-in-law had told me about her vintage-looking night-stands that she bought from a vendor there who painted beautiful, vintage pieces. I drove out to his studio looking for a piece for our small foyer in our old home and found the sweetest piece painting in grey. The piece had been painted with Milk Paint.

Milk paint?

I researched the product while the babies napped and decided I was just going to have to try it out on my own. I found eight, French wheatback chairs from a seller on Craigslist and decided to take a chance. I sent Brent to pick them up in Manassas on a weeknight. He begrudgingly made two trips, but it was worth it. I had my canvas. Now, I just needed to make the honey-colored, dated pieces beautiful.

18

"Fiona, move over, Lovie. Give you sister a turn."

Greta and Fiona were playing in the toy red Jeep parked under the portico just outside of the basement rooms we were living in. I was head to toe in paint as was the concrete patio where I had been working.

"Fiona, I'm going to count to three and then it's time out."

"Ok, but Mama I want it back after."

"Ok, I'll time you both."

I looked at my phone and set a timer in the hope that the girls could play nicely for the rest of the afternoon and I could work refinishing the chairs. Reid was born two weeks prior and was dozing in a bouncy seat by the side door in the shade of an old oak tree. Happiest baby on the block.

I turned back to the four chairs drying in the sun on the lawn. Two of them were shades of grey and two were a cream color. They had been completely transformed with the magic of Milk Paint, but I still was not convinced I had the look I wanted. That morning I opened the box from the Milk Paint Co, revealing several smaller boxes containing a powdered paint. The directions were to mix with water and a bonding agent. I tore through the kitchen drawers, searching for measure spoons and cups. I would sacrifice them easily for the project. I stirred and stirred and added more and more. The paint was thin and difficult to work with. But, I kept playing until I created a mixture that was thick enough to coat the seat of the chair. There were articles and websites with tips on how to achieve specific colors, but I didn't have the luxury of reading through content. Mama was trying to do a million things at once.

Brent and I had stained our own wood floors in our first house and although it was the messiest home-improvement process we went through, I knew that stain could lend a distressed appearance. We had purchased several cans in order to pick out the shade we wanted for our new floors. I wanted striped barn wood panels, but again, that was not in the budget. We would probably use the same Jacobean stain that we had used in all of our other homes.

I shook the sample can and peeled the lid off, revealing the dark, bubbling syrup.

"Mama, I'm hungry."

"Ok, Love. Fifteen minutes and it's lunch time. I'll make mac and cheese."

There were Cheerios and puffs sprinkled all over the patio just waiting for the dog to come lick them up. I was on borrowed time and had to rush. I took a used rag and dipped it into the stain and then rubbed it on one of the dry chairs. I took a step back and observed my work. It worked. The stain had offered the painted piece a hint of age, the distressed look that I was going for. I knew the chairs would work. All I needed now was to find a good kitchen table. I'd go back to Craigslist for the next five years to furniture my home.

"You should document your process."

It was a babysitter that had first suggested my blog. My business needed a name, one that signified where I was in my new life. Like most writers, I was always fascinated by the magic of birds - flight, freedom, swallows of birds moving together with instinct and ethereal knowledge. They were too magical to be ignored and moved like they were sending a message. Seeing a red or blue bird out my window meant God was watching me and that there were creatures outside in the world creating and spinning in their majesty. Birds were heavenly.

I was also safe now. Not just in a single room by myself, but in a whole house, a nest, and with people I knew loved me and supported me. When Brent came into my life, time and circumstance shifted. There became a before Brent and an after with Brent. He helped uncover who I was beneath the crusted scabs, wounds that wouldn't heal and scars that still throbbed red. He helped pull me from the wreckage, a burning house, so that I could stand on solid ground and walk away from the flames that continued to chase me. We were special and what we were building was special, like that of a blue egg contrasting the hard work that a nest takes to build, twig by twig.

I was creating beautiful things out of ugly pieces and the magnitude of the analogy was not lost on me. Rebirth. Oxygen. Air. Space to wander and be curious and think and dream.

So, I painted and I blogged. Painted. Blogged. Painted. Blogged. I was a mom first and a business owner second, but my two worlds intertwined in perfect unison as my kids romped around in the sunshine and I painted furniture in my driveway. I build a website and presence and was ready for my shot when *The Washington Post* caught wind of my activity.

19

I poured the three pounds of orzo into a clean, white bowl I had purchased at Target for the luncheon. Each cucumber was cut into a perfect square, matching the blood-red tomatoes and purple stained onion. I did a rough chop on the black kalamata olives, popping one in my mouth and letting the salty brine sting my tongue, making me salivate. I crumbled dry feta into the bowl and poured in the vinaigrette I had made with the fresh lemons from the grocery store. When all the ingredients were assembled, I pulled out my chef tongs and pulled at the pasta, turning the contents with my wrist. Pull, turn. Pull, turn. I did this a few more times until I saw the rainbow of colors dotted between the blades of orzo.

"Mama, can I have some? Can I have that?" Fiona standing by my side along with Kane, the dog, both waiting for crumbs to fall from the countertop.

"I'm sorry, Love, this is for Mama's special friends."

"What friends?"

"My friends that are coming today. Remember? They are going to take pictures of our house."

"Me? Are they taking my picture?"

"Well, I don't know. I sure hope so."

The editor for *The Washington Post* Lifestyle section had reached out the week before to confirm the article on Blue Egg Brown Nest. She had orchestrated a photographer and was bringing an assistant. We would have the interview over lunch.

I didn't know how these things worked and wanted to prepare a spread for the guests that were coming into my home. I had stayed up all night cleaning and sorting. Most of the rooms were completely decorated. Since I wrote daily on my blog, I always had projects and content. I would serve the orzo salad with chicken salad sandwiches on croissants and a tower of homemade macaroons.

"Mama, are those cookies for your friends too?"

"Here, Girls, you can each have one. Could you go find daddy and tell him that Reid is up?"

"What's up?" Asked Brent, coming into the kitchen. "The house looks amazing. You've done such a phenomenal job."

He hugged me from behind as I scrunched up my nose in doubt.

"I don't know what I'm doing."

"You don't have to do anything. Just how them your work."

"I guess, but what if it's total shit. What if everything just looks good in my head?"

"Stop. You don't give yourself enough credit. You've put so much work into the house and they are going to see that."

"I guess." I put Saran wrap over the orzo salad and put it in the fridge to marinate. "Oh, could you grab Reid?"

I glanced over at the baby monitor and saw Reid rolling around in his crib, sucking his fingers and cooing. Happiest Baby.

I walked the house, trying to observe my interiors with the eye of an outside observer. I had several of my own, painted vintage pieces and lots of little vignettes within eyesight. There were rooms that we not completed. I was still not making money to furnish the house the way I wanted it, but we had built this home as a young couple, I was writing about it and I had started my own business. I just hoped I was at the place in my life where my hard work and good choices were ready to meet this opportunity. As I found out the following week, I was.

20

The article came out on Thursday. Brent opened the paper to the Lifestyle section and saw a full-page cover of our dining room with a painted dresser in French Linen. My house was in *The Washington Post*. It was a six-page spread, including my biography, a description of my business, pictures of our home and a special image with Brent and my young kids – a picture that none of us would ever forget.

Brent was headed out the door when I pulled up my email at the desk in the kitchen. My inbox took minutes to load. I had over five-thousand new emails waiting for me. Five thousand.

"Brent?"

"Oh, my gosh, Chris. That's amazing."

"What are all of these?"

"Your new following."

I had a few hundred people following my blog and had started selling my refinished furniture, but it was nothing like the flood of people emailing me about *The Post* article.

"I'm going to need to get a sitter today." I sat down at my desk. My hands were shaking as I opened the first email, 'Hi Christen. I just read about your business in *The Post*. I am interested in painting my grandmother's coffee table. Is this something you'd recommend? If so, what color?'

I read three more similar emails all asking my advice and some wanting to hire me for design work or refinishing work. I could hear Reid starting to talk from his crib and knew I couldn't get through my inbox without help. I picked up the phone.

"Hey, Carrie. It's Christen. Are you able to come watch the

kids today?"

"Sure."

Carrie made it to the house within the hour and I carried my laptop up to the guestroom above the garage for extra privacy. I spent the next five hours in front of the computer answering reader questions and responding to the article. I was completely overwhelmed and fought back tears of gratitude. There was a community out there that was eager to connect with me and seemed to appreciate what I was doing. They loved my interiors and wanted my help to refinish their pieces like mine. They knew my name. They knew me by my name. Christen.

This was the birth of an identity for me. Could I really do this? Could I do something creative, write and raise my kids all at the same time? I could not believe that all these people had found me and seemed to admire me. I wanted to invite each one of them over, sit down on the little couch I had purchased with my own Blue Egg Brown Nest money, and have a cup of tea with them. I wanted to meet them all. I had too many emails to get through in one day and would spend the rest of the week responding to each and every one of them.

Nothing was the same after *The Washington Post* article. I made an LLC and started taking in clients all over the East Coast. I was buying and selling pieces and taking on pieces to refinish for people at my home. I also wrote every day. Writing and painting. My kids watched me work as we all grew up and up towards the sun.

Within a year, I had become a small business owner and published designer. I was in several design magazines a year, including *Cottage Style Magazine, Southern Living Magazine, Romantic Homes Magazine, Vintage Style Magazine, Arlington Magazine, freshstyle Magazine and a book publication of Southern Home.* I had grown used to people coming in my home and talking to me about my projects.

I hired a picker to find pieces for me and a driver to deliver. My kids romped around me while I painted for clients in my driveway. And I wrote. I wrote every, single day on my blog.

I wrote about painting, but also about family and love and God. I wrote about how blessed I was to be doing something I loved with my young family. I wrote about my gratitude for my readers. And then I opened up and wrote about my struggle with anxiety and depression...and my mom.

My readers fell deeply in love with me and I them. We connected on so many levels. I had women out there sharing their own stories of heart ache and pain. I had hundreds of emails a day, in fact. I would never meet all these people, but we were connecting over beautiful spaces, paint and what it was like to live in a broken world.

I was healing and it was a gift. I was moving out of the shadows of suffering first with my new husband, the babies I had fought to conceive and now my own identity as a business owner. I tried to push away the pain that tried to seep in through the crack in the doorway. I tucked my babies into bed at night and couldn't help feeling the tear in my heart as I thought about my mom and how she walked past the enormous buffet in the kitchen that was half painted that day.

She pulled in a deep breath, "Oh my goodness, you are painting that?"

She was mortified.

"Mom, no one wants a huge, brown piece of furniture anymore. I'm transforming it into something people will love in their homes."

"I would never paint a piece as beautiful as this."

My heart fell, but it didn't shatter. I didn't have her support for the furniture or the homes we built. She didn't try to understand or see our success, but I had thousands of readers out there that I knew loved me and I them.

I sucked in a breath and pushed down the feelings of rejection. I didn't have the words to defend myself and I didn't know that I was going to change her mind even if I could. So, I moved past the piece in the middle of the foyer, like an elephant in the room, and offered her coffee. She balked that I didn't have cream.

21

"I have a few copies of *Southern Style* that I just received if you'd like some."

"Ah, Chris, that's great." My dad said taking the books that included my work in the publication.

"Oh ok." She said.

"Look at mommy." Fiona pushed the book at my mom noticing her indifference.

I waited for her to fill me up, for the pit in my gut to be soothed with a compliment.

"That is very neat. I can't put it out though because I don't want my friends, well, you know."

She was telling me that she didn't want to seem boastful in front of company that came over if she displayed the book. I didn't have the words, just the familiar pain.

That night I thought to myself, "Why would it be so bad to brag about your daughter?" I had a nagging feeling in me that once I felt filled up enough, loved enough, I wouldn't need the attention I had garnered from my success. I kept working and selling and blogging, but the hole in my heart was not getting filled as I needed. My emotional needs were so enormous that nothing was going to fill them. There was a mother-shaped hole in my chest. I felt my depression creeping around me, waiting for an entrance, a chink in the armor. I knew the shadows were inching their way in just waiting for me to fall back into a familiar collapse. I had everything – the husband, the children, the home, the identity - but found myself starving at the banquet before me.

I continued to push myself and accepted a vendor position

at Luckett's General Store, a popular vintage shop, in the hopes that it would satisfy me. I rented a space on the porch and loaded up all my wares every Thursday to sell. I picked, painted and hauled pieces out to Luckett's every week and tried to claim my place amongst the other vendors. However, instead of feeling accomplished as I had been chosen from hundreds of dealers that were waiting on the Luckett's vendor waitlist, I felt exposed and vulnerable. I felt scared of doing a bad job or not selling the pieces I had picked or painted. I couldn't control the anxiety that was coming up and felt like I was on the verge of a free-fall.

I felt trapped just like I did when I was working. I was beholden to people and feared that at any moment they could reject me and throw me out, disown me. It was a feeling that was beyond my control and no amount of love from readers knocking on my door could get through. I wanted out. I wanted to pack up, go home and hide under a bed. I wanted to be done sharing myself with the world. I didn't feel good anymore. I felt cold and weak. I stopped blogging and I stopped painting. I upped my meds, joined a support group and started weekly acupuncture. But, I still found myself crawling into my beautiful, white four-poster bed and pulling in the curtains to block out the daylight.

When I was asked why I stopped everything by my beloved readers, I didn't have a good answer. I didn't know what to say. I just knew that everything felt hard and I was so very tired. I let my brain teeter into dark spaces imagining relief from the depression that was crushing me. The clouds moved in and I shut the door.

22

My dad had two heart attacks in two years. One of them was on Christmas morning when Abigail was coming into town with her family from New York City. We were on our way from Arlington to the house when my mom called us.

"Chris, Hon, Dad's not feeling well."

"Ok, what's wrong?"

My stomach dropped to my feet and my eyes welled with tears.

"Well, he's feeling some pain in his chest and just kind of, tired. I called an ambulance to come get him."

"Ok, we are almost to the house."

We pulled up and saw my dad being carried by stretcher into the back of the ambulance. I jumped out of the car, calling back to the kids, "Everything is alright. Papa is just going to the hospital. Watch your movie."

"Dad?" I said as I looked into the back of the ambulance.

"Hi, Hon." He said. "I'm just not feeling too well."

"Ok. I'm glad you are going to get checked out."

My mom was talking to the other EMT who suggested following the ambulance.

Abigail came up the driveway and handed my mom her purse. "Mom, I'll drive you."

"We'll meet you at the hospital." Brent said. "We will drop the kids at my parent's house."

Abigail and I had been fighting all morning about scheduling and duties for Christmas day. We were both exhausted and stressed. My mom and her had been fighting about my nieces making a mess in the family room, "Zach and I are trying to sleep in a twin bed with a pack n' play in the room!"

It was too much for anyone to handle, especially our family and we were imploding. By the time my dad had his second heart attack, something had to give

"You girls are making your dad sick!" My mom lashed out at me a few months after my dad's recovery.

"I made him have a heart attack?" I texted back. I was too scared to have a phone conversation or face to face, but I was quick with my words on text. "I did not give dad a heart attack."

But, what if I did? What if the stress from cold war and our deteriorating family system was killing my dad? What if I was killing my dad? I wanted to forget it all. Forget the therapy, forget the growing and changing and moving into the light, forget it all. I loved my dad deeply and wanted him to live. I would put my life on hold to save him.

I camped out at the emergency room, waiting with him while they performed tests. I didn't want to leave his side.

"Well, they got me all hooked up here, Hon."

"Yes, they do, Dad. It's good we came."

"Yea."

"The doctor came in while you were sleeping. He said it was a heart attack."

"Oh, he did? Oh wow. Ok."

"Yea, they are going to admit you they said."

"Ok. Where's mom?"

"She just ran out to get lunch, but will be back soon."

He had surgery the next day where they put a stent in his artery, opening up the pathways to his heart. It had become blocked and his arteries needed help to keep it open and blood pumping. I brought him treats from Starbucks and a blanket and sat with him while he ate his hospital food. We laughed about the types of desserts hidden under the plastic lid and guessed which one was next. The strawberry shortcake was his favorite.

23

"I don't remember you being there." Abigail said to me over the phone.

It was the most provocative, eye-opening thing she could have said to me. She didn't remember me being there. In the house? In the family? In the car when we were dragged to the doll museum and the Annapolis wartime museum where my mom packed egg salad sandwiches for us to eat in the car on the way home?

"Wait, what? Like in the house?"

"I don't know. I just don't remember you being around."

"Well, I guess I wasn't. I wasn't around."

"But, even when we were little, I don't remember you."

What was life like when I was a baby and Abigail a toddler? My earliest memory was of my mother and a beach. I went down to the shoreline, near the water where she was stretched out under the sun and I laid down next to her on the warm sand. I fell asleep in the sunshine and woke up to a nightmare. I remember the cold, powerful wave filled with sea gristle that flushed through my nose, eyes and mouth, taking me out into the ocean. My body rolled – one, two, three summersaults through the dark water, pulling me under. I thought I was going to die. The sea spit me out eventually, the tide receded as I crawled on my hands and knees out of the water's grip. I coughed up water and spit out grains of sand until I found my breath again. My head was spinning, and I reached out for my mother, but she was no longer there. She had left me asleep to be taken by the wave.

My mom had left. She had taken her beach towel and gone back up to the patch of sand by the dunes with the rest of the family.

"Where were you?" I said when I made it back to my family. I cried and cried, letting the tears and snot seep from my face.

"I was right here. I could see you."

"But, you didn't see me."

I was hysterical. Beyond comfort. She looked around at the other families and smiled as she wrapped me in a towel and said, "Shhh."

"I want to go home."

"We are not going home."

I cried some more feeling the trapped sand in the bottom of my bathing suit stinging my skin. "I have sand everywhere."

"Just go in the ocean and clean it off."

She had returned to read her book. I looked around at the blankets and umbrellas around me. Everyone was so calm. I was the only one that causing a fuss and I quickly felt embarrassed. I sat with a wet towel around me, the sand from my soggy bathing suit rubbing against my bottom. I spent the rest of the afternoon on high alert. Sitting straight up and keeping watch. I had learned a great lesson that day. I was never going to be caught off guard again.

Abigail moved to India. All the way to the other side of the world. And when she came back to visit, I felt like we were two little girls again trying to get along, appreciate one another and play nicely together in a world that we could never quite navigate. We were raised other and we were late to the party - late in trying to figure out our own place in the world. We were still trying to assimilate, and it was hard.

I knew her blue ocean eyes and her thick, black hair, the freckles on her nose. I loved her and I loved us. We were sisters locked away, fighting daily to free ourselves. And look at us – we did. It was as if an earthquake came, tore apart the earth, creating enough chaos to shake loose the lock and key, to fling open the doors so we could run. We each ended up on the other side of a crack in the ground, but we left the desert and found our promised lands. They were just on different sides of the world from one another.

She had three baby girls and became a painter. She surrounded herself with women that loved on her and made her fresh coffee every morning. And I fled only minutes away from Great Falls, but into a new city, a new reality, one that I had observed in other families and in books where peace is possible. Where I could expand and, most importantly, be curious about the world. It is a happy ending for both of us.

Dr. Evergreen said curiosity is the antithesis to black and white thinking. One can't be curious about the world when one is trying to organize information into only two groups. I've come to think that curiosity is a piece of Heaven itself. We were made to be curious about the world.

When my mother realized Abigail was not coming back, she asked her for a divorce. Abigail was their shining star and they poured and poured and poured into her. They gave her as much as they had to give. She was their joy, their entertainment, their lives. When Abigail went out to dinner with a friend, my dad would go along. When Abigail wanted a ride to the mall and a new shirt, my parents went with her and bought it for her. What a devastating irony it must have been when she left.

Abigail moved across the sea to live her life in a country packed with warm, brown women that met her with love. They fed her, drove her family and helped mother her children. I think my mom wanted that job even if she was incapable.

It reminded me of a *Twilight Zone* episode about irony, love and loss. There was a man that loved to read, but never had the time because he was always working and working. He was so sad and he loved books so much. Then one day the world came to an end, as it does in the *Twilight Zone*, buildings came crashing down around him and everyone on earth died except him. He looked upon where he landed in the rubble and realized it was the public library. There were millions of books in heaps all around him, enough to read for the rest of his days. He looked around for his much-needed glasses that had fallen off and as he stepped forward to search for them, he heard the crush of glass beneath his foot. He had broken the glasses he needed to read and would never be able to read any of the stacks of books scattered around him.

24

The nightmares returned at the reality of my parents aging and life marching on. We were not the close family we were taught we were. We were dispersed on our own islands, Abigail and I doing the best we could with what we knew. We were trying to save ourselves, grabbing at lifeboats in a broken sea.

I cried to my dad during that time telling him that I wished things were different. I didn't spit blame or ask for apologies. The time for reparations was over. But, I was still working every week, sometimes twice a week, in therapy. Why did I still feel sick and often empty?

I had a dream about vines and pussy willows and roots growing out of my private parts, my orifices, damp, dripping with caged mud and blanche worms. I woke feeling disgusted. I went through my day wiping them away from my chest to my stomach past my feet like my reiki master does when I lie on her table with my eyes closed.

I am a swamp.

I am growing swamp-like things out of my body like a cadaver lying in a field summoning the magots to feast. This is what it is like to write about the past and all that is inside of me still to be purged. I tried when I was young to expel it from my body, but I think it takes a lifetime and a tolerance for the mess.

Yes, Dr. Evergreen, it is worth cutting open my body once again and weighing my insides on a metal scale so I can account and write down the exact numbers and my observations and see what is in there. I need to see what is going on in there once again. And when I do, I will take great care to hold each piece, each organ, as if it were a baby because they are all babies that grow inside me, along with me, and live in the she that is my body albeit damaged and singed.

In this autopsy, I can see that they all did their jobs. So, well. So proud.

I can clean them, wash them white with snow, but a little slime-silted matter will stick and that's okay. It means I was alive. It means that I fought through to the very place I am now, to the Heaven that is this new family and home.

25

We were exhausted by the time we made our way onto the plaza from the Top of the Rock. I secretly hoped I would run into Hoda Kotbe.

"Can we do that?" Fiona saw the line of taxi bikes first.

I was still dizzy from the momentum of going up seventy floors in a cramped elevator and taking pictures out on the observation deck. It reminded me of when my dad had taken us to the Empire State Building, telling us that if we dropped a penny from where we stood and it hit someone on the head it would kill the person instantly.

Our hair was sweaty and stuck to the back of our necks. We had spent the morning unabashedly touring the city and taking selfies. We had already seen Battery Park, taken pictures in front of the Statue of Liberty and rode the sparkly fish at Seaglass Carousal within a few short hours.

"YES!" I exclaimed mirroring Fiona's excitement. Our feet were tired and a ride back to our hotel in the waiting pedicab looked like another novel experience on our weekend trip. Brent hesitated while the kids and I climbed in.

"Can we fit?" I asked pulling Reid close to me to allow for Brent and Greta to climb on.

"Sure, Ma'am."

"Get in, Brent!" I loved the feeling of being adventurous in contrast to Brent's cautiousness. I was anything but spontaneous, but the city in the middle of August was empty which meant we could unabashedly enjoy all it had to offer.

Brent begrudgingly climbed into the cab and sat on the hot leather seat. I could feel his embarrassment. "Well, he saw a live one coming." Brent said with sarcasm and he grabbed for the convertible top to hold on to.

"To the Peninsula!" I said with dramatic effect, pointing a finger forward.

Fiona squealed, her teeth clenched with excitement. Our biker pedaled until the little engine took over. We weaved in and out of the cars and the traffic as if we had been sprinkled with fairy dust. Reid and I laughed uncontrollably as we skirted by the lines of cars and pedestrians getting close enough to touch them.

"This is the best thing ever!" Fiona screamed.

It was the best thing ever.

Our driver witnessed our excitement, smiled and swerved even more. We howled and belly-laughed until we had to catch our breath and wipe our gleeful tears. We moved through the city streets like nothing could touch us and let the welcomed the breeze lick our hot faces. We were flying and it was our laughter carrying us higher and higher. I looked over at my squished family with pure delight.

The pedicab scooted up to The Peninsula entry way that was clustered with patrons and expensive cars. Brent pulled out his wallet. The kids and I beamed while taking a selfie with our driver who seemed to enjoy the ride as much as we had. Fiona asked if we could go again.

"That was better than any ride in Disney World!" Greta exclaimed. Yes, it was, my dear.

We packed into the hotel elevator and made our way up to the nineth floor where we crashed on the queen beds. Our clothes were still sticking to our skin from the summer heat and our feet were painted with dirt, but we were too tired to move.

"We have two hours until dinner." I said looking at my phone. Brent's eyes were already closed and Reid had jumped on his Switch. We were all stuffed into one room, clothes piling up near the bathroom door.

"Where are we going for dinner?" Greta asked.

"Ummmm." I pulled up the little itinerary I created on my

phone.

"Carmine's Italian Restaurant."

After a snooze, we all showered, changed into clean clothes and made our way back onto the street. Greta and Fiona linked arms and skipped down the sidewalk while Reid ran, jumping and pushing his feet against the skyscrapers like Spiderman.

I watched the girls walk independently in front of us and Brent grabbed my hand. We made our way past Trump Towers where tourists were gathered taking photos. I put my middle finger up to the gold signage.

"Look at the cats." The Gucci window was next to Trump and was decorated with life-sized cats.

"Stand next to them," I said to Reid.

I took a picture and posted it on Instagram with the caption, "I'll take the boy."

My heart was light. Brent bent down to kiss me, an acknowledgement that our little trip was a success and he too was enjoying himself. The city was busy and beautiful in a way that I had never seen before. I had never felt this safe and welcomed in New York. I had never felt like I could find pleasure in what it had to offer.

I had spent my entire childhood and into high school driving up to Queens with my family, me in the backseat of the burnt-red minivan arriving at Grammie Angelica's in the middle of the night. I smelled the spoiled garbage on the New Jersey Turnpike, a sign that we were getting closer to the Tappan Zee Bridge where we would cross into Queens.

We drove at night, after my Dad got home from work. We would sleep in the car. However, when we the cars started moving faster around us and the highway lights came at a quicker clip, I sat up with anxiety creeping up my spine. The city was dark and I closed my eyes tight as we stopped at the red lights with the dark shadows of people gathered in front of apartment buildings.

At eleven o'clock at night, the city was still wide awake. We passed basketball courts where men played under streetlight and strip malls with their aggressive metal gates that had been pulled down. Groups of people gathered on dark corners and under awnings for Chinese restaurants, their cigarettes glowing in the shadows. I was little, it was black outside and my dad seemed extra anxious. The message I received was that the city and everyone in it was dangerous. And it was when he was growing up, keeping himself safe on these same streets.

"I want everyone to dress down when we go into the city tomorrow." My dad would say when we would take the bus from Queens into Manhattan at Christmas time. He didn't want my mom carrying her purse and had us girls put a few quarters for the phone in our pockets in case we got lost.

I secretly hoped that we were going to see the Christmas parade or find Santa at one of the big stores. Instead, we walked and walked and walked until I had to run to keep up. I felt like I would either die from exhaustion or I would be kidnapped when some bad man would find me and grab me because I had dropped too far behind my parents. I remember grey clouds and food trucks, steam coming from metal boxes. My mom would usually stop in front of one and declare that she wanted a hotdog with the works.

We walked through Battery Park and took the ferry over to the Statue of Liberty. A vendor sold foam green crowns, magnets, key chains and I HEART NYC tee shirts. I wanted one of each.

"Look at those." I said out loud in case my Dad had not seen the twinkle in my eye.

"Uh huh." My dad said not even turning around.

Relief washed over me when we got to the base of the statue and viewed the line. It was all the way down the metal fence by the water. Abigail thread her arms into the front of my mom's coat as I bounced up and down from the cold. I wished desperately that my mom would see the crowd and say it was way too long. I was terrified to ride up on an elevator to the top. But, I knew I couldn't wait below where I could be murdered. We all stared at my mom, waiting for her to make the decision.

"I think it's too long. Let's just walk around."

Three hours later we were back at Grammie Angelica's house that smelled like salty meats and marinara sauce. I could barely keep my eyes open as she scooped ravioli onto a plate in front of me. The pasta warmed my belly and the relief that we had made it back to her home unscathed allowed me to relax. I asked to go to bed after we cleaned up the kitchen, turning down the coveted raspberry danish for dessert. All I had to do now was survive the next nine hours and hope that no one decided to put a bullet through the bedroom window.

26

"*Hamilton.*"

"What?" Their eyes grew to the size of large gumballs as they looked back and forth between each other.

"Are you kidding?" Greta exclaimed.

"Nope."

We had splurged and bought *Hamilton* tickets. Tickets to the musical were still extraordinarily expensive, but we had listened to the music in the car for the last two years and wanted to be a part of the excitement.

We finished up our vodka penne, paid the bill and made our way out in the packed streets of Time's Square. We passed mimes, vendors selling t-shirt and food carts.

"Let's get t-shirts!"

"What?" Said Brent turning back to me as I was following behind.

"Yes, let's totally get tee-shirts." I laughed at Brent's sour expression.

The kids clamored around the closest vendor's table. They each picked out NYC shirt and I took a picture of the three of them in front of the large neon billboards.

"Ok, we need to get in line."

We made our way to the back the line that snaked in front of the Richard Rogers Theatre. There was a woman in front of us that was carrying a yellow shopping bag with the M&M logo.

"Oooooo, M&Ms." I felt like nothing was off limits.

"Ma'am, where is the M&M store?" I asked.

"Time's Square."

"Come on guys." I said getting out of line.

"What? Chris, we don't have time!" Brent yelled after me and the train of children following.

"We are an hour early, Brent!" I kept walking.

We reached the two-story building and made our way up the escalators into a land rainbowed with candy. We made our way to the wall of M&Ms and I passed out bags to each of the kids so they could help themselves.

We selected blues and purples, hot pink and all the colors we had never seen before. I bought an "m" water bottle, Fiona got fleece pajama pants, Greta a key chain and Reid a gumball machine that spit out M&Ms.

"Alight, back to the line." I said over my shoulder, my own large yellow bag slung over my arm.

We went back to the line that was moving and headed into the dark theater. Our seats were in the third tier, but there were no complaints. We were at *Hamilton*.

More selfies.

The show started, "*How does a bastard, orphan, son of whore and a Scotsman dropped in the middle of a forgotten spot in the Caribbean...*"

Reid was rhyming the words with Leslie Odem Jr. until I tapped him on the shoulder, "Shhhhhh."

We found an unexpected and genuine thrill in our exploration of the city and drank it in with unabashed gluttony. It was no longer a place to be frightened of because it was not littered with criminals and crooks like I thought when I was a child. It felt like a playground. No, it felt better than a playground. It felt like freedom.

27

Brené Brown came down on a cloud from Heaven like the second coming of Christ, trumpets blaring, fireworks exploding and a chorus of angels singing Cat Steven's *Morning has Broken*. She came like Moses to lead me the rest of the way through the desert and into the promise land. And unlike the rich young ruler, I sold all my belongings, stood up and followed.

I fell in love with Brené Brown before she was Brené Brown. I listened to the audio version of The Gifts of Imperfection over and over as I carted kids to and from practices and out to Luckett's. The hour long drive out past Leesburg allowed her words to marinate inside of me, committing her research to memory. It finally felt like someone was talking to me in a real and personal way. I had read a ton of self-help books, listened to even more podcasts, and God knows how many sermons, but Brené was offering something different. She was willing to put herself in the story and talk about her own shame and vulnerability. She was in everything that she taught. She was honest, brave and a woman.

I was in the arena, Brené. Damn it, I had set up a tent and was living in the goddamn arena. And I was hated for it. My mother hated me for it. She stalked me like a wild, drooling, fanged animal hunts her prey, shaming me and my choices. From putting my kids in sports to building a new home. I was ready for it. I was ready for her to spew judgement at my new life choices, knowing that when you set up healthy boundaries those that benefited from the old set of rules lash out at any sign of change. She didn't stand by the sideline cheering me on, glowing at my personal improvement and health. She stood disapproving, suggesting I had fallen from grace.

I pulled my family from the mega church we had attended for over ten years when the messaging became so contrary to my heart. It was Peter all over again. It was the boy with the earring in the grocery store. It was my mother telling me to turn my back on people I loved because of what a man, a pastor, was teaching. I wasn't going to do it. The teaching did not describe the Jesus I believed in. My Jesus flipped tables in the synagogue.

I spend so many years under the thumb of teachers that hit and shamed and taught fear. I was betrayed by all the authorities in my life. My mother manipulated the Bible, telling me that God was not going to bless me if I went against her. And it was now time to react to what I was feeling about the church. I was older, an adult, and ready to listen to like-minded, loving people that wanted radiate love and acceptance.

I learned that being in the arena meant being ready for battle. There were times when I could fight and there were times that I had to lay my head on the dirt and cry. The more I turned from the ways of my family system, the more they misunderstood and rejected who I was becoming. Like Tara Westover in *Educated*, a woman that had to separate herself from her family in order to become more fully herself, educated, I too, felt the pain of walking away. Do I choose my own, unpaved path that will maybe lead to the mountain top or do I run back to what I know? Do I grow on my own, having faith in what I think is right? Do I move by faith not by sight?

Brené and Dr. Evergreen promised that if I stayed in the fight and committed myself to the change I wanted that I would create earthquakes in many of my relationships. However, I would also taste real freedom. And real freedom - from emotional abuse and chaos and shame and expectations and criticism and judgement were all I wanted. I was willing turn from the family I knew for the chance at true belonging and connection.

I recognized that my family was designed from fear. Abigail and I were raised with fear. If we stepped out of the lines, we'd fall into sin. But, didn't Jesus leave an entire flock to save just one little lamb from the cliff? The story that my family groomed me from no longer made sense. I didn't want to operate out of fear.

I knew there was more for me.

I chose friends who did deep dives, I disrobed and bared my vulnerability to the people in my life that I trusted and like the plant in Dr. Evergreen's office, I wanted to grow towards the sun. And no one had to tell me where the sun was, I was born with that knowledge.

I wanted truth-telling. I wanted authenticity even if it was scarce. I wanted to open myself up even more. What Brené was saying aligned with the deep feelings of who I was at a core level. And she was calling people to task. She confirmed all that I have known and introduced a new kind of healing to me and the rest of the world. She was creating a new culture of strong women that were inspiring and empowering.

I craved similar messages of freedom from a female authors and thinkers like Sue Monk Kidd, Jen Hatmaker, Nadia Bolz-Weber and Anne Lamott and devoured their books. Could there be leaders outside the church that were offering more relatable messages? Could this be what I've been searching for?

Maybe I was searching for these contemporary female Christians all along. Women that questioned the structure of the church with their very gender. Things they said spoke so clearly to me, like owning my own story, facing the trauma, rising up, embracing discomfort and freeing ourselves. I was more than all I had been taught to think. The compass in the center of my chest, the one that pointed to True North, burned. Metal on flesh.

28

My break from my conservative church was a slow burn that started with the birth of my daughter, new life. The birth of a baby was the rebirth I needed in my life – it was the most natural evolution possible. My heart and my body broke open and bringing forth life meant I was no longer just fighting for my own freedom in the world, but I was fighting for my babies. The stretch marks, soft belly and tired eyes were all the armor I needed.

A wild drum beat in my ears like rains from a hurricane on a metal rooftop, the wind pushing the trees sideways. I couldn't ignore it anymore. But, like any street fight, there was an underdog that needed to be brave enough to enter the fight and be willing to stay in it to the death, defeat the enemy and rise again. A phoenix.

There was a part of me, forty-years of me, that was groomed to think of God in very limited terms. I was taught not to question the teachers, which meant ignoring my instincts, curiosity and heart. I was taught by my parents, my school and my church that expanding out into the world was unsafe, unrighteous. But, I was starting to feel like there was no greater God-given gift than that of curiosity. I could be blessed, I could love God, and I could also be brave and continue to grow.

Look at my house on a hill, my healthy children, the love of my husband and my healing!

I started to trust that God wanted me to grow towards the sun and not shrink back in fear. I felt like all the wisdom I had accumulated throughout my life and in the scars on my body were accumulated for a greater purpose. God didn't give me a brain and a life so I could ignore every instinct I was born with.

29

COVID came to kill - separate mothers and fathers, babies and grandbabies, husbands and wives just like the end of days.

The news showed us dead bodies in Italy, lined up like wrapped baguettes in the street. We were told the virus was coming for us and we were not prepared. We didn't have ventilators in our hospitals or protection for our front-line workers. People were going to die in mass quantities.

I ordered extra toilet paper and stocked the freezer in the garage. We waited. The news included a tally on their broadcast of world cases and deaths along with US cases and deaths. Before anyone had officially announced that we were in trouble, 240 people had died in one week.

Trump addressed the country in what would become nightly press conferences over the pandemic. He put Pence in charge of a Covid-19 task force and invited the country's top epidemiologists to speak about the science of the virus. But, it still wasn't real. 320 people were dead. The tally kept moving upwards.

The country closed school on March 11, 2020 for fourteen days. We let the neighborhood kids play in the yard with one another still not sure what was the right thing to do. By the next day, March 12, 2020 we locked our doors. No one was going in or out.

I waited a few days before calling my parents.

"Hi Dad. I just wanted to check on you all and make sure you are watching the news." I said as I finished up my ride on the Peloton.

"Oh, yea. We are watching it," he said.

"Please tell me you are going to quarantine. They are very

specific about telling people over sixty and with compromised immune systems not to leave the house."

"I heard."

When my dad gave me short answers it was usually because he was preoccupied with waving my mom over to join the call.

"Chrissssssten?" She said in a soft voice. "Can I be a part of this conversation?" We had not talked much since my dad's birthday at the Cheesecake Factory back in February. "When we were young, we were taught to revere our grandparents. We would sit at our grandparents' feet." She was using a quiet voice, but it had started to shake with emotion. "Now it feels like the world is pushing us away, pushing us into our homes and away from our families."

She didn't want to be told that she was over sixty and at a higher risk, she didn't want to be told to quarantine and she didn't want to be told that she should not go to church or Zumba. And she especially didn't want me telling her what to do.

I felt her accusation through the phone. "Mom, I did not start Corona. I did not start this pandemic." I yelled, Brent scooting closer to me on the couch, listening to the heated conversation. "They just cancelled school. Brent's office closed."

The fire in my body felt like it was going to annihilate me. This was officially the worst thing that the world had faced. And here I was trying to convince my mom of the severity of the situation.

"This is not the way this conversation was supposed to go. I was sad."

"You are sad? We are all sad! Mom, they cancelled school. Are you listening to me?"

"Hon."

"I'm not the one making up the rules. Italy has shut down. People are dying by the hundreds. Are you guys watching the news?"

"You're not listening."

"No, you are not listening." I had gotten loud, my eyes blurring.

"I'm going to hang up."

"You are going to hang up?" I felt like my head was going to explode. "You are hanging up?"

"I'm hanging up now. You are just hurting me now."

"I'm hurting you?"

I heard the line click and shoved the heels of my palms into my eye sockets to stifle the hot tears. The frustration would erupt like lava for the rest of the night and my body would stiffen in a twisted rope of physical pain and exhaustion.

30

"I feel like I'm going to die right here and now."

I imagined my mom clutching her heart and falling onto the front lawn. I wonder if she actually fell to the grass and if she was surprised when two minutes into her collapse, she discovered that she was not actually dead but just lying on the ground. Would she stand up again and walk into the house to resume her day? Would she lay there staring at the sky? Would she pray that God would just take her to prove herself the victim and me the assailant? I went up to my room laughing wildly. This was the farthest she had taken her rage and there was nowhere else for her to go.

"Can we at least pray?"

"No, Mom. I'm not going to pray with you."

"Well, then you might as well divorce me. You should get a lawyer and divorce me right now. Why am I even here?"

"Why are you always so mean?" I met the volume in her voice. "We are not going anywhere. We are quarantining and if I had to get out, I am wearing a mask! Are you trying to get COVID? You could die. Dad could die."

"Well, then maybe I'll just die."

"Are you serious?"

"Well, what are we living for? We are just being pushed away."

"It's call quarantine!"

"You are telling me not to go anywhere and I'm sorry, that just won't happen. I can't do that, Hon."

The high pitch of her voice lowered to a quiet whine. There was no convincing her. I was going to have to lie on the bathroom floor in tears to eradicate this exchange from my body like the many times before.

I was quiet as I held the phone to my ear. "I'm going to go now."

She hung up.

31

This time was different. I did lock the door, but when Brent came to ask me if I was ok, I did not scream, "Get the fuck out." I was not on the bathroom floor, in the small room where the toilet was pushing my legs against the wall willing the drywall to break or my legs to break first. I did not let myself wonder about cutting myself or letting blood drain from my body like I had in the years breaking away from my family.

I pivoted.

I sat on the bed and thought to myself, I am not the monster. I am not the one that picked up the sword and started wielding it first. She said I was killing on the front lawn, in the warm grass, but something inside of me decided not to take the bait. I hung up the phone and used the energy to write. I put on Netflix and watched Chef's Table. The episode was about a man, a butcher's son, who grew up in Germany taking care of the cows in his father's pasture. He loved the animals so much that he wanted to become a veterinarian. Then, his father passed away and he had no choice but to pick up where he left off to support the family. He had to become the town butcher. I sobbed. I moaned at the menacing irony that left this man patting the sides of his beloved cows facia as they swung from hooks still warm and recently stripped of their hide. His only savior was his promise to the cattle that he would kill the animals in a loving way. Did he even believe it? He had to believe it. He held up steaks high in the air and brought them to the family table so that the people could honor the flesh before sinking their teeth into its salty texture.

I heard a small tap at the door.

"Do you want to watch the rest of that show with me?" Brent asked quietly.

"Ok."

He climbed into bed with me. It was six o'clock pm and still light outside. We pulled the white puff over our bodies and up to our chins. We had the rest of the night to lie in bed and watch episode after episode of *Yellowstone*. We had this space and time to just lie here. He was done with work, the kids were fed. A brilliant idea came to me. Popcorn.

"Can you make popcorn?"

"Do we have any?"

"Yes," I said. "It's in the pantry. Microwave."

He went downstairs for a few minutes and then emerged into the bedroom carrying a huge, metal bowl of warm, buttery popcorn. I smelled it first taking in the excitement of fresh popcorn in bed with a show. I picked through the pieces, pushing aside the white bits to get to the yellow soft buttered pieces.

Brent reached his hand in once I had had my fill. This was different. This felt so different. I washed my buttered hands and climbed onto my purple yoga mat that lived next to the side of the bed. I laid on my back and stretched my body straight and then twisted one way and another. When we had made it through four episodes, and it was time for bed I took the bottle of pills that my psychiatrist had prescribed for my nightmares and placed one on my tongue. Like manna. Like the bread of Christ. This is my body shed for you so that you may have life and life eternal.

I slept soundly and woke to the birds outside my window. There were no monsters in my head that night. I opened the shades and looked up at the blue sky. I thanked God for the day because He was still up there in the perfect blue sky. And over there in that green tree and somewhere in my chest only for me. Whispering only to me. Soothing only me. Letting me. Pushing me more towards the sunlight, more towards the me that has been in existence before time began. Like a compass setting fire to all the cells in my body and mind telling me yes, this is right. Follow this. It's already all here. It's always been buried, like treasure, right here.

32

"Call 911. Tell her to call 911."

"Susan, you need to call an ambulance." He said into the phone. "I know it is, we will pay for it."

"I'm going to drive over there." I said standing up, my anxiety escalating quickly.

"No, you're not." Brent covered the phone with his hand. "If anyone is going I am."

He was still on the phone with my mom trying to convince her of the seriousness of my dad's symptoms. He had a fever of 102 for the past three days, was coughing and felt physical fatigue so much that he could only lay in bed. She was planning on letting him rest while she prayed for his recovery.

"Ok. Call me back when you get him in the ambulance." Brent said into the phone before hanging up.

"I don't trust her. I don't trust her to get him to the hospital."

"Let's just see what happens."

"No. No. He had a fever for three days and she called it a low fever. He's been in bed." Tears started coming hot and fast, running down my face. Every symptom that he was describing was what I had heard as COVID symptoms for the past four months.

"I'm going out there to make sure he gets in the ambulance." I grabbed my keys and headed for the door.

"No, no you are not. I will go."

Brent walked out the door. When his car was out of the driveway, I grabbed my bag. "Greta, you are in charge." I pulled out of the driveway when my phone rang.

"I talked to your mom. He's in the ambulance and his vitals look good. That's a good sign. Your mom is going to follow it to

Reston."

I turned out of my street where I saw Brent in his car returning to our house.

"Where are you going?" He asked into the phone as he stared at my car.

"Reston."

I hung up the phone. I wasn't going to listen to anyone. I wanted to make sure the ambulance got to the hospital. I wanted to see my dad. I started sobbing on and off for the rest of the ride thinking of how I was never going to see him again. Hospitals were not letting family members into COVID patients' rooms. The news had stories every night of sick people dying alone, saying goodbye to their loved ones on the phone held by a nurse. This is what was going to happen. I was never going to see my dad again.

I couldn't control my breathing when I pulled into the Reston Hospital emergency parking lot. Brent had followed behind me in his car and parked next to me. There was an ambulance arriving.

"Chris! You can't go up there."

I ignored him and climbed up the grassy median to the circle drive where the ambulance had pulled up. I put on my mask and stood in front of the passenger side.

"Is this a relative?" The young paramedic asked me.

Brent answered, "Henry?"

"Yes," he said. "You can see him."

I shuffled around the back of the ambulance as two EMTs were pulling my dad from the back on a stretcher. He was in full head to toe PPE, his hair feathered in their swift movements.

"Hi Dad." I said with a trembling voice.

"Oh, Hon."

"It's ok. You are going to feel better."

The EMTs didn't stop but moved through a side door near the main ER entrance.

"I love you, Dad!" I shouted at the back of his head. He was not even through the doors before I burst into uncontrollable sobbing. I could not breath through my mask and I could not see through my stream of tears. Brent came up behind me and put his hand on my back.

"It's ok. He'll be ok."

I brushed his words away. I had watched the news for months. People his age who got COVID were not ok.

We found mom in the parking lot. She had followed the ambulance.

"They brought him in through the emergency area." I said before she spoke.

"Ok. I really thought he just needed to rest. I'm sure he doesn't have COVID." She said with her mask pulled down to her chin.

"Susan, you need to pull up your mask."

Brent and I backed away slightly. If Dad had COVID then my mom had COVID.

"I really think it may be something to do with his feet. His toes are awful. I told him this the other night. Let me show you a picture."

"I don't want to see a picture. Mom, he has all the symptoms of COVID. Why didn't you get him to the doctors for a test?"

"I don't think he has COVID, Hon. And we have an appointment with Dr. Ready tomorrow. He was going to see him tomorrow."

"Mom, tomorrow could have been too late."

"Well, I don't know about that. He was fine. He had a low fever. The only thing that started to worry me was that he couldn't get up and walk, but Dad doesn't move around a whole lot. You don't see him, but he doesn't do much."

She shook her head back and forth and turned her eyebrows up trying to compel me to understand.

A nurse came out. "Are you visiting a patient?"

We looked at each other.

"Yes, what is the protocol?" I asked.

"Only one person. Only one person and the same person can visit a patient during their stay."

"Oh, ok." My mom said pulling the mask down again. "I forgot my hearing aids. I should go in first?"

"He can only have one visitor." Brent tried to explain.

"We will take your temperature and then you can go see the patient." The nurse explained.

"What if it's COVID?" I asked.

"Oh, then no one can go in. He's here for a COVID test?"

"Yes, he was just brought by ambulance with COVID symptoms," I explained.

My mom shook her hand back and forth, "Oh, but he doesn't have COVID," as if she was going to get in trouble and decided to outright lie. But, it wasn't a lie either. She believed what she was saying.

"Let me get your phone number and we will call you when we get the results of his test. You can also call the emergency room."

Brent took her card and thanked her before walking away from the hospital entrance.

"Chris, Susan, move away from the door."

"What?" My mom could not hear us.

"The COVID test they are giving your Dad will take three to four hours to get results. That's what the hospital said when I called on the way over."

"Mom, you should go home. We will too. We can reconvene when we have an answer.

"I'm not going to go home," she said. "I need a Coke."

"Ok, well, let's be in touch in a few hours."

"I'm going to call Bob and ask him to intercede for Dad. He will do that for me."

I looked at Brent and curled my lips at the mention of her cousin's name. He was a fierce Christian and a confident to my mother in times of crisis. She talked about him like he owned the keys to the Kingdom and he was our ticket to getting all prayer answered.

Brent and I would also pray after we called Abigail. And we'd wait to hear from the doctors.

33

"Ok, guys. We are going to work on language arts."

Reid was sitting at the counter with his county issued iPad. I was puttering around the kitchen cleaning up breakfast and trying to follow along with the teacher. It was September 8, 2020 and the first day of school. But, instead of laying out their outfits and packing lunches, the kids woke up and logged onto their iPads to start their day.

The girls were both in middle school and I couldn't help but remember the time when I started Herndon Intermediate and the fear of mixing with all the elementary schools from around the county. We had to stand outside of the doors until exactly 7:20 when they custodians opened them and we flooded the hallways. We navigated our lockers and the classrooms and teachers. The lunchroom was total chaos that I didn't even try to open the bagged lunch my mom had packed me. I just went directly over to the vending machine and bought a cinnamon Tastykake. I threw the brown sack in the trash before anyone asked me why I wasn't eating the lunch I brought.

I stood in front of the cutting board assembling turkey and cheese sandwiches. I piled on the turkey and made sure it was next to the mayonnaise that was sprinkled with just a bit of black pepper. I put a piece of string cheese on their plate, cut up their favorite Gala apples and poured them each a glass of milk. Everything was laid out ten minutes before they came to the table for lunch.

"How did it go?" I asked as I sat down beside Greta in my usual spot.

"It's weird."

"Yea?"

I waited, letting her respond when she was ready.

"Yea, I mean, you can block your screen so you don't even really know who is in your class. Like, you can only see their initials."

"What? What does the teacher say? Doesn't she want to see you all?"

"I don't know. It's not required."

"So, do you see her?"

"Yes. We see her and anyone that unblocks themselves."

"What do you do?"

"It depends on the class. If most people are blocking themselves, I don't want to be the only that is seen."

The reality of online learning was getting worse. I thought about my girls in middle school and how they were meant to expand into their worlds and connect with new people in their new bodies. My son was in his last year in elementary school, the kings and queens of the school, and they were meant to stay in their room for several hours, stopping to do jumping jacks and move around when they switched subjects. This was not school. This was not connection. I thought about their sore eyes and necks and the depletion of social tools they would have when and if schools opened. What would their world look like?

34

Taylor Swift's cover of Tom Petty's *American Girl* was playing as I started my drive out to Great Falls. I could see how Taylor was an American girl and wondered if I was one too. I had had boyfriends, learned to walk in high heels and been disappointed by life in general.

I stopped by the gift shop on the corner near the 7-Eleven to pick up a candle and a little card game. I still tried to pick out the right gifts, something that would please them. Setting out on Route 66 to the Toll Road, I felt the unease in my stomach and hands as they shook with the anxiety of going over to the very same house I grew up in, the three windows in the front façade that was my room all those years ago. I had my disposable, pale blue face mask from a fifty-pack off I purchased off Amazon. We were all used to wearing them by now and I hoped my parents would have them on without me asking. I texted my mom this morning to see if they could sit outside for the visit. The answer was yes and I tried to trust that it would still be yes by the time I pulled up the driveway. I was full of doubt. The kids still buzzed around me sensing my apprehension at the morning's event. I very rarely left the house during COVID and if I did it was to go to the grocery store for all of thirty minutes.

I passed the corner where Dove lost her life. There were still four weathered white crosses for each of teenager that died, their names printed in black lettering. The loss and heartache after all these years felt like a preamble to how I felt about going home. Tears sprang to my eyes like they always did and I couldn't help but feel like I was driving right over the place where Dove's spirit started to leave her body.

I had to use the bathroom after taking all those pills this morning like I did every morning. I took so many that they no longer fit in the Monday through Friday single pill box. I needed the large one and refilled it often. I usually tried to wait to leave the house until I was sure I had emptied my entire bladder, but I didn't want to waste time in getting over there. I had already spent the week worrying about what it was going to be like to see my dad and how my mom was going to respond to me.

My dad was being treated for COVID at the hospital where they kept him for three weeks. She still denied that it was COVID at all, but we know from the medical records that this is what they were treating him for. My mom didn't believe it in just like she didn't believe in the vaccine. I'm not sure they watched the news, saw the numbers, considers the deaths. Maybe she thought those were the people that needed to be punished and this was their due, payback for sin like she said about Hurricane Katrina.

I stopped trying to convince her, rationalize with her, because it hurt too much. It did no good.

I knew she wanted me at the hospital, taking turns and responsibility over my dad. I waited for her to come to her senses and acknowledge my three young kids, her grandchildren that I had at home. I waited for her to consider the hospital rules and the safety of...me. It was still jaw-dropping that she didn't want me safe. It makes my shoulders pull upwards with tension knowing that she didn't consider that we could get sick and possibly die.

I know what she wanted. She wanted me to drop my life, come along side of her and support her, listen to her cries. I had done it before, every time there was a health crisis, every time. I would leave my family and fulfill all my duties as the daughter that was here, as the good girl. And I would listen to her. I would listen as she wailed and lamented about her own freedoms being cut short if my dad was too sick to participate in the life she wanted. She complained. She turned the terror of my dad losing his life into her loss. Please tell me her brain is broken because none of this makes sense. I was lost in a maze of crazy-making. She was trying to pull me in and I was not coming along for the ride this time.

I refused to participate, and she didn't like it.

I knew she wanted me to be there for her at the house when he came home as a support. But, I said no in spite of my guilt and her anger. I said no to her and yes to my family. It sounds so much easier said than done. Where was my mother that wanted me and her grandchildren safe? Nothing had changed for her. It was like she wanted me little, a little girl in her house at the ready.

I was driving a large SUV that fit my three kids and the dog, such a contrast to the little blue Honda I used to drive back-and-forth on the very same road, Route 7, passing the Potomac Vegetable Farms market and the garden center. There was construction everywhere as they were widening the road to accommodate all the new traffic coming from Loudoun.

Great Falls was not the sprawling green town that it had once been with acres of land and trees. There were lots with for sale signs and each spare patch had new homes built on it.
The closer I got to Fox Den Road the more nerves I felt in my belly. I turned onto the road that led to my childhood home where not much had changed. I passed Jennifer Walker with the beautiful black hair's red brick house. She was a year older than me at Woodlawn and the last stop the bus made in our neighborhood on the way in our school. I remember running into her at the outlet mall where we both pretended not to know one another.
Libby's house was the blue one on the right. I remember the homemade chocolate croissants her mother made for her and packed in her lunch once a week. I remember asking her at least two times if her mother had truly made them from scratch. How did she get the chocolate in there?

The Alden sign that my mom and the other home-owners near us had petitioned for to separate our half of the neighborhood from the other, newer half was still there. I remember how some of the neighbors talked about wanting the distinction be-tween our side of the street and the other side. I remember being in the car when my mom first saw the sign and how she stomped her feet on the car floor and let out an excited, "Yes!" as if she had won a battle.

The soccer field was on the left as the road wound around other homes that I no longer knew the residents of. Right be-fore the last curve, I saw the gully that I had played in with the other neighborhood kids and pretended we were little wood-land creatures that lived amongst the rocks. Grass had covered the rocks making it look like as simple buckle between Paige Winter's house and the brick one next to ours.

With my stomach churning, I turned into the driveway and saw Dad sitting on a lawn chair tucked behind his car. He looked as if someone had placed him exactly there, which my mom and physical therapist had.

I climbed out of the car and smiled as big as I could behind my mask. I presented them with Fiona's a plate of homemade rasp-berry thumbprint cookies, a sign colored by Reid and a baguette made by Greta.

"Ah, why thank you." Dad said as I offered him and my mom one.

"Oh, how sweet," mom said. "You can just put them on top of the car there."

"Dad, you look good." And he did. He had lost a bit of weight, but nothing much had changed since his stay in the hospital. It was easy to ignore the walker because I had actually thought it was a good thing, something that could help him get around more easily.

"Here, you take this chair," my mom offered.

I sat down and felt the slight breeze.

"Beautiful day."

"It is." I said noticing that it was not as hot in the shade of their large oak trees. I swore I felt the CBD that I had dropped be-neath my tongue kick in as I let my body sink into the chair six feet across from him. I let my mom putter around, putting the plate of cookies inside and getting her own chair.

My plan going in was not to discuss future plans or even how they were choosing to do things now. I was just going to sit and visit.

"You know, this whole thing has made me think a lot about my dad." Dad started, sucking in air and looking down at the ground with sorrowful eyes. "He was in the wheelchair for most of his life."

"Yup," I said. I was not going to rebut him and tell him that he himself was not in a wheelchair or that he didn't have spinal meningitis. I shook my head giving him permission to continue.

"You know, I think about him and how hard it was for him to get in and out of his chair to because I have to do it too now."

The leaves from the trees made a brushing sound as they touched each other. They were so tall. Taller than I remembered.

"The Lord kept him around long enough to see you. He loved his grandchildren. I remember him holding you and taking you for a ride on the ramp in front of the house."

I smiled.

"And my mom. He kept my mom safe for all those years. She was so strong. Do you know she was the fastest stenographer in all of the New York for years? I'd watch her get on the bus. Then we sold the house and used the money for the assisted living place near Cindy."

"Yes. We used to visit her."

"Ah, Cindy did such a good job taking care of her." He said mostly to himself. "Anyway, I have some books for you that I want you to pick out. Really good ones too. With those thick pages. Huge pictures. Art Nuovo, Art Deco. You're really going to like them."

"Yes, I'd love them. I remember those books." I replied.

My mom had come back outside and handed Dad and me a ruby-colored drink in a plastic glass with ice.

"Thank you, Hon," he said.

"Thanks." I placed my down on the driveway wondering if

she was going to feel badly if I didn't drink it. I had a moment in my head where I was going to take a sip so I wouldn't hurt her feelings. The cup stayed on the ground for the remainder of the visit.

"I was just reminiscing." Dad said to mom who had settled into her chair six feet away from both of us making up a little triangle.

"Oh yea?" She said and looked at me asking me with her eyes to note this comment.

"I'm writing a bit about my childhood and all these memories are coming to me."

I smiled and felt a closeness with my dad that we were both writing what we knew.

"Doesn't Dad look good?" Mom asked.

"He does. He looks great."

"He's still dealing with some lack of energy, but we have a little schedule for him that is working out quite well. I wake up at five o'clock. About five or five-thirty, fix him a little bowl of oatmeal, someone probiotic yogurt and maybe a little string cheese. I bring that up in a tray and get him to sit in a chair like this one. He eats and we listen to the sermon on the radio and just chill. Then we come downstairs for a bit. He holds onto the banister sideways, there's a whole method that we learned in the hospital. Dad's good at it. Then he sits in the sunlight on a chair by the front door and does some reading. He likes it."

I looked at my dad as she was talking. I saw his eyes smiling behind his mask, but he was quiet. I wondered if he did like sitting in the foyer on a chair.

"Then we have lunch and afterwards I go out to the grocery store or something," she continued. "For about a half hour or so. When I come home we go back upstairs and he takes a little nap. It's good for him because then he can get through the evening."

I nodded my head reminding myself that I was just here to listen. "Sounds like a good schedule."

She smiled and looked pleased.

I returned home the way I came, past the construction and the garden center, past my old church this time on my side of the street and Dove's cross on the opposite. I didn't eat breakfast and was starving. I wanted to sink my teeth into a large sub sandwich but had given up bread for the week.

I went up to shower and changed instead, saying hi to the kids in passing who were playing cards nicely together in the family room. I locked the door to my bathroom and quickly rinsed off with some scented body wash before turning on my noise maker and lying down on my bed, giving myself a minute to process. Ollie, the ginger cat who knew all, met me there. I felt heavy.

I wish things could have been different.

I wish things were different.

I knew I only had a minute before Brent came knocking at the door. I tried to will him away. I needed to be by myself. I didn't want to describe the morning.

I didn't descend from my room until an hour had passed and my stomach was making hungry sounds. Ollie had started whining for his food and the dog that had snuck in before I closed the door was getting restless. All the animals could tell time by the setting of the sun and feel in the air, even the fancy Persian with the pinchy nose on my white couch. It was time to eat.

EPILOGUE

They were called Yucatan birds. Each one moved with the tempo of the Mexican jungle. They were white like angels, their feathers silk.

The sun set behind the brush and right before the orange planet sunk into the ink of night, the birds came home. Every evening at the exact same time, the magnificent leader flew down the ribbon of the lagoon and picked a branch to settle on, burrowing its head into himself. Then, a steady stream of ethereal birds would follow, filling the sky. Their bodies swayed in flight until they reached the trees that welcome them. They shifted and nestled into one another and into the leaves and branches that held them close in their arms. The cluster moved in little waves putting each other to sleep until all was still. The pull of the moon, the ocean and all the rhythms of nature tucked them into bed.

No one taught them how to fly.

They used their feathers and bones and ligaments that they were fastened with from birth by their architect. And they knew from the dawn of their existence that they held this magic. They lived in the world fearlessly. Each bird trusting their good, strong bodies and the cradle of the sky - a soft, blue mother.

My healing came from the crooked smile of the server that offered us more coffee in the mornings and folded down our cool sheets at night. It came from the sway of the warm air, baptizing our bodies in the sunshine and dipping into one another.

We found sleep in the wide canopy bed where the native white birds cooed to each other outside the window, lulling us into deep and needed rest. They came every night, only at night, tucking themselves into the branches and creating a painting with their feathers.

And in the mornings the sun warmed our skin and welcomed us with its ever-present and brilliant shine. We filled our bellies with a rainbow of fresh fruit and green drinks in tall glasses and afterwards climbed onto our bikes shedding more of the past and the pain that had built up inside of both of us like stubborn, black tar.

I flung my straw bag into the basket between the handlebars. I didn't wait for Brent before finding my balance and pedaling forward. I went from a careful pace to a gleeful stride. I threw my head back and laughed, moving faster through the shaded path with abandon.

"Slow down, Hot Shot." Brent called out after me.

I laughed harder and louder letting the warm air fill my lungs. I was flying. Higher and higher. Up and across the bridge, over the wild lagoon below speckled with creatures that rose with the yolk of the sun. I pedaled up to the sky. Faster, faster until I was moving through the jungle, the air holding me so that I could fling my legs out and trust that I would be held.

I was a bird flying.

God was somewhere in the bamboo trees that I moved through, laughing with me and holding me in perfect balance. The blue sky covered me like a soft blanket, and I breathed in the scent of the sun-kissed flowers, each one growing towards the warm glow like it was born to; like it was born knowing how to move upwards towards the God that created it. He was all around and my heart beat in the perfect rhythm of the blue ocean. Just like the white birds above.

If you or someone you know has a mental illness, is struggling emotionally, or has concerns about their mental health, there are ways to get help. These resources are provided by National Institute of Mental Health.

National Suicide Prevention Lifeline

Call 1-800-273-TALK (8255); En Español 1-888-628-9454
The Lifeline is a free, confidential crisis hotline that is available to everyone 24 hours a day, seven days a week. The Lifeline connects callers to the nearest crisis center in the Lifeline national network.

Crisis Text Line

Text "HELLO" to 741741
The Crisis Text hotline is available 24 hours a day, seven days a week throughout the U.S. The Crisis Text Line serves anyone, in any type of crisis, connecting them with a crisis counselor who can provide support and information.

ACKNOWLEDGEMENTS

I have altered most of the names of people and places in order to respect and keep private their identities.

I don't believe many things in life are all good or all bad. I also don't believe there are any wasted experiences. Even the most painful ones have something to offer and often shape us into the people we are. Thank you, mom and dad for doing the very best you could with what you had. Dear sister, I love you and those wonderful moments when I feel deeply connected to you by our past and present.

To Brent, the love of my life, there are no words. You are everything.

To my children, you are all unicorns – magical and bright like the sun. You are important because you were born. I am just the woman you passed through. Each of you, my loves, are precious jewels that will go out into the world and shine just by being who you already are. Be brave. Be kind. Be curious.

To my extended family, I cannot name you all because I am too nervous that I would leave someone off the list by mistake. Thank you for including me at the table just as I am.

To the friends I made when I was young and scared, you are an important part of my history and I will never forget our precious time together. I have all our memories tucked in a special place in my heart. I think of you often and wish we could all meet face to face of a cup of tea.

To my golden girls, I am blessed by all of you. You have become my family and when we are together and I find myself in deep conversation or in a rolling belly laugh, I know I am seen. I am so blessed. I would not be in the healthy, whole-hearted place I am today if it were not for my deep connections with all of you.

To Rachel, my longest, dearest friend. Thank you for the over thirty years of witnessing and empathizing. I will always be so grateful for you and, of course, your shawl.

To Dove, I cannot wait to see you again in Heaven. Promise me we can run through the field of yellow wildflowers together with our play shoes.

Book Club Discussion Questions

1. If you wrote your own memoir what would the title be?

2. Name some of the main themes in the author's story.

3. What does "starving" mean to you? Have you had a time in your life when you felt starved for something emotionally? What did you do about it?

4. Were there times in your life that you feel misunderstood? Explain.

5. Have you had a time in your life when you have felt invisible? How did this make you feel? What did you do about it?

6. What was your childhood like? What was your relationship like with your parents? Do you wish it were closer? Explain.

7. What is the author's conclusion about God and the church? Does she have one?

8. Discuss how the church represents itself in 2021.

9. What role do birds play in the author's story? What is their importance and where do they appear?

10. The author discusses how having her first child helped give her courage. If you are a parent or have children in your life, do you agree?

11. COVID has affected everyone. How did it affect the author's relationship with her parents? How has it affected you and your family members? Were you surprised by their reaction to the pandemic? Explain.

12. Do you feel like we are talking about mental health as much as we should be?

13.   Do you think the author succeeded in what she set out to do?

14.   What is the most important point the author makes in this book?

ABOUT THE AUTHOR

Christen Bensten

Christen Bensten is a mom of three living just outside of Washington, DC. She graduated from the University of Mary Washington in 2000 where she received a BA in English Literature. She started her blog and small, women-owned business, Blue Egg Brown Nest (blueeggbrownnest.com) in 2002, which gained national recognition.

When she is not writing, reading or painting furniture, she is fostering loads of kittens that are also looking for safe, loving homes.

Connect With Christen Bensten

I would love to meet and connect with you, share a cup of tea and hear your story.

For more, follow me at
christenbensten.com
@christenbensteauthor

For my dear, Blue Egg Brown Nest readers and new readers, I will see you at
blueeggbrownnest.com
@blueeggbrownnest

Made in the USA
Middletown, DE
07 April 2021